Muncie, India(na)

THE ASIAN AMERICAN EXPERIENCE

Series Editors
Eiichiro Azuma
Jigna Desai
Martin F. Manalansan IV
Lisa Sun-Hee Park
David K. Yoo

Roger Daniels, Founding Series Editor

A list of books in the series appears at the end of this book.

Muncie, India(na)

Middletown and Asian America

HIMANEE GUPTA-CARLSON

UNIVERSITY OF ILLINOIS PRESS
Urbana, Chicago, and Springfield

Library of Congress Cataloging-in-Publication Data
Names: Gupta-Carlson, Himanee, author.
Title: Muncie, India(na) : Middletown and Asian America /
    Himanee Gupta-Carlson.
Description: Urbana : University of Illinois Press, 2018. | Series:
    The Asian American experience | Includes bibliographical
    references and index.
Identifiers: LCCN 2017031763| ISBN 9780252041822 (hardcover :
    alk. paper) | ISBN 9780252083440 (pbk. : alk. paper)
Subjects: LCSH: South Asian Americans—Indiana—Muncie. |
    Immigrants—Indiana—Muncie. | Gupta-Carlson, Himanee.
    | Muncie (Ind.)—Ethnic relations. | Muncie (Ind.)—Social
    conditions. | Muncie (Ind.)—Biography. | Lynd, Robert
    Staughton, 1892–1970. Middletown.
Classification: LCC F534.M9 G87 2018 | DDC 305.8009772/65-
    dc23
LC record available at https://lccn.loc.gov/2017031763

Contents

Acknowledgments

This book is about Muncie, Indiana, the small city famed for its typicality. I grew up in Muncie in the late 1960s and 1970s, and left in 1981 with no intention of ever returning. However, when I decided in 2000 that I would make the city the site of my doctoral research, my relationship with Muncie forever changed. Over the many years that it took to write, revise, and re-revise this book, I made dozens of trips to Muncie while residing first in Honolulu, then in Seattle, and finally in Saratoga County, New York. I benefited from the insights, commentary, and support of numerous people along the way. This reminds me that even when a written work bears the name of a single author, the product is the result of many.

In Honolulu, I was guided as a doctoral candidate by Michael J. Shapiro, Kathy E. Ferguson, Sankaran Krishna, Nevzat Soguk, and David Stannard. I also gained valuable insights in these years from professors Geoffrey White, S. Charusheela, Monisha Das Gupta, and Jagdish and Miriam Sharma, and support from many University of Hawai'i colleagues and friends, including Grace Alvaro Caligtan, Melisa Casumbal-Salazar, Maigee Chang, Jenny Garmendia, Kathleen Hurtubise, Diane Letoto, Jackie Palmer-Lasky, and Melly Wilson. I owe especial thanks to Eundak Kwon and Bianca Isaki for their close reads, edits, and comments on the initial project.

In Seattle, creative writers of many genres helped me re-envision the project as a book, including Wendy Call, Ferdinand DeLeon, Waverly Fitzgerald, and

Edward Skoog. I am grateful to the Richard Hugo House for creating a space for me to connect with so many writers and to the Artist Trust of Seattle for accepting me into its inaugural Literary EDGE program for writers.

In Saratoga, my SUNY Empire State colleague and friend Menoukha Case read and commented on nearly every chapter in the book, probably twice. I owe her a special debt. I also thank Michele Forte for talking me through several re-articulations of various chapters as I prepared the manuscript for submission. Numerous faculty professional development grants, an individual development award from the United University Professions, and acceptance into two college-sponsored writers' retreats also helped me not only bring the book to completion but also share the work in progress at academic conferences.

I was fortunate to have been accepted into the Wabash Center for Teaching and Learning in Theology and Religion's workshop for Pre-Tenure Asian and Asian American Teaching Faculty in 2011–12. There, I met David Yoo, who not only offered splendid advice on publishing within Asian American studies but also introduced me to Vijay Shah, then an editor with the University of Illinois Press. Shah enthusiastically supported my proposal and put the manuscript under contract. Dawn Durante continued Shah's work, and I thank her for her kindness and her patience. I also thank Julie Gay for her close copyedit of the final manuscript. Other scholars who played a crucial role in helping me bring the book to completion are Tamara Ho, Jigna Desai, and the anonymous reviewers who offered tough yet supportive comments.

The fifty-one individuals I interviewed for this project gave me time, stories, food for thought, and memories that I carried with me throughout the entire process of writing this book. I cannot thank this group enough, and I wish I could name them individually without betraying the confidentiality instilled by academic protocols. I can, however, name the five people who traveled with me almost constantly on this journey: my parents, Naim and Shailla Gupta; my sisters, Nisha Gupta and Anju Gupta-Lavey; and my husband, Jim Gupta-Carlson. Their stories are the core of the book, and their love and support have been vital to making it a reality.

Finally, I wish to acknowledge the support I received from the Center for Middletown Studies at Ball State University and the many people in Muncie itself for providing me with time, references, and memories to tap. Without Muncie, there would not be this book. Muncie has become a city that I am now happy to call my hometown.

Muncie, India(na)

Introduction

Wind tugging at my sleeve
feet sinking into the sand
I stand at the edge where earth touches ocean
where the two overlap
a gentle coming together
at other times and places a violent clash.[1]

—Gloria Anzaldúa, *Borderlands/La Frontera:
The New Mestiza*, 1999

Stillwater, Minnesota
October 7, 2005

I heard a quiet, rhythmic drum tapping as my fiancé Jim and I approached a Holiday Inn party room on the night before our wedding. My parents had rented the room for the Indian premarital party known as a *sangeet*, and as we walked in, I saw a familiar sight: large white sheets spread over a carpet on which women in saris and salwar kameez were seated comfortably cross-legged. A longtime family friend was drumming on a tabla. She had emigrated three decades earlier with her husband from Ahmedabad, India, to Muncie, Indiana, where our families met. With her were my mother, two aunties, and several South Asians from Muncie who had become an informal part of our family in the four-plus decades that we had all been collectively a part of the United States. Friends and family mingling like this had created a diaspora kinship pattern of lineage and love that prompted so many of them to come from wherever they lived in the United States to celebrate my marriage to Jim, the grandson of Swedish and German immigrants who had settled in Minnesota in the early twentieth century.

Jim gripped my hand tightly. A celebration composed of elements of my Hindu Indian heritage was new to him. He told me with his eyes and with his fingers clenched around mine that he felt out of place. His nervous grip added to my worries about the tensions I sensed in the room. I looked around and saw Jim's parents, sisters, brothers-in-law, nieces, and nephews on chairs at the edge of the sheet-covered spaces of carpet. I imagined that they too were uncomfortable. I translated the discomfort into disapproval, and this had the effect of filling me with shame over our Indian ways.

I felt anger, too. I could recognize the upsurge in my emotions as a familiar reaction to being othered in a predominantly white and Christian-dominant America. As a forty-two-year-old American-born woman and a daughter of the first immigrant Indian family to settle in Muncie, Indiana, I had spent almost my entire life in the United States. I realized intellectually that marriage outside one's race, ethnicity, and religion might constitute a social risk, even if it was the twenty-first century and even if the number of interracial, interreligious and nonheteronormative couples within my own circle of friends was immense. The anger helped me fight the humiliation, but the painful grip on my fingers meant neither would completely dissipate.

Jim's grandparents left Sweden and Germany for Minnesota in the early twentieth century. As teens and young adults, his grandparents made the Minneapolis/St. Paul area their home. At the time of our wedding, his parents were still living in the house in which Jim grew up, a few blocks from where his father was raised during the Great Depression.

My paternal grandparents, both deceased, had lived their adult lives in the village in India where my father was born. My maternal grandparents spent most of their lives in New Delhi, where my mother grew up. I met my paternal grandparents only once, in 1967 as a five-year-old, and my maternal grandparents I saw a handful of times before they passed away in the 1990s. My parents were well educated and of a well-placed caste. They were married in 1959 and left India for the United States in 1961. In 1966 they moved to Muncie, a small industrial city that had begun evolving in the 1960s into more of a college town centered on Ball State University. Muncie had been studied since 1924 for its all-American typicality, a portrait that often masked the presence of its nonwhite residents, including African Americans, newer immigrants, and individuals who traced their ancestries to Asia. My parents had lived in their married life at nine different addresses in India and the United States. My father meticulously logged these addresses on the back of a photo of himself and my mother as newlyweds until the photo fell apart. Once they arrived in Muncie in 1966, however, their moving stopped. They began calling themselves Americans and referring to Muncie as their home.

On this night, we were in Stillwater, Minnesota. The wedding ceremony was to take place the following morning in Minneapolis in a garden dedicated to the American poet Henry Wadsworth Longfellow near the base of the Minnehaha Regional Park waterfalls, close to where Jim grew up. We wanted our wedding celebration to integrate our cultural heritages in a way that mirrored how we saw ourselves, as a diffusely entangled whole defined by varying genealogical threads of race, ethnic identity, and religious background that define America, too.[2] We planned an evening reception that would feature Indian appetizers, a meat-and-potato dinner, and a Swedish wedding cake for dessert. Our gifts for our guests included grains of wild rice traditionally harvested by the Indigenous Americans of Minnesota and small saffron packages from Kashmir. We had tucked these favors into handmade ceramic pinch pots. We had traveled from Hawai'i in the hope that our celebrations in the heartland of the Midwest where we both had grown up and where most of our family lived would bring all of us together.

Braiding difference, however, is hardly simple. I looked at the people at the sangeet. Most of my relatives and Indian family friends were seated on the floor, eating Indian samosa and bhel puri snacks and painting intricate designs on each other's hands with the mehndi paste made from henna dye, clay, and water. Most of Jim's relatives and family friends were dressed in suits and ties and sitting in chairs, watching from the sidelines. In the film *Selena*, a Mexican American singer who speaks no Spanish graciously greets members of the Mexico City media, who had expected her to speak their language, and wins them over with her smiles and kisses on cheeks. I would have liked to be so charming. The only problem was that in this America, the person who was in the position of being the other did not have a way to assert control. My body was marked by gender, race, ethnicity, and religion. I was the bride: the brown bride, the Indian bride, the Hindu-born bride marrying into a white Lutheran Covenant family of Swedish and German roots.

Earlier that day, my parents had performed a *havan* as a symbolic removal of obstacles. The havan is a ritual that in our family's custom involves burning ghee (clarified butter), herbs, and sugar. It is said to cleanse the environment. I had felt that the ritual would provide a symbolic gesture that we were starting married life fresh. During the ceremony, Jim's sister and brother-in-law had stood near the edge of a circle that had formed around us, their arms crossed. I gazed back, worrying that I had done something wrong. However, when I averted my gaze, I saw two of Jim's former Navy friends watching the ceremony with smiles on their faces. Afterward, they approached me.

"That was beautiful," one of them said. "I saw the two of you together, married."

The comment bolstered my spirits. A jar of the ghee essential to the ritual had gotten lost. I had hastily purchased a bottle of Wesson vegetable oil at a convenience store to use in its place. I had laughed off the substitute, saying God would understand, but I knew that my mother felt the replacement to be a personal affront. Originally, we were going to perform the havan at my sister's home outside St. Paul. A flash flood two days earlier forced us to find an alternate locale. My mother had contacted the Hindu temple and Indian cultural center in Minneapolis, but Jim and I vetoed this idea because we wanted to do the ceremony at a religiously neutral site. We chose the Minnehaha Regional Park because it was near water, in nature, and where our wedding was to take place. Despite the site's recognition of the indigenous peoples who resided in the area before European Christian settlement, watching Jim's sister and brother-in-law made me feel as if there could be no neutral ground. Regardless of the long tradition of advocating for freedom of religion, religion in America by the eighteenth century had become either Christian or non-Christian. There were no in-betweens. Yet the reassuring comment from Jim's friend helped me remember that not every Christian was cut of the same cloth, just as every Hindu was not.

We told our guests that the sangeet would be a casual event. Jim prepared for it by changing out of the kurta pajama he had worn for the havan and putting on a pair of blue jeans and a Hawaiian-style aloha shirt. I changed from an orange and gold salwar kameez into a bright blue and purple one. A close family friend in New Delhi had designed the dresses as well as the floor-length fuchsia wedding lengha I was to wear the next day. I chose these styles as wedding attire for a variety of reasons: I was proud of the fact that I was not only of Indian ancestry but was also marrying a man of my choosing. I also was proud that I was marrying not as a young woman in her early twenties unprepared for such a big step but at age forty-two, at a point where I thought I had grown more comfortable being myself. I wanted my dress and my wedding to be emblematic of the self that I felt I had become—a self that moved comfortably in the pluralistic America that my generation of both South Asian and non–South Asian peers had helped create. On the surface, my strategies had worked. The fluorescent lights in the hotel room shone on the sequins covering my dress, causing me to glitter. Inside, however, I felt turmoil.

In the community of children of Muncie South Asians, I was among the eldest of the American-born generation. Although most of the immigrant generation had remained in Muncie, those of us who were American-raised had grown apart and away from Muncie. We saw each other rarely, if at all. In becoming part of a multiracial and multireligious America, I had grown distant from my roots and felt more familiar with non-Indian ways of marking life rituals than vice versa. That loss of intimacy with Indian roots had made life easier at times in the United States. At other times, it caused me to be shocked and to feel hurt when comments about the irregularity of Hinduism would be voiced in my presence, reminding me of how a hegemonic system of a Christianity dominated racially by whites asserts control over American life. This system has caused such religious holidays as Christmas and Easter to be regarded as normatively secular and has organized such ordinary events as the workweek around a day of rest marked as the Christian Sabbath. These seemingly invisible ways of being have long vested Christians in the United States with an unearned and unacknowledged privilege while disempowering the followers of other faiths as subordinate.[3] This sense of subordination is something I sense that every non-Christian has at least once felt in the United States, perhaps more keenly when one is also nonwhite.

Jim and I had lived all over the United States, and Jim had traveled during deployments around the world. Both of us also had adapted ourselves to Hawai'i's traditions and ways of life after having lived in the islands for a number of years. Aware of our ethnic, religious, and cultural differences, we wanted to integrate them. We planned the ceremony to include the singing of a mantra (or hymn) to the deity Ganesh (the figure of Hinduism most relevant to my family) and the reciting of a verse from Corinthians (which Jim and I had found while thumbing through a Bible during a church service in Honolulu). However, my desire to hold the pre-wedding havan and to have my father sing the Hindu mantra in the next day's wedding ceremony had provoked disapproval. Jim's sister had told me that singing the mantra would be like praying to a deity and as such would be a sin. She advised that we separate the rituals by religion, and hold separate services. The phrase I had learned early in school—"separate but equal is inherently unequal"—was so ingrained in my brain that separation was not an option.

Jim told his sister to relax and that we could all stand together as a family for the twenty minutes that the ceremony would last. But Jim also had needed convincing from me that the ceremony would not be too Hindu or too foreign because he too had felt wary of worship that differed from the faith in which he had been raised. I tried to dispel his fears by characterizing the rituals I wanted to include as nonreligious practices: I told him that a mantra was more like a song than a prayer and that the havan would invoke spiritual blessings, not deities.

My future father-in-law helped quell Jim's fears, telling him that America was about cultural diversity and that it was good to learn new things. Jim's mother also was kind and supportive, saying that she didn't see a problem with anything Jim and I had wanted to include in the ceremony and that if a pastor had approved our plans, everybody else should be able to.

Someone hugged me from behind.

"You look beautiful."

It was my twenty-four-year-old cousin, the American-born son of my mother's youngest brother, my uncle, or *mamaji*. My mamaji had emigrated from India as a young man in his twenties when I was twelve. Unlike my quieter father, he was boisterous and jovial. I could remember him sitting at our kitchen table in Muncie, ignoring my stares as he devoured one fresh green chili pepper after another and swallowed glass after glass of water in between. Now my cousin, joyous like his father and seemingly oblivious to my anxieties about my future in-laws, started asking about the marathon Jim and I had run just a week earlier in the Twin Cities. He saw the moment as an opportunity to converse with his elder didi and took advantage of it.

Soon, an auntie called me over. She and my mother had toe rings, bangles, and a collection of stick-on bindis from which they wanted me to select. I settled on the floor beside them and let them adorn me. My auntie put rings on my toes. My mother coaxed numerous glass bangles onto my arms. Nrita, the twenty-three-year-old daughter of one of our Muncie friends who grew up in Muncie two decades after I had, when there was much more access to popular Hindi music hits and images of teen idols coming out of India, showed up a few minutes later with her mehndi kit. She prepared to decorate my hands and bare feet with the paste; as she set to work, I thought of the multiple ways that those of us who grew up Indian in the United States had made ourselves American, balancing our fondness for the savory flavors of a samosa with the lusty tang of a white wine. I remembered the martini and the steak salad I had shared the night before with a white friend who was relishing the opportunity to wear a sari at the post-wedding reception. She had urged me just to have a good time and not to worry about what others might think. And I remembered the bar where we sat was in Jim's former neighborhood, where many of the regulars were friends of his parents who were delighted to meet the new daughter-in-law.

"It's your day," my friend declared. "Be the bride."

I was not just a bride, however. I was a writer, a scholar, and feminist-minded thinker. I was aware of weddings as being patriarchal rites that subsume women at least symbolically into subservient roles. I knew that "being the bride" could mean being demure and nonconfrontational, and that my age, my opinions, and many of my actions were not conforming to that role. At the time my wedding was taking place, I was also working on a doctoral degree, a process that invites one to engage in the practices of questioning conformity. I was studying how people who were of Indian, Pakistani, and Bangladeshi ancestry and were of Hindu, Muslim, or other faiths practiced in South Asia (including Christianity) negotiated their relationships with those who appeared more typically American, in the sense of being racially white, ethnically of European descent, and Christian in religious affiliation. I had done ethnographic fieldwork on those relationships in Muncie, my hometown, and met Jim after returning to the University of Hawai'i to complete my doctorate.

The U.S. Navy had deployed Jim to Pearl Harbor. When we began dating, he described himself to me as a "born-again Christian" and said that it didn't matter to him if I was not. As we made our wedding plans, I did not think they were relevant to my research until his sister's comments about keeping religions separate came to us through e-mail. Her e-mail arrived as my mother was offering suggestions for adding more orthodox Hindu elements to the ceremony. Arguing with my mother while feeling intimidated by Jim's sister led me to start seeing how Jim and I marrying in a way that I thought was very American (interracial and interreligious) was not that at all. In the social circles we moved in, bringing different races and religions together was fine. For some of our family members, it was not. The intimacy of this dilemma forms the core of this book.

Nrita began mixing water into the mehndi powder, creating a dark-green paste that she loaded into a plastic cone. She began to decorate my bronze hands as if they were a cake, warning me not to wriggle and spoil the design. Soon, two teenage girls—the nieces of my fiancé—plopped down beside me and started peppering me with questions: What's the meaning of mehndi? Do toe rings have religious significance? Why do Indians hold a sangeet? I cringed as the girls' hands reached for my salwar kameez and started stroking the silky folds and fingering the beads and sequins embroidered into the design. I did not want to be rude, but I didn't like this touching.

I knew the girls' questions were not meant to create harm, but I did not know how to come up with easy answers. I was afraid that the ceremony would appear a spectacle that they would mock later. I wanted the girls to remember the wedding not as culturally foreign and alien but as a part of the America that all of us inhabited. I also did not want to create the impression that what we were doing to celebrate the Hindu elements of our wedding had any more weight than that of putting up a Christmas tree in December, a ritual my family had always understood as Christian but enjoyed doing. So I told them the activities were traditions my parents had brought with them from India, ones I had wanted to be a part of our wedding. My explanation seemed to satisfy them but could not rid me of my fear that the girls saw me as a version of the 1893 World's Fair foreigner.

My mood shifted again as Nrita's father clapped his hands and announced that it was time to dance. Boisterous beats of bhangra began to boom through the room. The Punjabi-style dance music and the infectious energy got everyone on their feet. At his cue, the mother of the bride began dancing with the father of the groom, and the father of the bride with the mother of the groom. My sisters followed, and then Jim's navy friends. Soon, numerous others were on their feet. The dancing broke the tension, and Jim's nieces began asking if they could have their hands decorated with mehndi too.

After the sangeet I sat with my parents, sisters, and several Indian friends from Muncie who were staying at the Holiday Inn. Before Jim left with his parents, he told me that his mother, sisters, and nieces had gotten their hands decorated with mehndi, and that some had asked for the image of a fish. And so a symbol traced in secrecy throughout Christianity's history of survival amid persecution ended up on their palms. This marking offered a reassurance that, in their America, Christianity would continue to predominate.

Himanee Gupta-Carlson and Jim Gupta-Carlson celebrating their wedding nuptials on October 8, 2005, at the Minnehaha Regional Park in Minneapolis.

American-Born Indian

Like my wedding, this book has grown out of my experiences of being American born and of Indian heritage simultaneously in the United States, experiences I have lived for more than a half-century. Sharing these stories has created an opportunity to write a different kind of history of a South Asian immigrant community in the United States. I root this history in the small, tight-knit community of South Asians who grew up around my parents in Muncie, Indiana, my hometown. However, this history is about all of us. Muncie is the town that became a representation of typical America with the publication in 1929 of Robert S. Lynd and Helen Merrell Lynd's *Middletown*. That book and a follow-up report, *Middletown in Transition* (1937), were the first substantive social-science studies conducted of American people. The books set the stage for subsequent studies through the twentieth and early twenty-first centuries. The legacy of that scholarship has had the effect of keeping *Middletown*'s rendition of the culture it documented as a representation of what was typical of America, and of the town where the Lynds did their study as a personification of that typicality. Well into the twenty-first century, Muncie remains an epitome of typical America.

What most of the Middletown studies did not do was take seriously the racial, ethnic, and religious diversities and accompanying tensions that have long—if not always—been interwoven into the cultural ways of life in American communities, large and small. The legacy of this failure has been its enabling of a particularly biased perception of what is American to define how life practices like weddings such as mine become subject to criticism and disdain for the nonnormative white American Christian other. This book strives to unravel that legacy. It calls attention to the everyday ways this disdain is enacted and highlights how such actions assert a religiously and racially defined sense of nationalistic supremacy that perpetuate deeply ingrained hostilities in the United States against the nonwhite, non-Christian other.

My parents moved to Muncie in 1966, thirty-seven years after the first Middletown study had become a national bestseller. I was three years old at the time. My sister Nisha was an infant, and my mother was pregnant with my other sister, Anju. My parents were among the first immigrants from India to arrive in Muncie and have been the longest continually residing Indian immigrants there since. I was born in Iowa City, Nisha in Cleveland, and Anju in Muncie. We grew up in a predominantly white, middle-class, Christian neighborhood where we made many friends and interacted with neighbors who were kind and generous. Still, at times, our neighbors viewed us as different culturally from them and could not include us fully in their understanding of what being an American meant.

Like the aggressive taunts of "Hindu, Hindu" that many young Indian American children in larger cities have been subjected to on school buses and playgrounds, recollections of being asked if we were "black people" or if we worshipped cows lingered well into adulthood, alongside other fonder memories of playing dodgeball in the concrete squares of our neighborhood streets and of climbing trees and jumping on and off swing sets in our backyards. Such remarks make a subtle but important discursive link to the derogatory manner in which Indian and other Asian immigrants were historically treated. Nativists in the early-twentieth-century era of anti-immigrant hostility, for instance, used the term "Hindu" pejoratively to label all Indian immigrants as a menace to a white America. While neither the children expressing the taunts nor those victimized by them might be aware of the historical referent to Hindu, persistence of the term as pejorative continues to convey a racially coded indication that nonwhites are not always welcome.[4] For me, these mixed memories created a legacy of confusion, causing constant questioning as to whether I was Indian, American, both, or neither, and what the implications of fitting or not fitting into any or all of those categories were.

I learned about the Middletown studies as a teen. I was unaware, however, of how they, like much of the social science literature of the first half of the twentieth century, had been written to omit nonwhites, non-Christians, and new immigrants. Such omissions have long been part of America's long-standing legacies of racism, religious othering, and immigrant exclusion.[5] Had I been aware of those exclusionary practices and able to understand them, I might have viewed the overt distance that childhood peers placed between themselves and me as more than my incapability to fit in. Instead, I blamed my parents' being different from the Muncie norm as the cause of my problems and strove to disassociate myself from them and their cultural roots as much as possible. I rebelled against my mother's immigrant desires of success to see her eldest daughter in medical school and to marry a young Indian man of my parents' choosing by leaving Muncie as soon as I finished high school to pursue a bachelor's degree in journalism.

I completed my degree at Northwestern University and began working as a newspaper reporter in 1985. Restless and unwilling to settle down into any one place, I moved from newspaper to newspaper, working in Boise, Idaho; Belleville, Illinois; Fort Worth, Texas; Wilkes-Barre, Pennsylvania; Kansas City, Missouri; and Seattle, Washington. A midcareer fellowship for journalists in 1995 brought me to Honolulu, where I began a transition away from my journalism career by enrolling in graduate school at the University of Hawai'i. Being in Hawai'i helped instigate this shift because the experience of living in an Asian majority society allowed me to see my place as well as my parents' place in Muncie in a larger geopolitical and historical context. In doing so, I began to understand why I had always had a difficult time reconciling the connotations of warmth and belonging that conventionally accompany the word *home*.

Hawai'i is known officially as the fiftieth state of the United States and as a vacationer's paradise. The academic colleagues, community organizers, and political activists with whom I interacted while at the university defined Hawai'i more appropriately as the kingdom that the U.S. government overthrew in 1893, forcibly annexed in 1898, and converted to a state in 1959 via a popular ballot that gave its residents no choice but to join the union or remain a territory. Hawai'i, while a state, has remained a colony well into the twenty-first century with corporate and military interests predominant in its economy. I came to see Hawai'i and the indigenous Hawaiian people as sharing an affinity with the peoples of South Asia, even as I, along with many of my peers in Hawai'i, understood the position of the South Asian individuals who had emigrated to the islands as being in the more problematic category of upwardly mobile Asian settlers. Although Hawai'i's population is majority Asian, persons of South Asian ancestry are a small fraction of that demographic. South Asians also arrived in the islands more in the late twentieth century rather than the late nineteenth and early twentieth centuries, when large plantations run by Americans recruited hundreds of Chinese, Japanese, Korean, and Filipino laborers. South Asian individuals, like some of the descendants of the plantation-era Asian settlers, often were seen as prioritizing their social and economic well-being at the expense of the islands' indigenous peoples and resources, and of staking a claim to Hawai'i as their home without questioning how their historic roots to the islands had usurped the indigenous Hawaiian peoples' of their lands.[6]

From this vantage point I could see how European settlers had built an America and defined it as "theirs"—religiously, ethnically, and culturally—in a similar way to what the white plantation owners had done to Hawai'i. The European settlers had used the forced labor of imported slaves alongside indentured servants of less well economically placed Europeans and the uprooted and exterminated tribes and nations of peoples who already were inhabiting the western hemisphere. I also could see how modern émigrés, while continuing the violence, also faced a different kind of violence through European descendants' refusal to acknowledge them as a part of their America. Many South Asian American residents of Hawai'i whom I met resembled my parents. They were individuals who had come from their home countries with middle-class backgrounds in search of better educational and economic opportunities for themselves and their families. They, like my parents, sought an identity independent from the British colonialist shadow that fell over their histories.

Studying American history and political culture in such a politically charged environment as Hawai'i led me to interrogate my place in Muncie and the United States as well as my relationship to India. On the mainland as a young adult journalist, I had felt that I possessed a hyphenated Indian-American identity within a broader identity of Asian American. The hyphenation signified a conjoining of an ethnic nationalist sense of self, tied to genealogy and heritage, with a citizen-oriented sense of self, tied to birthplace and place of residence. In Hawai'i, as a mainland transplant, I felt American and Indian, and unhyphenated. I felt that there was little connection between the two selves beyond the idea that neither held a strong historical or cultural tie to Hawai'i. I felt unwelcome at times and loved at others. These contradictory sensations put me into the skin of my parents and got me to imagine what being an immigrant from another country might feel like in the continental United States. It also made me wonder how they and other South Asians saw themselves in an America defined by the rubric of typical America that the popularity of the Middletown studies had established.

Methodology

The chapters that follow reflect an autoethnographic approach to examining my memories of growing up in Muncie alongside the stories of past and present members of the immigrant and American-born generation of Indian, Pakistani, and Bangladeshi residents. I build these collective stories into my analysis of some of the key texts in the Middletown archive. I also lean on the practices of discourse analysis to make meaning out of the stories and in many cases to unearth "silences"—understandings of social realities that often are suppressed by more dominant views.[7] The term autoethnography calls attention to how this book is both ethnographic (in the sense of creating a text of a particular group of people in a specific place) and autobiographic (in the sense of this story being partially my own). The writing I share emerges from ongoing reflection of how I place myself against the historic, political, and sociocultural themes the book explores and how my sense of self, as the researcher and as a person, is informed and transformed through this work.

Scholarship on the research and writing practices of autoethnography describes how the methods I use are aimed at challenging the distanced relationship between a researcher and her research topics and informants to establish a "more intimate and more emotionally rich narrative."[8] Autoethnography, as a form of scholarly research and writing, encourages such reflection by allowing readers to "feel the truth" of the stories that a narrator shares as well as those that her project informants have shared with her.[9] I share stories that others have shared with me via interviews and other conversations, stories that I also have attempted to contextualize within larger narratives of race, ethnicity, migration, resettlement, cycles of life, and desires to worship as one pleases, freely and safely. Part of my task of contextualization also involves looking at my own experiences in relation to their, as well as my, evolving understandings of how I comprehend and relate to the larger themes that form this study.

My use of discourse analysis also shapes my methodology. I conducted interviews as loosely structured conversations centered on a few open-ended questions. I used those interviews to create texts that readers could, in the style of discourse analysis, understand as constructed truths. I listened to audio recordings of the interviews to construct stories based on what my interviewees told me, and then listened again and again—often years later—to the stories in order to discern how they might support particular societal narratives of truth, how they might contest those truths, or how they might ignore them altogether. In the process, I have made meanings out of stories as a way of highlighting the oppressive structures of race and religion particularly, but also gender, ethnic superiority, and class that exist in America and seek to maintain dominance over more inclusive ways of knowing. I hope the meanings I construct can open a dialogue on a more just society for the future.

Some of the processes of discursive control are easy to see: for instance, the Lynds' removal of African Americans and foreign-born residents from their studies of Muncie, and the insinuations that occurred during my wedding, highlight how it is reinforced that if one is not white and/or Christian, one is a foreigner and potential contaminant. Others are more difficult to unearth. All strive to establish and sustain social justice. In doing discourse analysis, one comes to realize that discursive truths rely on those suppressed perspectives for their existence. If the discursive truths had no other truth to compete against, they would cease to exist. In unraveling the meaning of such ideas as "the typical American," one becomes more attentive to those suppressed truths.

The Interviewees

I use the terms South Asia and South Asian to refer to my group of interviewees in Muncie as a whole; I use either national or regional ethnic terms to describe the individuals when speaking of them specifically. The primary data are drawn from the lengthy, open-ended interviews I conducted with thirty-one individuals as well as four discussion groups I organized. A total of fifty-one individuals participated in the project as interviewees, discussion group participants, or both. I conducted my initial interviews in 2003–04 and remained in touch with most of the participants in the years after, even as some left Muncie or passed away. The thirty-one participants I interviewed individually included members of eleven families, with representatives of three generations: the initial immigrants themselves along with their children and, in the case of one family, the parents. The initial immigrants were in their late forties through early seventies at the time of the interviews; several of the discussion group participants, however, were in their mid-twenties. The main interviewees arrived in Muncie between 1966 and 1994, while several discussion-group participants had come as late as 2001. Among the interviewees were my parents and sisters, whom I identify, along with my husband, by their own names. I have used pseudonyms to identify my other interviewees or have referred to them anonymously in an effort to keep their identities confidential.

Tables 1 and 2 in the appendix provide information about the individuals who participated in this project. These demographics offer a representative snapshot of the community of South Asians in Muncie and its evolution over four decades. A most notable feature of the demographics is the affluence of the community. Although I did not gather specific income data, I would classify nearly all the participants in my study as either upper middle class or wealthy.

The first South Asian immigrants to establish long-term homes in Muncie were professors hired by Ball State University in the 1960s and 1970s at a time when the institution's student and faculty populations were beginning to grow more international in scope. This group of immigrants generally arrived in the United States several years before moving to Muncie as postgraduate students. A second group that began to arrive in the 1980s included a large number of physicians. Ball Memorial Hospital drew them to Muncie at a time when deindustrialization in the Northeast and Midwest had left many medical centers in rural and inner-city urban communities in need of physicians. Following these two groups of immigrants was a third group: a steadily increasing population of healthcare professionals, computer scientists, software engineers, and information-technology specialists. These individuals began settling in Muncie in the late 1990s, and by the early twenty-first century they accounted for a large share of the city's new South Asian immigrants.

The community members' positions in middle-class professions mirrors the general norm of South Asian Americans nationally, who are shown in census and other demographic data as being highly educated and more affluent than other Asian American and ethnically defined groups in the United States, with a median household income among Indian immigrants that by 2015 had reached $103,821, a figure well above the $55,000 figure for the overall U.S. population.[10] These general characteristics are problematic in that they obscure issues of financial distress and class differentiation that exist within South Asian American communities on a national scale. While I do not regard my findings as an indication of a lack of such differentiation in Muncie, it is beyond the scope of this book to delve into such differences.

The economic prosperity of the interviewees did not make them immune to societal discrimination or blind them to the realities of how religious and racial hegemonies had resulted in their feeling inferior or unwelcome in America at some point in their lives. The experience of being cast as a "foreigner" or "outsider" in the Midwest reflects not only how discourses on the United States are put forth to the world but also how immigrants learn to establish their own sense of place within that portrayal. How each interviewee dealt with such experiences are all stories that collectively help to deepen the understanding of how we might imagine an America of more racially inclusive and religiously reciprocal relationships.

Most of the émigrés in my study came from India, but the group also included individuals who traced their ancestry to present-day Bangladesh, Nepal, and Kenya. Most of the émigrés had come to the United States as young adults, but two were more elderly and had left India after their children had established lives in Muncie and could serve as sponsors for their visas. Nine of the eleven families whose members I interviewed had come from India. They traced their ancestry to a wide array of ethnically and linguistically defined geographic regions, including the northern states of Himachel Pradesh and Punjab; the central plains states of Haryana and Uttar Pradesh; the western state of Maharashtra; and the southern states of Andhra Pradesh and Tamil Nadu. The émigrés from the tenth family were born in the region of pre-Partition India that eventually became known as Bangladesh. Members of the eleventh family emigrated from Kenya, where the immigrant generation was born. This couple traced their ethnic lineage to the pre-Partition Indian region of Punjab, where their grandparents in the 1840s had been born. Their ancestors left Punjab to work in the British Empire's colonial apparatus in Africa, and soon after my interviewees were born, the section of the Punjab from where their families had come had become known as Pakistan. Participants in my discussion groups included individuals from other states in India such as Assam and Gujarat as well as one individual from Nepal.

These intricate geographic differences illuminate the ethnic and religious complexity of the South Asian community not just in Muncie but also throughout the United States and beyond. The South Asian community as a diaspora group has been multiethnic and religiously diverse from even the earliest years of South Asian immigration to America, with more than three dozen differing ethnic, regional, linguistic, and religious affiliations included in the umbrella term of South Asian America. That rich range of diversity, however, is often obscured in governmental census classifications of peoples from India and the other nations of South Asia that have tended to emphasize commonalities in national origin and biologically defined racial similarities while eliding differences in regional, ethnic, and religious affiliations.

At the same time, the relationships I found to exist among the members of the community revealed both how the logic of statecraft and the general economic prosperity of the group had created a sense of national and ethnically defined unity among at least the India-born research participants who fell under an umbrella of being Indian—and often proudly so. The immigrant members of these families came from all over India. When they moved to Muncie, they became friends. In doing so, they would refer to themselves individually as being Punjabi, Bengali, Kannadiga, and so forth, or of hailing from a city such as New Delhi, Bombay, or Bangalore. At the same time, they also referred to themselves collectively as Indians. The Muncie group of émigrés also had little trouble referring to themselves collectively as South Asians, a term that refers to individuals from India, Pakistan, Bangladesh, Nepal, Bhutan, and Sri Lanka. These correlations between individual identity and ethnic and geo-political affiliation highlight one way that South Asians in Muncie and in the United States make sense of their place in America as individuals with specific ethnic affiliations as well as persons categorized as racial and often religious minorities. It also underscores how the experience of living not in a larger metropolitan community on the East or West Coast but in a smaller city in the Midwest might encourage these individuals to view ethnic or linguistic identities that hold relevance in India as well as larger South Asian communities in the United States or elsewhere as less important when the collective number of immigrants is smaller.

The Muncie South Asian community, while predominantly Hindu, includes Muslims, Sikhs, Christians, and Jains among its members. Yet many of my interviewees had adapted their lives in Christian-dominant Muncie in a manner that seemed almost to evoke a biblical message delivered to exiles in the Book of Jeremiah of making the nation to which one relocates your own: "Build ye houses, and dwell in them; and plant gardens, and eat the fruit of them. Take ye wives, and beget sons and daughters; and take wives for your sons, and give your daughters to husbands, that they may bear sons and daughters; and multiply ye there, and be not diminished. And seek the peace of the city whither I have caused you to be carried away captive, and pray unto Jehovah for it; for in the peace thereof shall ye have peace."[11] This call to seek peace in the place where one arrives resonates with my marriage to a man born outside the religion and the cultural heritage of my family as well as the relationships South Asians have forged with others in Muncie. The tension accompanying this quest for peace has been a part of my life as I have worked to navigate a path between my ties to my family in the United States and India, my love for my husband, and my relationships with nearly everyone else.

This book also examines the experiences of some of the children of the Muncie South Asian émigrés, primarily those born between 1959 and 1971. All of these individuals were in their early thirties through mid-forties at the time that I interviewed them, and had moved away from Muncie. Most were married; several had children. I felt that the stories of their lives resonated with my own memories of Muncie and, at the same time, differed somewhat from the experiences documented in much of the scholarly literature on South Asian Americans of what is often referred to as the 1.5 generation (individuals who immigrated to the United States as young children) or the second generation (those born of immigrant parents in the United States). These groups of South Asian Americans have been characterized as possessing a global awareness that encompasses an understanding of themselves as racialized Americans as well as having a sense of belonging to a larger transnational migrant community.[12]

Consciousness of a transnational affiliation often comes through friendships with persons of a similar immigrant background. The children of the immigrants who arrived in Muncie between 1966 and 1974 did not recall growing up with this kind of interaction with South Asian peers. They also received little expo-sure to aspects of their cultural heritage outside of that in their own homes. As a result, they often came to understand themselves in a racialized sense as nonwhite and non-Christian without the awareness that there was an entire world of people like them. The implications of this lack of awareness became especially clear to me when I traveled to India in 1992 at age twenty-nine and walked with my mother and one of her sisters through a crowded shopping district in the Rajouri Garden neighborhood in New Delhi. As I gazed at women who looked "almost exactly like me," I realized that this was the first time I had felt as if I did not stand out as unusual or foreign.

South Asian American Studies

If I had asked my parents in the 1970s who had come to the United States from India before them, their response likely would have been that they knew of no one except for a handful of other college students. Little was known about the presence of South Asians in the United States. By the late 1990s, South Asian American studies had grown into an academic subfield of the interdisciplinary fields of Asian American, ethnic, racial, and American studies, as a result of a range of studies published in the 1980s and early 1990s.[13] Subsequent work has offered deeper, multifaceted insights into the experiences of both the earlier, pre-1965 immigrants and those of the later decades of the twentieth century.[14] What follows is a summary.

Individuals from nations now known as India, Pakistan, Bangladesh, Nepal, Bhutan, and Sri Lanka began visiting the United States as early as the 1780s. By the late 1800s, hundreds each year were entering the country as college students, manual laborers, maritime merchants, lumberjacks, and farmworkers. These émigrés were settling in rural and urban industrial communities alike throughout the United States. While the largest numbers of these immigrants resided in small agricultural communities in California and the urban immigrant enclaves of New York City, some found their way into predominantly black or Hispanic communities in the South and Midwest.[15] The numbers of such early immigrants grew until the early twentieth century, when anti-Asian hostilities in the United States culminated with federal and state policies that severely restricted the legal entry of these immigrants. The end of World War II, along with the end of British colonialism in India and the ensuing establishment of new nations on the subcontinent, ushered in a new era—and with it a seemingly more tolerant attitude toward South Asian immigrants, particularly those representing an educated elite. With this change, the estimated population referred to at times as "Hindu" and at other times as "East Indian" ancestry in the United States rose from 2,405 in 1940 to 8,746 by 1960.[16]

These numbers began to look miniscule by 1970, when the 1965 Immigration Act formally took effect. The act was passed by Congress and signed by President Johnson some five years after President Kennedy had famously urged Americans, "Ask not what your country can do for you—ask what you can do for your country." The law was not intended to change America's dominant racial stock or national character, but in reality it did. Heralded as a landmark moment in American immigration policy, the law eliminated the race-based criteria for naturalized citizenship, which had been in place since 1790, as well as the quotas on the numbers of immigrants the United States would accept from specific countries. The 1965 law made educational background, skills, and technical expertise the primary qualifiers for immigration and had an enormous influence on how young, educated, middle-class, and upper-middle-class adults in such developing nations as India and Pakistan began to view their lifelong professional prospects. With the booming economy and vast resources of the United States, many began immigrating or planning their educational lives around immigrating. By 2015, an estimated 13 percent of the U.S. population was foreign born,[17] a large percentage of whom came from Asia, partly because the act's favoring those who were highly educated and from more economically prosperous backgrounds also limited the conditions of arrival for less well-positioned immigrants, including agricultural and other laborers from Mexico and other parts of the Western Hemisphere.[18]

By the mid-1980s, the impact of this change on the American landscape was quite clear. The U.S. Census Bureau, which began formally categorizing persons of Indian ancestry as Asian Indians in 1980, estimated the population of this group at 387,000 in 1980 and at 787,000 ten years later. The population continued to double roughly with each decennial census, and stood at nearly 3.5 million as of 2015. The U.S. population of other South Asian peoples has increased at a comparable pace. Those self-identifying as Pakistani grew from 153,533 in 2000 to 390,861 in 2010; as Bangladeshi from 41,280 to 154,286; as Sri Lankan from 20,145 to 51,259; as Nepalese from 7,868 to 86,526; and as Bhutanese from 183 to 14,466.[19] While the figures vary with each nationality, the overall numbers show persons of South Asian ancestry to be one of the fastest growing demographic groups in the United States—an estimated 4.3 million residing in the United States as of 2013.[20] By 2014, immigrants from India—barely noticeable before 1960—were the third-largest group of foreign-born residents of the United States.[21]

The growth in the South Asian population in the United States has come largely through new immigration, with a growing number of South Asians arriving with temporary work status and no guarantee of being able to establish permanent residence. Immigrants from South Asia increasingly have entered the United States with a strong base of technical education and professional training to take jobs in high-tech industries that often are well paid but temporary. The 1990 Immigration and Nationality Act more than tripled the number of permanent residency visas issued on the basis of occupational skills in response to demands from multinational corporations. That act, through establishment of what is known as the H-1B visa category, also substantially increased the number of temporary foreign-worker permits such companies could seek. This category is a three-year temporary work visa for college-educated immigrants that allows for the possibility of becoming a permanent immigrant. This program has been used particularly by Indian immigrants and has produced much of the South Asian immigrant community in the United States in the early twenty-first century.[22] As of the 2010 census, seven out of ten Indian immigrants in the United States had arrived after 1990.[23] The H-1B visa group of immigrants joins those who began arriving in the late 1970s and ended up in more service-oriented, lower-wage occupations. The latter group often came as a result of family reunification policies that enabled the initial post-1965 immigrants to sponsor relatives. The Muncie South Asian community both reflects and contradicts this portrait.

Asian Americans and the Midwest

Immigration policies from the mid-twentieth century through the present have helped establish a more demographically diverse America. Still, Euro-American and Christian cultural practices of the early twentieth century persist in defining the Midwest as white, Christian, and conservative. Asian Americans have resided in the region since the early twentieth century, but their presence drew little scholarly attention until the early twenty-first century. Such lack of attention creates an aura of invisibility for the community I study. That sense of invisibility frames how my experiences as well as the stories I have crafted from the experiences of my interviewees speak about being South Asian American in the Midwest.

Most of the scholarly work on South Asian America published in the mid-1980s through early decades of the twenty-first century has focused on larger metropolitan areas on the East and West Coasts, with some studies done on such noncoastal communities as Chicago and Atlanta. These studies also put more emphasis on the South Asian communities being studied within the particular locales, rather than on specific aspects of the geographic locale itself or of the relationship between South Asian communities and the broader locale. The studies paid little attention to the experiences of individuals in smaller cities such as Muncie that also were attracting South Asian immigrants.[24]

To some extent, the neglect of the smaller-town experience was understandable. Large metropolitan areas were and continue to be the places where thousands of South Asian immigrants, along with hundreds of thousands of the other immigrants who enter the United States annually, go most often in search of jobs and education. Immigrant South Asian merchants and business, religious, and community groups in such large metropolitan areas have been able to take advantage of having a large South Asian population to reproduce the religious and cultural structures and practices so commonly found in diaspora: temples, mosques, gurdwaras, and other houses of worship; dance and language classes; and ethnic restaurants and specialized grocery stores.[25] The bustling commercial neighborhoods of Jackson Heights in Queens, New York; the long stretch of Indian, Pakistani, Bangladeshi, and increasingly Afghani shops along Devon Avenue in Chicago; and large South Asian–dominant suburban communities like Edison, New Jersey, and Herndon, Virginia, offer ample evidence.

Muncie, like many smaller, nonsuburban communities throughout the United States, does not have such spaces. As a result, one cannot see a South Asian community unless one starts to look. This sense of invisibility has required a delicate balancing of anger, awareness, and adaptation on the part of the South Asian American individuals who grew up and/or reside in Muncie and informs their understandings of what it has meant to be South Asian in the United States in ways that might overlap but at the same time contradict the experiences of those in more cosmopolitan areas. Because I grew up within that shadow of invisibility myself, the balancing act also has informed how I have written about South Asians in Muncie as a community in the Midwest. If one is marked as different—in a racial sense, in a cultural set of practices, and/or in religious affiliation—the affect (or felt knowledge) of this sense of being different can be an isolating experience. That feeling of isolation might affect even those South Asian Americans living in areas with large communities of other South Asians around them, but it is particularly acute when one's understanding of self in an ethnicized sense comes primarily from parents who, as new immigrants, might themselves be trying to figure that question out. This sense of isolation gripped me during my wedding, until anger helped me recall that many forces of racial, ethnic, and religious hegemony were at play and gave me a way to respond in a manner that demonstrated awareness of those forces and the effect they were having on me, even as I sought to keep my own anxieties to myself.

Asian American studies scholars acknowledge that the emphasis on bicoastal and metropolitan immigrant experiences has resulted not only in a rendering of such communities elsewhere as invisible but also in what might be overly simplified understandings of the intricacies of racially white and religiously Christian dominance. In doing so, emergent scholarship offers new ways to understand how individuals of Asian ancestries disrupt longstanding stereotyped understandings of America as white first and black second. Jigna Desai and Khyati Y. Joshi, for instance, note that in America's South, the presence of the Asian American body disrupts and shifts understandings "of Black and White in a region in which this binary is writ large." This disruption calls attention to foreign-ness and globalization within "a space assumed to be parochial and isolated."[26]

Literary and cinematic works that began to emerge in the 1980s have captured this sense of disruption: Bharati Mukherjee's 1989 novel *Jasmine*, about a young female émigré, and Mira Nair's story of an Indian family who settled in Mississippi after being forced to leave Uganda, released in 1992, are two examples. Abraham Verghese's memoir, *My Own Country: A Doctor's Story*, published in 1995, went even further by offering a nonfictional account of life as an Indian immigrant doctor in rural Tennessee. Verghese shares a story of a suit salesman of Indian origin who would come from Hong Kong and travel through the United States in search of potential customers for business attire stitched by Indians residing in Hong Kong. The salesman would find a telephone book and search the yellow pages for Indian restaurants. Finding none, he would look up common Indian last names, such as Gupta or Patel, in the white pages. A phone call to one of those individuals would decide where he would eat dinner.[27]

While the Midwest and the South are different regions, the experience of being Asian and "not from a coast" bears similarities in each of these areas. For instance, I could remember my mother bringing Indian dishes to Muncie potlucks, much as Mukherjee's character in *Jasmine* did in the small Iowa town where the novel was set. The racial positioning of Indians within and between whites and blacks depicted in *Mississippi Masala* echoed aspects of the racial organization of Muncie society. And my parents received phone calls similar to those made by the suit salesman of Verghese's book throughout the late 1960s and 1970s. These calls often came from new Ball State students or new Indian immigrants who became dinner guests, then acquaintances, and later close friends. These anecdotal experiences also illustrate the point that Surinder Bhardwaj and N. Madhusana Rao made in an early 1980s geographic appraisal of Indian Americans in the United States as being "scattered all over."[28]

A sense of South Asian America as existing not just in cities but also in widely scattered pockets within small towns across the United States helps illuminate how increased attention to the experiences of South Asian Americans and other Asian Americans in smaller communities away from the coasts might help deepen our understandings of America as a whole. Pawan Dhingra, for instance, documents how Indian motel owners in Ohio have sought entrepreneurial success and professional fulfillment against the background of a region that has long "served to define a traditional 'American' character of a supposed commitment to family values (rarely defined), individual rights, independent determination, and military pride."[29] Such complications reveal how the Midwest, often romanticized for its bucolic rural landscapes or caricatured as racist and backward, is more complex than these stereotypes might suggest.[30]

Examining how South Asians and other immigrants interfaced with localities defined by the racial and religious structures that have shaped communities like Muncie throughout the United States also provides a way to consider how racial hierarchies defined solely on black-white terms alongside the dominance of Christianity have organized Midwest American life, and how the children of South Asian and other Asian immigrants have dealt with these issues. Such analysis evokes the question that Leslie Bow raises in her examination of the placement of diaspora Chinese communities in Mississippi during the early civil-rights activism in the South. Bow asks: "How did Jim Crow accommodate a supposed 'third' race, those individuals and communities who did not fit into a cultural and legal system predicated on the binary distinction between colored and white? Put another way, where did the Asian sit on the segregated bus?"[31]

My experience as a child and teenager in Muncie did not include much interaction with South Asian Americans outside my family. I had little exposure to immigrants of other ancestries or to those who can trace genealogical relationships to Native American tribal organizations and nations. Racist red-lining policies physically separated African American communities from whites and created economic stratifications. African Americans lived predominantly in neighborhoods on the south and east sides of Muncie. which were more working-class enclaves, whereas whites resided to the north and west in neighborhoods that ranged from being middle class to highly affluent. That separation of white and African American communities has persisted well into the twenty-first century in other ways, with many churches maintaining racially discrete congregations. Although there has been some racial intermixing, the economic profile of Muncie has long equated wealthy with white. The white-dominant neighborhoods in the northern and western parts of the city near Ball State University were where my parents and most of the other South Asian families resided. This isolation from other nonwhite ethnic groups meant that I grew up mostly around whites, affirming in a sense the image of Muncie as Middletown that the Lynd studies portrayed.

Looking Ahead

Chapter 1 introduces Muncie as Middletown. Chapters 2 through 5 explore the themes of racial, ethnic, cultural, and religious difference, and how members of Muncie's South Asian community made sense of their lives and crafted a sense of their selves amid the tensions that accompanied such differences. Chapter 2 introduces the stories of my parents and their oldest South Asian friends who were among the first to arrive in Muncie. Chapter 3 includes stories my sisters and two other women shared of attending Muncie's elementary, middle, and high schools as the only nonblack or nonwhite children in the late 1960s and early 1970s. Chapter 4 looks at how two Muncie-raised South Asians and I experienced high school life in Muncie in the late 1970s through early 1980s against the backdrop of a controversy that erupted in 1982 over a documentary film, *Seventeen*. Chapter 5 examines the contributions to community building that South Asian immigrants who began to settle in Muncie after 1980 made, focusing particularly on the experiences of two medical doctors and their spouses.

Chapter 6 and the Conclusion return to the theme of religious difference that I opened with. Chapter 6 explores how members of Muncie's South Asian community who are Hindu and Muslim articulate relationships with their home nations as well as the Muncie community against the backdrop of a broader U.S.–based South Asian diaspora community that tends numerically to be Hindu dominant. The Conclusion analyzes a dispute in Muncie between evangelical Christians and an interfaith coalition over how to celebrate the 2003 National Day of Prayer and goes on to propose a template for imagining a more racially and religiously pluralistic America through a rearticulation of tolerance.

In describing the first Middletown study as "a metaphor for the invisibility of people of color in the social science literature during the twentieth century," Yolanda Moses alludes to the lack of representation of nonwhite Americans in social sciences and academic literature. Moses, who is African American, explains that she read *Middletown* in the 1960s without the privilege of knowing that Muncie had an African American community.[32] I hope the experiences I share will help eliminate that exclusion for future generations.

CHAPTER 1

Creating a Typical America

The Middletown Studies and Muncie

> Genealogy is gray, meticulous, and patiently documentary. It operates
> on a field of entangled and confused parchments, on documents
> that have been scratched over and recopied many times.
>
> —Michel Foucault, "Nietzsche, Genealogy, History," 1971

August 1, 2003
Muncie, Indiana

The United Airlines flight attendant announced that our aircraft was beginning its descent into Indianapolis. I tightened my seat belt and took a deep breath. My parents were to meet me at the airport, and I was to drive with them to Muncie. I had flown from my home in Honolulu, across the Pacific Ocean and over the U.S. continent, with plane changes in Sacramento (not far from where some of the first immigrant South Asian American communities formed in the early twentieth century) and Chicago (where more than 150,000 South Asian Americans were residing in the metropolitan area by the early twenty-first century[1]).

I had traveled this route over the Pacific and across the continent many times before to visit my parents. But this time I was to stay in Muncie for four months. I would interview my parents, my sisters, and more than fifty family friends of South Asian ancestry who lived or once had lived in Muncie. I was hoping to find out what it meant for them and for me to call this place—this place that had come to represent a certain meaning of typical America to so many others—home.

I looked down through the airplane window, imagining the cornfields disappearing into urban sprawl below. The humid air of late summer felt as if it were blanketing me, enclosing me with memories of the past. Muncie, like so many all-American cities, had evolved out of tribal communities taken over by white settlers. Two branches of the Delaware tribe set up two villages in the late eighteenth century. The White River, which winds through the city, separated these settlements, with one to the north and the other to the southeast. Land-claims disputes between the tribes and whites erupted after the American Revolution and War of 1812, and following the Battle of Tippecanoe and Treaty of St. Mary's in 1818, the tribal peoples who were indigenous to the area were involuntarily relocated to America's West. After the federal government opened the area around Muncie for white settlement, pioneers of European ancestry cleared the heavily forested land and by the late 1820s had established a small agricultural community. A first family, the Gallihers, settled in Muncie in 1840 and established a church, First Baptist, in 1859.

African Americans moved into the area from the South and other parts of the newly established United States, as the whites were sowing their ethnic European and religious Christian roots into Indiana soil. The African American ancestors hailed from Europe, Africa, and indigenous America. Many came to Indiana, which was established as a free state in 1816 even as its constitution denied citizenship rights to nonwhites. For the African Americans, Indiana was an escape from slavery and a place for better lives for themselves and their families. In 1865, as the Civil War was ending, Muncie was incorporated as a city and the Delaware County seat.[2]

The discovery of a large vein of natural gas in 1886 began to transform the town's economy from agricultural to manufacturing. By the 1890s, Muncie had been nicknamed the "Magic City" and was regarded as an up-and-coming place to live, close enough to Indianapolis, Dayton, and Chicago to take advantage of these cities' commerce routes but far enough away to escape exposure to their reputed immorality. Christianity was strong among Muncie's citizens. Revivals occurred often, and fifty-three churches had been established to serve Delaware County's population of 30,131 by 1890. Before the nineteenth century drew to a close, Muncie had become home to seven glass factories, fourteen steel and ironworks plants, two carriage works, four washing-machine factories, two hub-and-spoke factories, and a pulp company. In addition, 326 city lots had been purchased for what would become Ball State University.

Muncie, by the early twenty-first century, was a county seat, a college town, and an agrarian center of commerce. It also was a residential refuge for thousands of workers who commuted the seventy miles to Indianapolis—the twelfth-largest city in the United States, and the residence by 2010 of 12,669 Asian Indians. Indianapolis was home in the early twenty-first century to car racing and professional sports and historically to one of the nation's largest Ku

Klux Klan branches. Some descendants of the Galliher family still called Muncie home.[3]

As the plane began its final descent, I started to feel anxious. I was only going back home. Yet, doing research in a typical American town to which I held a personal and highly conflicted tie was laced with a politics that I found difficult to articulate. My mind went back to a memory of being on the playground outside my elementary school during recess. I was a first-grader and had made fun of a boy who was in kindergarten. The boy responded by spitting all over me, his saliva coating my face and getting lodged in a lace collar on my dress. For years afterward, any mention or sight of spit would cause a physical revulsion in me. That reaction was how I had felt about Muncie, and at times in my twenties I would declare that if I ever went back to the city, it would be to spit all over it. I no longer had a desire to spit on Muncie, but I feared my memories might repulse me in similar visceral ways.

The plane landed. I made my way to the front of the aircraft and crossed the portal into the terminal, where my mother was waiting. My father pulled up to the baggage-claim area, and after gathering my bags we drove out of the urban sprawl of Indianapolis together into the still-ubiquitous cornfields that characterize east-central Indiana. Just before sunset, we arrived in Muncie, a twenty-four-square-mile place that, amid a world of difference, still took pride in being "typical America."

Introducing Muncie

Muncie has been a site of academic study and popular curiosity and a place with a history of conflicted race relations for a century. It also has been my hometown. The texts by Robert S. Lynd and Helen Merrell Lynd that made Muncie famous—*Middletown: A Study in Modern American Culture* (1929) along with its sequel study, *Middletown in Transition: A Study in Cultural Conflicts* (1937)—form the foundation for not just the rich archive of studies on Muncie as Middletown and Middletown as Muncie but also for the vast popular reputation for typicality that Muncie through the twentieth and early twenty-first centuries has acquired. What makes this archive curious is what the Lynd team included in *Middletown*, and most significantly what they left out. Their practices of inclusion and elimination highlight the hostile racist and anti-immigrant climate of the era. The all-American norm that emerged in this era has had a long-term effect of limiting our understanding of Middle America to being primarily white, Protestant, and unreceptive to change.

Another way of understanding Muncie is through its history of race relationships, which longtime community activist Hurley Goodall, Ball State University students, and other scholars and writers have reconstructed through oral histories and interviews, photographs and newspaper articles, and other primary source documents. This history suggests that perhaps Muncie was typical indeed of the America of its time, though not in the way *Middletown* conveyed.

Between the lines of these two depictions of Muncie are other stories: of Jews and other non-Christians and of immigrants and their children, as I am. As a result, the Muncie that this chapter crafts is more than a simple phrase like "typical America" can sum up. It is a space that is complex. This complexity is due in part to the blending of autobiography, ethnography, and discourse analysis that forms the methodology for this book and sometimes produces results that are murky, at best. For as Michel Foucault writes in his essay "Nietzsche, Genealogy, History," "the successes of history belong to those who are capable of seizing these rules, to replace those who had used them, to disguise themselves so as to pervert them, invert their meaning, and redirect them against those who had initially opposed them; controlling this complex mechanism, they will make it function so as to overcome the rulers through their own rules."[4] In this sense, history becomes a discourse that one must take apart to discover what was suppressed.

Foucault intertwines the work of genealogy with that of history, creating a helpful frame for examining Muncie as a space where histories of different peoples, voices, and perspectives might collide and overlap. In this sense, the *Middletown* archive becomes important to understanding not only what the history of Muncie was but also what that history was not. Genealogy is typified by trails of descent, lineages, and legacies. For Foucault, it is, as the epigraph suggests, "gray, meticulous, and patiently documentary. It operates on a field of entangled and confused parchments, on documents that have been scratched over and recopied many times."[5] Upon genealogies are written histories. These narratives of the past gain societal acceptance as "truths" because they are orderly. But once written, we often fail to see the ambiguities within those histories, unless we start to look within the fields of "entangled and confused parchments" for what might lie underneath the scratching over and recopying to which Foucault refers. In highlighting at least some of these ambiguities, this chapter shows how Muncie has become a palimpsest upon which America's typicality is continually written.

Creating *Middletown*

"The aim of the field investigation . . . was to study synchronously the interwoven trends that are the life of a small American city. A typical city, strictly speaking, does not exist, but the city studied was selected as having many features common to a wide group of communities. Neither field work nor report has attempted to prove any thesis; the aim has been, rather, to record observed phenomena, thereby raising questions and suggesting possible fresh points of departure in the study of group behavior."[6]

Robert S. Lynd and Helen Merrell Lynd open *Middletown* with these words. They were the first researchers on record to study Muncie and into the twenty-first century remain the best known. Robert Lynd (1892–1970) was born in New Albany, Indiana, near the Kentucky border, and grew up in both New Albany and Louisville. The son of a banker whose family had emigrated from England in the eighteenth century, he served as a Methodist minister at a Wisconsin oil camp and as an editor for *Publisher's Weekly*. Helen Merrell Lynd (1894–1982) also grew up in the Midwest in LaGrange, Illinois, and, after her family moved to Framingham, Massachusetts, attended Wellesley College. She met her husband in 1919 while hiking in New Hampshire. The two began to date and were married in 1922, after she finished her master's degree in history from Wellesley College and he began studying at the Union Theological Seminary.[7]

Their lives intersected with that of Muncie when the Institute of Social and Religious Research in 1923 (formerly a part of John D. Rockefeller Jr.'s Committee on Social and Religious Surveys) commissioned Robert Lynd to conduct the study that eventually became *Middletown*. Lynd was allowed to select a city of his choice, and after some deliberation, he chose Muncie. He and his wife arrived in 1924 in Muncie. Accompanying them were two statisticians (Faith Williams and Dorothea Davis) and a stenographer (Frances Flourney). The group divided up the work of researching Muncie and for eighteen months resided in rooms rented from Muncie residents.[8]

In a collection of writings and interviews she gave that was published in 1983 in *Possibilities*, Helen Lynd described working in Muncie: "The Institute of Social and Religious Research of the Rockefeller Foundations wanted someone to go out and do a study of the religious life of a small town. I don't know who suggested Bob do it."[9] For her, the project started out as a plan to stay in Muncie as her husband did his work. Eventually, she took on a half-time appointment and undertook many of the interviews that helped set *Middletown* apart from other studies of the time.

"We would always make a point, if a casual conversation seemed to offer something interesting, of writing it down as soon as we got home," she recalled. "Some of the most interesting material came from things that couldn't have been charted in advance."[10]

The Lynds and their research team arrived in Muncie at a time when the United States was in the midst of an unprecedented level of racist violence and a nativist backlash to new immigration. In 1917, five years before their arrival, the Russian Revolution had occurred, resulting in an anti-Communist hysteria throughout the United States and an extreme restricting of immigrant entries. In the same year, the U.S. Congress overrode a veto by President Woodrow Wilson restricting the entry of immigrants who could not pass a literacy test and allowing for those who spoke of revolution or sabotage of the government to be deported. Thousands of immigrants were seized two years later, and hundreds were deported for expressing alleged anarchist or procommunist sentiments. By 1924, anti-immigration panic had resulted in the nullification of citizenship rights granted to Asian immigrants who had married natural-born or naturalized U.S. citizens; the revoking of rights of nonwhite immigrants to own land in several states; the rendering of prior legal entry of Latinos over the U.S.-Mexican border illegal; and the establishment of a barred zone restricting new arrivals to the United States to individuals from primarily northern and western Europe. Newcomers from Asia, southern and eastern Europe, and Africa were effectively kept out, and several states and municipalities made efforts to deport individuals from those parts of the world who were in the United States. To be nonwhite in those years meant living with a constant threat of racial animosity, if not outright violence.

Neither Robert nor Helen Lynd saw themselves as documentarians or agents for change. They preferred to call themselves "amateur sociologists."[11] Yet, in the 1920s, at a time when legal segregation, lynchings, and race riots were erupting across the country, the historical backdrop provides an important context for understanding how and why *Middletown* became the kind of study it was. Burgeoning academic disciplines in the United States such as sociology and anthropology were moving away from a fascination with what has been described as the "primitive other" toward a deepening preoccupation with establishing an understanding of the "American self."[12] "It was, of course, a coincidence that the Lynds embarked on their Muncie fieldwork in 1924," Sarah Igo writes. "But in the context of renewed nativism, eugenic designs, and postwar patriotism . . . a scientific description of the United States, trained not on urban problems but on a white midwestern town, could serve as a compelling cultural arbiter. Like national origins quotas, facts about life in an average community might stabilize and consolidate America."[13]

The *Middletown* researchers sought to show how everyday Americans lived, to reveal what matters concerned them and motivated them to act. Modeling the practice of cultural anthropologists of the early twentieth century, the Lynd team organized the project into six categories: "getting a living," "making a home," "training the young," "using leisure," "engaging in religious practice," and "engaging in community activities." They adapted methods of participant-observation that anthropologists had developed to study work and commerce, marriage and divorce patterns, child-rearing values, schooling, movie and theater-going habits, reading choices, clothing styles, shopping habits, automobile use, church attendance, local politics, social services, and athletics, among other topics. The team members pored through local newspapers, visited the city's high school and surveyed students, sang at church services, and attended Rotary Club meetings. They counted and documented the items on household kitchen shelves, measured ownership of washing machines and cars, and conducted lengthy interviews.[14]

"I did a lot of the work on the press and the records of various organizations," recalled Helen Lynd. "Bob went to the Rotary Club and high school ceremonies. The interviewing of ordinary people came later. Faith Williams insisted, 'We're getting generalities. We need to talk to individuals.' It was one of the best things we did."[15]

The methodology for the *Middletown* research was so systematic that it remained the standard for ethnographic study for the next fifty years. However, it also produced a text that was not acceptable to the Rockefeller institute that had commissioned it. The Institute for Social and Religious Research had intended to publish the study as a report on religious practices. As the Lynd team shifted the focus away from an exclusive look at religion toward a broader examination of behavioral patterns and cultural habits, the institute grew skeptical of the project's outcome. When the final manuscript was submitted, the institute rejected it.

Robert Lynd, however, was able to submit the document as a doctoral dissertation to Columbia University, with contributions that resulted from his co-authorship with Helen Lynd differentiated from his solo writing with a blue pencil.[16] The couple then took the study to the trade market. Harcourt, Brace, and Co. publishing house released it as a 534-page book in 1929, marketing *Middletown* as "the latest and most indispensable word in the new American vocabulary." The book, priced at $5, became a bestseller, going through six printings in its first year of publication and earning enthusiastic reviews in newspapers across the country. Libraries and bookstores could not keep copies of the text on their shelves.[17]

No one was more surprised by the book's market success than the co-authors themselves. Both the *New York Times* and *New York Herald Tribune* produced front-page reviews, with *Times* reviewer Stuart Chase declaring, "This book should be inscribed on tablets of stone and preserved for future generations." As Helen Lynd recalled, "Brentano's window was filled with nothing but *Middletown*. Bob's family was in Florida. They went to the hotel where they had lunch and someone said, 'That was such a fine review of your son's book this morning.' Mother Lynd said, 'I couldn't find it. I looked all through.' She'd looked in the section of little reviews, not on the front page."[18]

Becoming Typical America

Middletown is not a fast read, either for scholars or for a general reading public. It is long and almost unwieldy in its collections of statistics, survey data, and complex sentences accompanied by lengthy footnotes. Yet the picture of American life that Robert and Helen Lynd managed to convey through their statistics, anecdotal stories, and personal commentary is captivating in its frank, straightforward narrative. The statistics and the analysis carry a folksy, persuasive tone that enticed Americans. For the first time, Igo notes, Americans who saw themselves as "ordinary" had a study that was not about "degenerates, delinquents, and defectives" or an exotic group of "primitives" from Asia, Africa, or the Pacific but instead a book that was all about them. They took in every word vicariously, seeing *Middletown* and its people as representations of themselves.[19]

Robert and Helen Lynd wrote that with the discovery of natural gas in 1886 "the boom began which was to transform the pastoral county-seat of Muncie into a manufacturing city." In 1890, the population of Muncie was 11,360. By 1920, it had swelled to 36,524. That transformation, Robert and Helen Lynd wrote in *Middletown*, "comprehends for hundreds of American communities the industrial revolution that has descended upon villages and towns, metamorphosing them into a thing of Rotary Clubs, central trade councils, and Chamber of Commerce contests for 'bigger and better' cities." Gone in this metamorphosis was what Americans today might consider markers of a simpler life: family dinners, evening walks, and casual conversations on the front porch. Industrialization "changed living patterns," causing "women to work outside the home" and "harnessing men to machines."[20]

Despite these sweeping changes, the book contained what readers who sought a more "back-to-basics" understanding of life could read as a note of comfort and hope. The American people of Middletown for the most part were not conscious of the structural socioeconomic changes in their societies, according to Robert and Helen Lynd. They remained loyal to their families, were optimistic that life was changing for the better, were dedicated to improving the lives of their children and future generations, firmly believed in Jesus Christ and his divinity, and were devout followers of the Bearcats, the high-school basketball team that had won numerous state championships. While the Lynds themselves meant for this portrayal to be a criticism of Middletown's naiveté, many American readers and media commentators took it as a reflection of the American self, a self that, like any other human, was imperfect but ultimately all right.

Reviewers praised *Middletown* as a book that touched the heart of America and its people as representing the texture of the nation itself. Readers embraced *Middletown* residents' experiences as suggestive of their own. They indulged in such findings "that workers rose earlier in the morning than their employers; that schoolgirls preferred silk to cotton stockings; that the newest homes in town lacked parlors; and that belief in hell was weakening."[21] When the city's High Street Methodist Church rebuilt its facility following a fire, a copy of *Middletown* was placed in the cornerstone. The Chamber of Commerce cited the book as evidence that Muncie was the ideal American city, and the editor of the afternoon newspaper wrote, "If you have not read *Middletown*, you have not taken proper stock of yourself."[22]

Scholars of Middletown argue that it was not the book *Middletown* that made Muncie famous for being typical but rather the popular lore that grew around it. And, indeed, the Lynds themselves disputed the typicality of Muncie by writing that "although it was its characteristic rather than its exceptional features which led to the selection of Middletown, no claim is made that it is a 'typical' city."[23] However, media coverage and the market popularity of the book quickly established Muncie, which media commentators soon revealed to be the true identity of Middletown, as typical America, symbolically and literally. Muncie became a market-research and product-testing site as well as a place for news media to consult residents about their opinions on current events.

"Paul Lazarsfeld said recently that a statistical study had been done to determine the most typical American city, and it turned out to be Muncie, 'Middletown,'" mused Helen Lynd. "We certainly never made any claim that it was a specifically typical city."[24]

What *Middletown* Left Out

In the era of anti-immigrant hostilities and racist violence in which they wrote, the Lynd team filtered out African Americans from their study as statistically insignificant. They chose Muncie as their model for studying America partly because Muncie, unlike much of the rest of the United States, lacked a large foreign-born population. Helen Lynd explains these choices by stating that "Bob didn't want a city with a large foreign population or a racially-mixed city."[25] In

Middletown, itself, Robert and Helen Lynd more formally justify their decisions with this statement:

> In order to secure a certain amount of compactness and homogeneity, the following characteristics were sought:
>
> (1) A city of the 25,000–50,000 group. This meant selection from among a possible 143 cities, according to the 1920 Census. A city of this size, it was felt, would be large enough to have put on long trousers and to take itself seriously, and yet small enough to be studied from many aspects as a unit.
>
> (2) A city as nearly self-contained as is possible in this era of rapid and pervasive inter-communication, not a satellite city.
>
> (3) A small Negro and foreign-born population. In a difficult study of this sort it seemed a distinct advantage to deal with a homogenous, native-born population, even though such a population is unusual in an American industrial city. Thus, instead of being forced to handle two major variables, racial change and cultural change, the field staff was enabled to concentrate upon cultural change. The study thus became one of the interplay of a relatively constant native American stock and its changing environment.[26]

These decisions made Muncie appear a much whiter community than it actually was and established a barometer for understanding the typical American as non-foreign born at a time when most urban communities in the United States had large immigrant populations.[27] The decisions also set forth a widely accepted popular understanding of a typical American as white in a racial sense, European in ethnic nationalist origin, and Christian (largely Protestant) in religious affiliation.[28] These exclusions have drawn heavy criticism since the late 1970s, even as scholars and popular commentators have defended the Lynds' decisions as representative of their time or as being conditioned by the original study that the Rockefeller institute had asked Robert Lynd to conduct. Yet, despite the attention that has been given to these distortions, the image of typical America that *Middletown* crafted and that its popular following perpetuated persists. One might ask why. A possible response is to look again at the climate of racial and anti-immigrant hostility that characterized the United States in the 1920s, when the book made its debut alongside the emergent desire among Americans, whomever they might have been, to know themselves.

During these years, African Americans were systematically denied rights to vote or congregate in whites-only public spaces on the basis of Jim Crow laws. Immigration laws and policies that had been steadily enacted at least partially out of a belief in the inability of Asians to assimilate into a white northern and western European racial stock culminated with the 1924 Johnson-Reed Act. This act and other policies resulted in the nullification of citizenship rights granted to Asian immigrants who had married natural-born or naturalized U.S. citizens; the revoking of rights of nonwhite immigrants to own land in several states; and the establishment of a barred zone restricting new arrivals to the United States to individuals from primarily northern and western Europe. Migration of Latinos across the U.S.-Mexican border that had previously been termed as legal was reclassified as illegal; newcomers from Asia, southern and eastern Europe, and Africa were effectively barred from entry; and efforts were made in several localities to deport individuals from those parts of the world.[29]

Immigrants from the Indian subcontinent, then a part of the British Empire, experienced both legalized discrimination and racial violence. Mobs of white workers attacked Indian immigrants in several small lumber-producing communities in the Pacific Northwest from 1907–10.[30] The state of California enacted an alien land law in 1913 prohibiting nonwhite immigrants who were ineligible for citizenship from buying land or leasing for more than three years. And in 1922 the U.S. Supreme Court declared in the *U.S. v. Bhagat Singh Thind* case that Asian Indians, by virtue of not being white, were ineligible for citizenship.[31] These incidents paralleled racist incidents and policies against Chinese, Japanese, Korean, and Filipino immigrants.[32]

This backdrop offers one way of understanding Robert Lynd's disinterest in a city with immigrants and a racially diverse demographic. For Muncie was, as longtime civic leader Hurley Goodall has pointed out, "a microcosm" of the nation. "Everything that happens here," Goodall has said in reference to Muncie, "is happening all over the country."[33] Although Goodall, born in 1927, was describing Muncie and America in the early-twenty-first century, the comment calls attention to a series of discursive thought patterns that emerged in the social-science disciplines of the early twentieth century, particularly in sociology as it was coming to be defined by scholars working out of University of Chicago under the leadership of Robert Park. These patterns of thought not only mirrored the racist and anti-immigrant hostilities of the American public environment but also created a means by which both the normative white and all others could come to know themselves.[34]

From these patterns of thought emerges a portrait of a nation whose majority white Anglo-Saxon Protestant population felt under attack from those who were other to them. That attack could be repelled in part by governmental policies such as the landholding and voting laws, segregation policies, and anti-immigrant restrictions being enacted at the federal level as well as in many state and local settings to prevent nonwhites in the United States from enjoying the freedoms of expression, movement, and entrepreneurship that whites could take for granted. The attack also could be neutralized through academic practices that used the presumed objectivity of social-science research to establish a way of understanding the American as normatively white, of northern or western European ancestry, and as primarily Christian. Within these frameworks, even if nonwhites and non-Christians were always a part of American life, their histories and experiences could be disregarded as being not the norm. Disregarding African American experiences as irrelevant to American life was simple, based upon this logic.

Choosing Muncie as the site for *Middletown* because it lacked a large foreign-born population also meant the Lynds' study of industrialization excluded a "critical ethnic dimension that was otherwise nearly universal in America," as Richard Jensen has observed.[35] Such a dismissal of that ethnic dimension also could be rationalized within these sociological frameworks. In the 1920s, the fields of sociology and anthropology were beginning in the United States to move away from a fascination with what had been described as the primitive other toward a deepening preoccupation with establishing an understanding of the American self. To know the American self, however, required an understanding of the non-American body as foreign-born and as "exotic and representative of a faraway place," as Henry Yu argues. With federal and local laws restricting the participation of Asians and others of non-European ancestry in American life, sociologists could simultaneously establish parameters of what was "un-American" to create an understanding of the American.[36]

Other streams of intellectual life mirrored the academic discourses. As Igo shows, many writers and visual artists of the 1920s and 1930s sought to articulate an American way of life. *Middletown*'s market popularity allowed for a bridge between the scholarly and the popular to form. What made *Middletown* stand out was its tone: impartial, seemingly unbiased, grounded in statistics.[37] What also fed the interest was the excising of the black and foreign-born body from the conception of the American self. The elimination of race and ethnicity from the equation freed the Lynd team from having to deal with the racial and ethnic tensions that cut across almost every aspect of American society. They were free to create a study in which they could focus on what they described simply as cultural change. In doing so, the meaning of American culture came to be equated with the nation's dominant race. This equation allowed histories of the suppression of indigenous peoples by European conquerors and family genealogies that include racial miscegenation that resulted from interracial marrying as well as such practices of antebellum-era plantation rapes by white masters of female slaves to be pushed to the background of the grand historic narrative of the nation's birth and development. This description of culture also enabled future researchers to associate a sense of American culture with the characteristics of a white majority, and to cast depictions of any other demographic within the nation as aberrant of the norm. Yu asserts that while people of Asian, African, and other non-European ancestries have long been regarded in American social thought as either a racial problem or racial solution, both of those conceptions depend on seeing the nonwhite as other to the American self.[38]

Middletown's success prompted publishers Harcourt & Brace to encourage Robert Lynd to do a follow-up study. Lynd, who was by that point a professor of sociology at Columbia University, returned to Muncie for six months in 1935 and conducted the research for *Middletown in Transition*. The book, also co-authored with Helen Lynd, was published in 1937 and portrayed the impact of the Great Depression on Middletown residents. The Lynds in this book acknowledge that the greatest, most polarizing factor in Middletown was not an economic division between business and working classes as they had proposed in *Middletown* but rather a racial line that divided the city geographically and socially. A city map accompanying the text illustrates the racial line, showing white and Negro communities as distinct and set apart. In a sense, Muncie had two communities, the Lynds reported, separate communities that did not interact.

However, because the research team had so studiously ignored the African American community in 1924–25, Robert Lynd lacked the baseline data—and perhaps the interest—to develop any kind of profile of the African American community and of the race relations in Muncie a decade later.[39] The two studies helped established Robert Lynd as one of the nation's leading sociologists, and at Columbia University he trained some of the next generation of Middletown scholars. This legacy led to a series of subsequent studies in the 1970s through the 1990s whose researchers also used the 1924–25 data as their basis.[40]

Middletown's Others

"I'm a native of Muncie."

It was January 2003, and Hurley Goodall was introducing himself to a group of Ball State University students gathered at the Virginia B. Ball Center for Creative Inquiry. Goodall, an African American and retired member of the Indiana State House Assembly, was seventy-five years old at the time. He had been a Muncie resident his entire life. The students were about to embark on a new study of Muncie, led by anthropologist and former Ball State faculty member Luke Eric Lassiter. The following words, which Goodall penned and read aloud, opened the book that resulted from their project, *The Other Side of Middletown: Exploring Muncie's African American Community*.

"In 1929, Robert S. Lynd and Helen Merrell Lynd [published] . . . what they called an 'objective study' of American society," Lassiter quoted Goodall as saying.

> The method they used was to come and live in that American community, observe the people, the institutions, and forces that made the community work. The effort was also designed to show how communities change over time, but also how certain things did not change. The choice of the Muncie community was determined, in part, by population . . .
>
> And this is the part I'm interested in . . . a homogeneous native born population, a small foreign-born and Negro population that could basically be ignored.
>
> That was the standard the Lynds set. So, in essence, the African American community here . . . was completely ignored by that study. And, hopefully, some of the things you'll be doing will fill that void.[41]

By the 1990s, academic journals were publishing articles documenting Muncie's multiracial profile. These articles along with a collection of oral histories of members of Muncie's Jewish community and a memoir by Gregory Williams on the experience of growing up biracial in Muncie in the 1950s had begun to correct the distorted view that the Lynd studies established. The students' project went further. In a semester-long course, the students took the Middletown texts and, with the help of some of Muncie's African American residents, examined each arena of community life among the town's African Americans that the Lynd team had studied. The portrayal of Muncie they produced was of a city that seemed like two cities, divided on the basis of race, from the 1890s through the early twenty-first century. That division, observes Goodall, was not the choice of the African Americans. It resulted from a legacy of segregation that conveyed a sense that African Americans were not a part of an all-American Muncie.[42] What follows is a history of that community, drawn from the students' work as well as other sources.

The first documented African Americans to settle permanently in Muncie were Edward and Mary Scott, who migrated in 1845 from Virginia and North Carolina, five years after the white Galliher family established their settlement in Muncie. Edward Scott was listed in an 1860 census as being one of five black barbers in the county. An African American church, African Methodist Episcopal Church, was established in Muncie in 1868, and a second church known as Second Baptist was established in 1872. According to other population records, land deeds, letters, and newspaper clippings, individuals of African ancestry began entering Indiana shortly after it was incorporated as a free state. The first African American pioneers came primarily from the South and were either runaway slaves or former slaves who had been granted their freedom. From 1860 to 1867, before a black-exclusion law was enacted by the state, approximately eleven thousand African Americans migrated to Indiana.

By 1880, the African American community was well enough established to draw a visit from orator and civil-rights activist Frederick Douglass, who visited Muncie at the invitation of a black political organization to campaign for President James A. Garfield. A community of slightly fewer than two hundred residents was concentrated in an area south of the central business district, known as Industry. That community more than doubled to 418 residents by 1890. A second community, known as Whiteley, began to form in an area northeast of Muncie after the city began to industrialize. Whiteley was initially built as a factory town and was annexed by the city of Muncie in 1919. By the 1920s, that neighborhood was the most racially integrated part of the city.[43]

As more African Americans migrated to Muncie in the 1940s and 1950s, Whiteley and Industry grew increasingly African American in their demographics. City planners, seeing a way to contain the growing African American community, proposed prohibiting blacks from living or establishing businesses elsewhere in the city. Although community protests successfully shelved the plan, the unofficial divisions remained. As Phyllis Joanne White, a longtime Whiteley resident, recalled, "It was so ironic because the white friends that we were friends with during the day in school, laughing and talking, would come out in Whiteley and drive through calling us all kinds of names. They would come out and call us 'niggers' during the night."[44]

Retrieving Other Histories

Unlike the rich body of scholarly articles, media commentary, and archival resources that surround the *Middletown* studies, much of what is known of Muncie's African American experience comes from what Goodall and other elderly members of the African American community in Muncie themselves can remember or have saved. Goodall, for instance, amassed forty boxes of notebooks, articles, and photographs in his attic before donating them in the early 1980s to Ball State University's Stoeckel Archives. These materials document both his life and that of the African American community in a manner that is fascinating and personable yet incomplete. This calls attention to Michel Foucault's observation of genealogy as a technology of operating over documents scratched over and recopied several times. It suggests that histories like those of the African American communities rest in fragments buried into the silences of a resultant, widely accepted mainstream document. Yet Goodall's collection, like the longstanding practices of passing on knowledge in indigenous American communities via oral storytelling, presents a counter argument by showing that other pasts are perhaps intact. The challenge lies in understanding how to make sense of these histories. On one hand, they help fill gaps by retrieving experiences left out of the dominant narratives of American life like *Middletown*; on the other, they raise different questions about what these documentarians, by their recounting histories that often are personal to them, left out.

From *The Other Side of Middletown*, for instance, we learn that Goodall was born in Muncie on May 23, 1927, two years before *Middletown* was published, one clear indication that amid the white Muncie that the Lynds' text portrayed, African Americans were present. We learn that his father, Hurley Charles Goodall, died when young Hurley was three, leaving his mother, Dorene Mukes Goodall, alone to raise three boys. The youngest of the three sons suffered polio as a small child and died in an automobile crash in 1943, while the eldest dropped out of high school to join the U.S. Navy and died in combat during the Korean War. Goodall, the middle son, graduated from Central High School in 1945. During his junior and senior years there, he also worked a 2 A.M. to 10 A.M. shift at a foundry, Muncie Malleable, before starting classes at 10:30 A.M. After finishing high school, he joined the U.S. Army, and the monthly stipend he sent home made the family self-sufficient for the first time. All these events are just as typical of Muncie life as the stories that *Middletown* contained. What makes them stand out? One factor might be that Goodall chose to use his own lifelong successes to subvert the dominant narratives on Muncie and share his side of his community's story.

Goodall enjoyed a distinguished civil-service career after World War II. He returned to Muncie Malleable to work full time while completing classes at Indiana Business College, Purdue University, and Michigan State University. He became one of two African Americans hired by the Muncie Fire Department in 1958 and was the first African American elected to serve on the Muncie Community Schools Board of Education in 1970. In 1978 he was elected to the Indiana House of Representatives and served as a state assemblyman until 1994. In 1992 he became a visiting scholar with the Center for Middletown Studies, which was established at Ball State University in 1980, and worked in that capacity to compile Federal Writers Project interviews conducted in 1937–38 with African Americans in Muncie whose families had experienced slavery.[45] He continued to communicate with the students who helped write *The Other Side of Middletown* after the study was published.

Goodall has described his life as being about breaking barriers. Studying the documents that Goodall saved and reading such texts as *The Other Side of*

Middletown alongside other works on racial and religious minorities reveal that the barriers in Muncie that Goodall helped break were stiff. His boxes of documents and memories show a racial climate in Muncie of intense hostility not just in the 1920s but also through much of the late twentieth century. Into the 1960s African Americans were barred from most restaurants and theaters. They continued through the 1970s and often into the early twenty-first century to attend separate churches and to form separate clubs and organizations. The social conditions for African Americans until the 1960s mirrored the segregation practices of the South, according to the interview transcripts compiled by Goodall and analyzed by historian Jack Blocker. Yet African Americans saw the conditions as less insufferable in Muncie compared with elsewhere because there was work and because the presence of other African Americans in the city created a network of relative safety. Citing the oral histories, Blocker observes, "They came because a sister had said that good wages were to be had in Muncie or so a father could find work in a marble factory."[46]

African Americans were not the only nonwhites moving to the industrializing small cities of the Midwest at this time. People from the Indian subcontinent, other parts of Asia, and South America also were traveling, often in discreet ways, to such industrializing localities as Youngstown, Ohio; Gary, Indiana; and Detroit and Dearborn, Michigan. Little is known of these early migrants, as they often passed themselves off as black or Mexican to avoid hostilities directed toward people of Asian ancestry and often did not collect the kinds of historical documents that one could use to re-piece their histories. Yet we do know that the lure of decent wages in Midwest factories established a network that allowed for Indian seamen, among others, to find work in the region during the 1920s era of anti-Asian restrictions. While such men often resided in the United States illegally and thus kept themselves in the margins of society, they did find homes and build communities, often in the African American neighborhoods that were segregated from whites. In his book *Bengali Harlem*, Vivek Bald has recounted the lives of several such immigrants. One man, Mustafa "John" Ali, Bald writes, jumped ship in Baltimore in the early to mid-1920s and spent the next decade moving: Baltimore; his native village in Bengal, India; Chester, Pennsylvania; Buffalo, New York; Detroit, Michigan; and Gary, Indiana.[47] Gary is about two hundred miles north of Muncie.

One key challenge of reading Muncie's histories on individuals of nonwhite or non-Christian ancestries is trying to decipher what experiences and viewpoints might have been omitted for reasons of personal safety or legal status. For instance, the Ku Klux Klan controlled Muncie's politics in the 1920s and maintained a strong presence in the city. Yet, published works on Muncie's nonwhite communities suggest that the Klan did not affect Muncie's racial and religious relationships adversely, even as such incidents as cross burnings were reported well into the late 1970s. Elder Jewish residents of Muncie who were interviewed in the mid-1970s have recalled how they would find Klan robes and hoods in the closets of their non-Semitic friends while playing in those friends' homes after school. They also remember being taken by their parents downtown to watch parades where Klan members were among the marchers, and from time to time of reaching out to business associates or personal acquaintances who were Klan members to help them resolve difficulties with police or local laws.[48]

Many longtime African American residents also recalled the Ku Klux Klan in *The Other Side of Middletown*. At the same time, many of them noted that the Klan gave African Americans a reason to build community with each other in order to protect themselves and their families. That sense of solidarity for self-protection may have further separated the African American and white communities. However, in oral histories, African Americans have indicated that while the Klan presence was clearly apparent, the organization itself did not engage in much racist violence in Muncie. "They used to assemble right down here on Broadway," one interviewee recalled. "There was an auditorium there and a rink. They'd use the skating rink and things. And they'd use that to meet there. But, the Klan never did anything around here. Had a parade."[49]

On the surface, these comments suggest that the Klan was a benign presence. However, the very fact that a white-supremacist organization had a presence in Muncie, no matter how benign, brings attention to how Muncie kept its nonwhite population in its place. Using seemingly harmless public events like gatherings at skating rinks or holding parades shows not only that the Klan was present in Muncie but also that the race and religion with which they affiliated were in charge. It reinforces how their presence was normalizing of white Christian dominance. During the years that the Lynd team did its research, members of the Ku Klux Klan were welcomed by the Chamber of Commerce and held seats in Muncie's city council while community organizations, public parks, and churches were segregated by race. Klan members marched through downtown in 1922 and 1924, with the mayor and police chief leading the second of these assemblies.[50]

A careful reading of *Middletown* suggests that the Lynd team too was aware of the Klan's presence. While the index to *Middletown* lists only three references to Negroes, it includes eight to the Ku Klux Klan. Both terms also appear several more times throughout the book. An examination of how the terms are used offers much insight into how the racial politics of Muncie mirrored those of the nation it was said to represent. The mentions of "Negro" are often made as notations that responses from African Americans were excluded from surveys, questionnaires, or other data-gathering methods. Robert and Helen Lynd used footnotes to indicate that Negro churches were not included in chapters on worship and religion, and they noted at the top of a chart tabulating high-school responses to a questionnaire that Negro students' responses were removed before the compilation. The questionnaire asked high-school students to respond with "true," "false," or "do not know" to such statements as "the white race is the best race on earth"; "the United States is unquestionably the best country in the world"; and "the Russian Bolshevist government should be recognized by the United States government."[51]

The references to the Klan, on the other hand, are in the main body of the text, highlighting its normative presence in Middletown's life. Robert and Helen Lynd described the Klan as a formal lodge that residents belonged to as well as a social organization akin to a civic or religious group. They also noted that Middletown was a pro-Klan town, and observed at one point that corruption in politics was due to elected officials' affiliations with the Klan. These references built to a sustained three-page discussion of a Ku Klux Klan rally near the end of the book in which the authors quoted people proclaiming that "Jesus Christ is the leader of the Klan" and that while Klan members "are not against the Negro," "Rome fell because she mixed her blood."[52] Such references reinforce the whiteness of the typical American and the deliberate exclusion of African Americans, non-Christians, and the foreign born.

Both Robert and Helen Lynd were known to be socially progressive individuals, with Robert Lynd sharing a sentiment of other sociologists of his time that racial discrimination was wrong and that a diversity of peoples would make America stronger. Their son, Staughton Lynd, who became known in the 1960s for his anti–Vietnam War activism, has described his father as a former "pick and shovel laborer" who "preached in the school house Sunday nights," and his grandmother on his mother's side as being a schoolteacher who refused to let her students salute the American flag "because, she said, it isn't true that there is justice for all."[53] Yet the casual and multiple ways in which the Klan comes up in *Middletown*'s text suggest that while the organization's primary targets nationally—African Americans, foreign-born residents, and non-Protestant Christians—were not felt to be a part of typical American culture, the Klan's own activities were normalizing some idea of an American way. The effect of that normalization was felt by some of the students who worked on *The Other*

Side of Middletown. Luke Eric Lassiter shares one example in the book's closing pages:

> [The students] eyes were opened several times throughout the semester as the black students told story after story about, on the one hand, their own experiences with the kind of racism they had themselves faced at work, in the community, and in the university; and, on the other hand, how this was similar to and different from the kinds of racism their consultants talked about. This was brought home most powerfully when a white Ball State University faculty member complained to several of the white students that our research was ignoring the "real" black community—the "real" black community, that is, of criminals and drug dealers, who were the same age, the faculty pointedly said, as one of the black students in the class.[54]

That the Middletown studies screened out inhabitants of Muncie deemed to be nonnormative began to draw scholarly criticism only after Robert and Helen Lynd had passed away. By then, the Middletown archive's rendition of what was a typical American had been indelibly inscribed into the popular mindset. From an early age, I recognized that being the child of Indian immigrants made me nontypical of Muncie, even though I also was a child from Muncie. I could represent Muncie at the World Affairs Institute or at the many swim meets and musical competitions in which I took part. When I traveled to other localities on high-school trips or with my family, I could say that I was from Muncie. But I could not be *of* Muncie itself. This incapability to be of Muncie meant little to me as a child because I had no idea of what the lack of such beingness was rooted in. It did, however, trouble me on an emotional level, creating a sense of internalized racism in that I often wondered whether it might be possible to change my name, the color of my hair, or the hue of my skin. That incapability to fit has never left me entirely, and it was one of the emotions that played out decades later as I encountered the religious and cultural xenophobia expressed during my wedding. Even then, I felt incapable of formulating a coherent response.

As a child, I also had come to realize that despite my Indian ancestry, I was an other to the born-and-brought-up-in India Indians who saw me and spoke of me, often quite fondly, as their American relative. My family lived in India for approximately one year when I was ten, and while that year was filled with generosity and love, it also contained a vein of incomprehensibility. I did not speak a language other than English, and I had not grown up with any experience of day-to-day life in India. For those reasons, I could not easily see my family members in India as related to me, and they could not see me as Indian like them. Just where, if anywhere, did I belong?

I carried that question with me for many years after I left Muncie and lived in larger, major metropolitan areas where the numbers of South Asian Americans were greater. Even in these communities, however, the question of where one fit could not be resolved. These communities often were composed of newer immigrants who had arrived in the United States after 1980. As I grew aware of the sometimes-derisive ways in which these newer immigrants looked upon South Asians who were not from India or the other nations of the subcontinent, the question of fit became one I felt compelled to address.

What Indian Community?

In September 2003 I attended a Small Cities Conference sponsored by the Center for Middletown Studies. During lunch, I joined a table of conference attendees, one of whom was among the center's founding members. He knew of my father, and he asked me about my project. I said I was doing a study of the Indian community. He began to laugh and exclaimed, "What Indian community?"

This dismissal of the presence of an Indian community in Muncie highlighted the normativity of whiteness in articulating American culture while also erasing the lack of a differentiation between a majority group and a sole group. That norming, however, was not just a practice of scholars from the Center for Middletown Studies or those representing the more dominant racial group. It also persisted in interdisciplinary fields that emerged in the academy in the 1970s to counter such hegemonic representations. Scholars working within Asian American studies, for instance, have begun to show interest since the start of the twenty-first century in experiences of Asian Americans who had earlier migrated to and built lives in communities outside of New York, California, and Hawai'i.[55] For many such scholars, the discovery of such communities came only when they themselves moved outside of California and began to meet Asian Pacific Americans who had lived in the Midwest, Deep South, and other regions in the United States' "middle" for decades.[56] The presumption that there were no such groups in areas like east-central Indiana had bothered me before I returned to Muncie. I presented my project proposal at a number of academic venues for about a year before going to Muncie, including at talks in my university's department and a scholarly conference. One concern that questioners consistently brought up was the small size of the South Asian population in Muncie as well as the small size of the city itself. Muncie, despite being perceived as a large locality by residents of the farming communities surrounding it, was far from the cosmopolitan metropolises that had been drawing many of the post-1965 immigrant arrivals. It was often suggested that I either expand my study to consider all nonwhites and/or immigrants to Muncie or move my site to a location where a larger South Asian community existed.

These concerns resurfaced when I arrived in Muncie. During my first few weeks, I spent time driving around the city and hanging out at the mall and in coffee shops, hoping to watch and get comfortable with the city that was home to the people I wished to interview. My excursions were random and, as I started later to realize, influenced by how I, too, had perceived Muncie geographically. Those perceptions were informed by how I had traversed the city as a teenager in the late 1970s, at a time when popular conceptions of the city were influenced in part by Muncie's presence in the Steven Spielberg film *Close Encounters of the Third Kind*. Just as the film conveyed an impression of Muncie as small-town and predominantly white, the Muncie of 1978–80 was like the Muncie of 1929. It was racially segregated, with the African American residents living primarily on the city's south and east sides. Those were areas that those who, like me, had grown up on the predominantly white north and west sides had little reason to go to. Because my trips home after high school had involved family visits, I generally had not deviated from those paths. I usually stayed at my parents' house and in their immediate neighborhood. When I went out, it was usually to go with them to restaurants, grocery stores, and shopping areas of their choice. I rarely explored Muncie by myself.

That changed when I returned in 2003 to do my research. As a resident, albeit a temporary one, I sought to find places where I could run for exercise, coffeehouses where I could write, and stores where I could buy personal items that were more to my tastes than my parents'. I wanted also to get a feel for the town, to see how it had changed, if places like the elementary-school playground where I had been spat on still could provoke revulsion in me. Exploring Muncie alone produced many pleasant experiences, such as the discovery that the maple saplings my parents had planted in the yard of their first home had grown into trees more than thirty feet high and that the family who lived in that house had a child whose kindergarten teacher some thirty-five years later was the same one that I had had. Yet the explorations also were frustrating because I often ended up getting lost. Over time, I realized that landmarks from my childhood that no longer existed or new signs on a building were showing me that the city, in two decades, had not quite remained the same. Having to stop at gas stations or convenience stores to ask for directions also showed me that the inhabitants of Muncie had changed.

Many people with whom I struck up conversations had moved into the city after I had left. Some people I met knew of my parents and their hobby shop; others remembered my younger sisters, who had attended Ball State and Indiana Universities and had been married in the town. But how many people of Indian ancestry lived in Muncie? One, maybe two? Few gave it much thought.

Questions about the small size of the community mounted as I began to share my project with old childhood friends, some of the South Asian residents I hoped to interview, and others. Some people, like my father's former Ball State faculty colleague, questioned the existence of a South Asian community. Others wondered what Muncie's demographic difference from the larger, more cosmopolitan U.S. cities that had drawn huge numbers of South Asian immigrants in the late twentieth and early twenty-first centuries would reveal about South Asian Americans. Still others confused Indiana with India, thinking that I was not actually in Indiana to do the study but en route to India, a seemingly natural place for a researcher of Indian ancestry to have grown up.

"Indians in Muncie?" an old school friend responded. "Where? Who? Isn't it just your family?"

"I think you're talking about a sub-community," another friend offered, in an effort perhaps to be helpful. "There's not really a community here from what I can tell."

Similar questions came from individuals of South Asian ancestry whom I approached to ask if they would agree to be interviewed. Most agreed to share their stories. Yet they too were puzzled as to why I would choose Muncie as a site for my study. "What can we tell you that you don't already know?" asked many potential interviewees. One response from a longtime family friend was particularly illuminative. She said, in an ironic resonance with the *Middletown* authors' defense for filtering out the African American residents as statistically insignificant: "Oh good, I get to be a statistic."

Over time, I came to realize that these comments and my anxious reactions to them before and during the project were quite meaningful. They reinforced the image of Muncie as typically American, making it quite difficult to see it in a way that was other to how it had been historically portrayed. Like the confusion between Indiana and India and the questions of whether a study of South Asians in Muncie would be representative of South Asian America, the surprised responses to my statement that I was studying the Indian community in Muncie hinted of a resistance to understanding America's past and present as multivocal, polycultural, and sociopolitically heterogenous. It was easier to think of America as the Middletown studies portrayed it: racially and culturally homogenous with subculturally defined groups of people small enough to ignore.

Trails of Descent

"Muncie, Ind. is the great U.S. 'Middletown' and this is the first picture essay of what it looks like." These words open an eleven-page spread of photos taken of

Muncie by the American photographer Margaret Bourke-White and published by *Life* magazine on May 10, 1937.

Life editors introduced the photo essay with these words: "Muncie, Ind. is the most interesting small town in the U.S. For 12 years, it has been surveyed, studied and talked about more than any other city its size in the world. Sociologists use it as a specimen, advertisers as a test tube." The essay praised Robert and Helen Lynd for bringing the world's attention to Muncie and attributed the importance of *Middletown* as follows: "*Middletown* made Americans gasp with wonder, recognition and surprise. For the first time they saw clearly how U.S. citizens live, work, play, think and talk." The editors went on to describe how they sent Bourke-White to Muncie and how she returned with a "yard-high stack of pictures."[57]

Bourke-White's photo essay has been credited for Muncie's association with typical America among a mass audience. *Life* editors wanted to accomplish just that. In explaining why the magazine chose to devote so much of its editorial space to photos of Muncie, the editors stated: "LIFE here presents 11 pages of [Bourke-White's photographs] in the belief that they are an important American document. . . . Here, set down for all time, you may look at the average 1937 American as he really is."[58]

If the popularity of *Middletown* established Muncie's role as a representation of what was typical of America, the *Life* photographs deepened the imprint for the decades to come. The *Life* editors' description of Bourke-White's photo essay of Muncie as an important American document reinforces that view. The images show Muncie streets and Muncie houses; people at home, work, and in leisure activities; members of the elite Ball family and the poorest of the poor. The images do not show African Americans or other individuals of color.

Well into the twenty-first century, Muncie has continued to be known for its typicality. As Bruce Geelhoed has put it, the small city continues to "typify American beliefs, customs, and traditions," with divorce rates, robbery rates, the numbers of books checked out of libraries, costs of living, per-capita income, and presidential voting patterns mirroring national norms.[59] Even as Robert and Helen Lynd themselves discounted the power that *Middletown* had had on shaping America's understanding of itself, the immense popularity of the book spoke to the allure that "knowing ourselves" can present. Igo writes: "[By] acting as anthropologists of contemporary culture, the Lynds—in a particularly authoritative way, and at a critical juncture in national life—had created a new social scientific object: 'average America.'"[60] That object is what we are left with.

CHAPTER 2

Marring Typicality

South Asian Immigrants in Muncie

Across the border in Mexico
stark silhouette of houses gutted by waves,
cliffs crumbling into the sea,
silver waves marbled with spume
gashing a hole under the border fence. . . .

I walk through the hole in the fence
to the other side.

—Gloria Anzaldúa, *Borderlands/La Frontera:*
The New Mestiza, 1999

August 23, 1966
Muncie, Indiana

Shortly after midnight, a blue Plymouth Valiant sedan, obviously used, pulled into the parking lot of a motel. The driver was a young Indian man dressed in casual slacks and a button-down shirt. With him was a petite woman, five months pregnant, wearing a sari and carrying an infant in her lap. A young girl was in the back seat, asleep.

The man turned off the engine and, in a soft murmur, said a few words in Hindi to the woman. She reached into the glove compartment and handed him a tie. He opened the door and stepped out into the thick, humid air. He looked up at the stars studding the summer sky for a moment and then looked all around him, imagining the green-gold cornfields rolling for miles around the American university and the small town, closing his eyes perhaps to the strangeness of his brown skin and black hair against this landscape in the Heartland. With vigor, he knotted the tie around his shirt collar and entered the motel to arrange for a room where he and his family could spend the night.

The woman sat quietly in the passenger seat of the Valiant, waiting for her husband to return. The drive from Cleveland to Muncie had tired her, but, feeling the responsibility of caring for both her husband and her children, she had done her best not to let her fatigue show. Now, she wanted to stretch her stiff body and lie down. Just a few more minutes, she told herself. Just a little while longer.

A rustle from the back seat prodded her alert. The girl had awakened.

"Where are we, mommy?" she asked.

"Beta, we're in Muncie," the woman responded.

"What's Muncie?" the child persisted.

"Muncie," her mother said, "is where we've come to stay now."

"Home?" the daughter asked.

Her mother hesitated for a few seconds. And then she replied, with a slight tentative tone in her voice, "Yes, home."

· · ·

This couple was my parents. I was the girl in the back seat. My parents, Naim and Shailla Gupta, were part of a group of a few thousand young South Asians who, beginning with the end of the British Empire in India in 1947 and the breakup of the subcontinent into newly independent nations, chose to leave their villages and cities for opportunities abroad. Those who came to the United States usually found themselves in the cosmopolitan coastal cities of New York, San Francisco, and Los Angeles or in other large metropolitan areas such as Chicago, Atlanta, and Dallas. For a handful, the paths from the subcontinent crossed the cornfield-studded lands of America's Midwest and ended in small cities like Muncie.

My parents and the other South Asian immigrants who came to Muncie in the first few years after the 1965 Immigration Act was signed were similar to others who entered the United States between 1946 and 1969, the year the 1965 law officially took effect. They were young and well educated. They were deeply patriotic and proud of their home countries, which just two decades earlier had won independence from a century of British rule. As children of a newly independent India, they were enticed by what America was offering: education that would allow them to develop stronger skills, and jobs that would provide them the kind of professional advancement that the proud but economically poor home nations of their birth could not. Unlike the generations of Indian agricultural workers, seamen, and traders who had entered the United States before 1920, the post-1965 émigrés tended to be professionals who fit a stereo-typed depiction of Asian Americans as "model minorities." Even in the cases where these immigrants were cash poor because of the U.S. government's stringent limits on how much money the newcomers could bring into the country, they represented an antithesis to the impoverished African American communities as well as the historical perceptions of untrustworthy Asian immigrants that much of America's national discourse had reviled. From the perspective of those in their home countries, these émigrés often were seen as daring and sophisticated for risking life and livelihood to pursue opportunities abroad.[1]

The South Asians who arrived in Muncie between 1966 and 1975 came primarily to work at Ball State University, which was built on the northwest side of the city at the turn of the twentieth century and established as a teacher-education college in 1930. Enrollment and curricula expanded dramatically after World War II, and the college became a research university in 1965. Before the 1960s, Ball State had attracted as students young men and women of agricultural backgrounds. The college had preferred to hire faculty members who also had been brought up in Indiana, believing that outsiders would not fit its culture. The surge in enrollment and transition to university status, however, created such a demand for faculty that the university began recruiting nationally and abroad.[2]

• • •

My parents had driven to Muncie from Cleveland, Ohio, where my father, by virtue of what my mother described as "the luck of the Irish," had acquired a green card allowing for permanent residency in the United States by walking into a government office with his University of Iowa diploma. He had completed his doctorate in educational psychology a year earlier, four years after he and my mother traveled by train from New Delhi to Bombay, where they boarded a ship bound for London and then a plane for the United States.

As my parents left India, their necks covered with garlands that their parents and brothers and sisters had draped over them, my father promised his mother two things: that he would never eat meat and that he would never become a Christian. My mother promised her parents, six sisters, and three brothers that she and her husband would come home soon. Nearly everyone thought my parents' journey to America would be temporary. Although my parents' families were accustomed to seeing adult brethren leave home, no one in either of the families had left India, as far as anyone could remember. Someday, everyone was sure, Naim and Shailla would come home for good.

By the time my parents arrived in Muncie, they had been away from India for five years. I was born in Iowa City in 1962. My sister was born in early 1966 in Cleveland, where my father had taken a postdoctoral appointment. Soon after, my mother became pregnant again. A tenure-track position as a university professor awaited my father in Muncie. Within a year of their arrival, I was enrolled in a preschool at a Presbyterian church near the university and my parents had made a down payment on their first home, a ranch-style house in Halteman Village, a subdivision built by the city's prominent Ball family on the northwest side of town. Halteman Village, located adjacent to the university and isolated from the lower-income African American and working-class white neighborhoods on the south and east sides of the city, had become a neighborhood of choice for the new university faculty and professionals migrating to Muncie, despite a cross burning that had occurred in the neighborhood when the first African American family purchased a house in the community in 1965.[3]

Over the next five decades, my parents became a sort of first family in Muncie. My father was the first Asian Indian professor at Ball State University to receive tenure as well as, in subsequent years, a promotion to full professor. My socially active mother was a member of a university-wives club, my elementary school's parent-teacher association, and the Unitarian Universalist Church of Muncie. She also was a Brownie Scout troop leader and later the owner/operator of a hobby-and-craft shop that had existed in Muncie since the 1940s under the name of McKnight's until she and my father changed it to the Gupta Hobby & Craft Center. She was a source of delightful craft projects and gifts to many of Muncie's children as well as a shoulder to cry on for numerous young South Asian women who in the ensuing years would arrive in Muncie as she did—as wives accompanying their husbands, wherever their jobs might take them, across the globe, all looking for ways to feel at home.

My parents built lives in Muncie that extended more than five decades. Their children completed high school, earned undergraduate and graduate degrees, and married. My father retired from the university in 1993 and helped run the shop until my parents closed the business in 2004. America had become home by this point to their three children, two grandchildren, and numerous nieces, nephews, grandnieces, and grandnephews born in this country after relatives my parents sponsored joined our family in the United States. When the twin towers of the World Trade Center collapsed on September 11, 2001, my mother was on the telephone collecting reports on the safety of our family members who were living all over the United States.

In spite of the normalcy of their actions, my parents stood out in Muncie as different. The saris my mother wore and the bindi she applied as a makeup dot to her forehead drew stares from Muncie residents and comments about her choice of style, marking her as someone who seemed to belong to a world other than theirs. My father's dark skin and unmistakably foreign accent led the university that eventually would employ him for twenty-six years to tell him shortly after his appointment to the faculty that, as a non-U.S. citizen, he could not apply for tenure. He challenged the assertion and won. His experience illustrates how traces of the veiled racism that had long characterized American life would surface in wrongful treatment of the South Asian immigrants nationally who until the mid 1970s had little awareness of the legal recourses available to them.[4] Yet nobody outside of a few departmental colleagues knew of this victory. My father kept the story to himself until one night, while visiting my parents in 1996, I expressed anger over what it had felt like to grow up brown and foreign-looking in a community as white as Muncie. My father shared the story of his struggle with tenure as a way of letting me know he understood what it was like.

As my parents began building a life in Muncie, other immigrants of South Asian origin joined them. Tilak, who came from what today is known as the southern Indian state of Karnataka, accepted a position in the mathematics department at Ball State after completing a Fulbright scholarship at the University of Minnesota. He arrived in Muncie in 1967, and his wife, Subhadhra, and his two young daughters joined him a year later. The family lived briefly in Buffalo, New York, before returning to Muncie in 1971 to live permanently. Mushtaq, from what is now Bangladesh but was then East Pakistan, arrived in 1969 with his wife, Haina, their three daughters, and an infant son. Mo, a professor of mathematics from the north Indian state of Himachel Pradesh, and his wife, Dula, came in 1971; the couple by 2003 had raised three sons to adulthood in Muncie. Deepak, a doctor of Marathi descent growing up in the southern Indian princely state of Hyderabad, settled with his wife, Roshini, in 1972 in nearby Marion, the site of a 1930 lynching of two African American males by a mob led by the Ku Klux Klan. Their daughter and two sons all grew up in Marion before the family moved to Indianapolis. Kamal, a professor of accounting, relocated to Muncie in 1973 with his wife, Sushma, from Oxford, Ohio, where he had taught after migrating from the southern city of Bangalore. Their daughter was born and grew up in Muncie.

The cornfields that lay behind my parent's house in 1967 were dug up, and in 1970 a new complex, Scheidler Apartments, was built to accommodate a growing number of married Ball State University students. Many of its inhabitants were international students, including some South Asians. By 2000, the South Asian community that these scattered families from the South Asian diaspora of the 1960s and 1970s brought into being in Muncie had grown to include seventy-nine residents identified by the U.S. Census as Asian Indian. By 2010, that figure had doubled to 159, as the Asian Indian population became the second-largest Asian-defined demographic in the United States.

The South Asian community of Muncie has remained small by big-city standards. Well into the twenty-first century, little in the physical structure of Muncie existed to mark the presence of such a community: no temple or other house of worship, no community center, no Indian restaurant, no fixed gathering place. Only temporary spaces and fleeting images could offer indications that a community existed: a room borrowed for an evening at the Unitarian Universalist Church for a South Asians of Muncie Association meeting; a lecture hall reserved at Ball State University for a guest speaker from Hyderabad or a dance performance for a troupe from Rajasthan; lights on the homes and sandbags in the driveways of Indians' homes on the night of the Indian Diwali festival; the glimpse of a doctor's face that looked South Asian in the emergency room at Ball Memorial Hospital; the once-monthly presence of ladies in saris serving sandwiches with a food bank in Muncie; occasional gatherings of families at Thai Smile, one of Muncie's few vegetarian-friendly restaurants that served spicy food.

I was among the children of this community in Muncie. As part of the first generation of South Asians to grow up in this town that had come to be defined as typical America, we learned in a rudimentary way to cook Indian dishes as well as to bake 4-H butter cakes; to speak a little bit of Hindi, Bengali, Punjabi, or Kannada as well as to order a meal at a restaurant in Indianapolis in French; and to practice the religious rituals that our parents taught us to associate with our "mother lands" even as the ringing of church bells each Sunday morning reminded us of the community of which we were not entirely a part. We were a part of an all-American society as schoolchildren and, later as teenagers and young adults, as civic participants in community orchestras, piano recitals, swim meetings, service projects, and similar events. But our nonnormative skin tones, hair colors, and ways of understanding and practicing religion kept us apart from the dominant culture. In the Muncie that *Middletown* and its legacy portrayed, little room existed to fully embrace, let alone acknowledge the demographic differences that the 1965 Immigration Act helped create.

Mushtaq affectionately refers to my father as being the "Christopher Columbus" for the Indians and other South Asians in Muncie, and to himself as being among the pioneers who followed. His words inadvertently erase—like the Middletown studies did—the displacement of tribal peoples by European colonial settlers and the importation of African slaves that enabled the construction of a white America. At the same time, his words describe himself as a not-fully-welcomed member of the present-day white America he migrated to. Like my parents and many of the other South Asian émigrés in Muncie, Mushtaq attained a high level of respect for his intellect and scholarly achievements and received a prestigious award for contributing to Indiana's cultural heritage. But he never felt himself quite fitting the role of true Munsonian. Nor did many of these immigrants' children, most of whom grew to adulthood in Middle America before journeying away, as their parents did from India and other countries earlier, to pursue jobs and start families of their own.

This chapter looks at the lives of these South Asians. I look first at how the concept of a simple but highly charged word—home—has come to be a part of how these immigrants view their place in Muncie and the United States and their relationships with their home countries as contingent and lacking permanence. The instability of a sense of home that these immigrants articulate interacts with understandings of Americanness that have upheld the white Christian body as a prevailing norm. Against this norm, I delve more deeply into the stories of three elder immigrant couples who were among the first to settle in Muncie permanently. I suggest that individuals like these South Asian Americans in Muncie built lives and formed communities that were like the African American community in one critical sense: small and vibrant within themselves, virtually invisible to those outside them. Unlike African Americans, most of the South Asian Americans, however, had the economic and educational privileges of being able to build homes in Muncie without the outwardly hostile sense of racial animosity that events like the cross burning in the neighborhood where my parents chose to live illustrate. Yet as the initial claim that my father could not attain tenure shows, these groups were not immune to the effects of that racism, even as racism was a topic that the individuals I interviewed rarely brought up. This sense of racism might be detected in the ambivalent ways in which my interviewees spoke of home.

No Home

"Where is home?" I asked a dozen people gathered in my parents' living room. "What does home mean for you?" Most of those gathered were South Asian émigrés in their late twenties through early forties. They had come to Muncie in the 1990s and early 2000s, long after our family arrived. Demographically, they represented a different group of immigrants from the university professors, research scientists, and mathematicians who had come to Muncie to take jobs at Ball State University in the 1960s. This younger group included computer scientists, information technologists, medical doctors, and software engineers. While some were employed by Ball State, many more were affiliated with the adjacent Ball Memorial Hospital, health-services companies, or information-technology firms that in the early twenty-first century relied on skilled immigrant labor.

I had invited the participants to join a group discussion to help me understand general attitudes among Muncie South Asians toward citizenship and national identity and to learn how they articulated their place in Muncie as South Asians. My hope was that the manner in which the participants conversed with and responded to each other would illuminate these points. Later, however, I realized that my questions had provoked dialogues less on Muncie and America and more on how the participants had come to perceive the idea of home abstractly as something that would be forever out of reach to them. In this sense, the dialogue evoked a sense of how ideas of home and homeland have consistently underscored the daily lives of South Asians in diaspora.[5]

"I cannot say what home means," responded one participant, a twenty-nine-year-old woman who had grown up in New Delhi and had married a young Indian émigré who had taken a research-and-development position with a corporation based in Muncie. She was quite lonely in Muncie until my father happened to see her at the local Staples store. Perhaps remembering how he, too, had felt alienated and alone in Muncie, he had greeted her by speaking Hindi. "I have never been to my home, unless you mean my home to be the place from where I came. My home is now in Pakistan. Obviously, I cannot go there."

"Why not?" I asked.

I knew one possible answer to this question. Many Hindu and Sikh Indians whose families had lived in what is present-day Pakistan before the British colonial administration had carved the country off from what England ruled as India to create a Muslim-majority state did see Pakistan implicitly as off limits. The 1947 Partition that occurred at the end of the British Empire in India had resulted in the establishment of two separate nations—India and Pakistan. This geopolitical change resulted in a dislocation of some 14 million individuals and an estimated 1.5 million deaths. Memories of the horrific violence have continued to inform the attitudes of many India-born individuals toward Pakistan, as this individual's comments illustrated, in the sense of never being able to cross the boundary to an ancestral home.

She took a while to answer my question. In the meantime, the buzz of conversation in the room began to rise. I jumped in.

"What are you saying?" I asked one of the other participants, a twenty-seven-year-old who had grown up in Mumbai.

He hesitated, as if he realized that he was treading on what might be a delicate issue. Then he said, "Well, why would anyone want to go to a home in Pakistan anyway? Why should anyone who is Indian do Pakistan a favor by making a visit?"

A few others laughed, a little nervously.

"So, what is home about?" I pressed. "Why shouldn't she go, if she wants to go? She can get a visa. Pakistan isn't bad. In fact, it is very nice. I've been there. I went there in 1996. The people are friendly, the food is incredible, and if you have a personal tie, it can be even more special just to see where your family once lived, the . . . history, that transpired."

Others in the room began murmuring. Our conversation shifted away from home and more into the "difficulties" that a Hindu might face in a Muslim-dominant country.

I persisted. "What is home? What does home mean for you?"

"I think you set us up with a trick question," interjected another participant, an information systems specialist from Chennai. "There is no way that we, as immigrants, can ever define home."

As I listened and re-listened to the dialogue on tape and went through a set of writing exercises that I had asked the participants to complete, I found myself wondering if my question indeed had been a trick question. Most of the South Asians I had met in Muncie were hard working, friendly, and prosperous. Their lives revolved around their houses, families, jobs, and friends in Muncie—many of whom, if not all, were South Asian also. They socialized at each others' houses and spoke via email or telephone, often on a daily basis. They characterized themselves as satisfied and content, and rarely seemed to dwell on unpleasant things.

Nevertheless, some element seemed to be missing. Did Muncie feel like home to them? My experience of growing up in Muncie had left me with a sense that it could not feel like home because I could not feel American in some normative sense of what an American was defined to be. I wondered how, if at all, my experience might be reflected among this group of immigrants. Was it important to feel at home? Was that feeling a precondition for complete happiness to fill the self, for friendships to form, for communities to thrive? The dialogue that emerged from my persistent questioning seemed to point ultimately to how a lack of home had become a facet of the participants' senses of beingness. In doing so, the dialogue resonated with many historic and sociopolitical factors that have shaped contemporary migrant experiences and helped illuminate how the contemporary evolution of a global South Asian diaspora has touched both Muncie and the lives of the city's South Asian residents.[6]

Living All Over the World

The era of global migration that came in the wake of World War II and the beginning of decolonization movements throughout Asia, much of Africa, and the Pacific led to one of the most dramatic transformations in the world. Many scholars have characterized this transformation as resulting in massive movements of people and highly visible shifts in the diversity of local communities. Erika Lee, for instance, writes: "Contemporary immigrants come as part of new global patterns in which people are moving around the world, sometimes to multiple places over the course of their lifetimes, in search of better lives for themselves and for their families." These moves, as Lee notes, might start off as temporary but over time become permanent. They also can become circular, with immigrants moving between home and host countries. All of these patterns force immigrants to learn "how to situate themselves in a changing world."[7]

The concept of home, as discussed by these South Asians, offers a sense of how the broad economic, cultural, political, and social effects of these changes have touched their individual lives. The concepts show how émigrés of highly diverse ethnic, linguistic, regional, and religious backgrounds come to identify themselves in nationalistic terms as a result of migrating from one nation to the next. It also speaks to the logic of race in organizing diverse peoples on the basis of homogenized ethnic and national categories, particularly in terms of persons of color. At the same time, the sense of home as inaccessible speaks to how a sense of being "homeless" in a white-dominant United States brings these immigrants into closer contact with one another, creating a sense of solidarity among themselves, at least. These feelings come despite—or because of—the economic security that these migrants' class and educational statuses both before leaving their home countries and after settling in the United States have given them the luxury to enjoy. In a sense, the articulation of home affects how these South Asians place themselves in Muncie and the world and how they interact with one another.

How does a sense of belonging form among a group of people who regard themselves as having no place to call home? Johanna Lessinger compares her experience of doing research in India first in 1971 and again in 1991: "In the India of 1971 only a handful of middle-class people or entrepreneurs had been abroad to work or study." Twenty years later, Lessinger notes, the city of Madras (renamed Chennai) had evolved into a cosmopolitan center "full of high tech and export industries." "Accompanying these changes was a vastly increased level of overseas migration. Virtually every middle-class family, and many working-class families as well, had relatives and friends who had lived abroad for extended periods or who had left India for good."[8] Both the ideas that a home is lost to an Indian if the geographic locale lies in present-day Pakistan and the sense that immigrants who leave their home countries lose their homes forever can be understood as part and parcel of a society of peoples whose lives are characterized by such mobility.

Lessinger's findings mirror the comments of many newcomers to the United States from India, Pakistan, and Bangladesh whom I have met over the years. Early in my life, in the late 1960s and early 1970s, these newcomers seemed unfamiliar and at odds with the cultural way of life they encountered in the United States. By the early twenty-first century, they could more quickly adapt to a newer way of life and, depending on such factors as their age, often seemed more familiar and in tune with the popular culture of the United States than I did. When I would speak with such individuals, I would learn that most had gained some familiarity about the United States from a much more globalized mass media as well as through information provided by family members or friends living abroad. These factors underscore the size of South Asian diaspora—about 40 million people by the second decade of the twenty-first century. In this sce-nario, it is difficult to be a person of South Asian ancestry and not have at least one connection to a family member or close friend residing in a country differ-ent from both their current place of residence and the one in which they were born.[9] Many South Asians report in the twenty-first century that they spend much of their life planning as young adults for a possible relocation abroad.

Increases in immigration to the United States reflect an aspect of this plan-ning. Despite these increases, South Asian American communities have been slow to form as distinct enclaves in all but the largest metropolitan areas. Geog-raphers Surinder Bhardwaj and N. Madhusudana Rao found that the post-1965 wave of Indian immigration had produced the most geographically dispersed ethnic group in the United States, with more than half of the forty-eight con-tiguous states housing significant Indian populations as of 1980.[10] This dis-persed pattern of settlement has continued into the early twenty-first century. While Indians constituted the third-largest immigrant community in the United States, only nine metropolitan areas housed communities with more than fifty thousand people as of 2013. Indians lived throughout the nation in all but a half-dozen states.[11]

This dispersal has set South Asian Americans somewhat apart from other Asian American and European American communities in the United States. Although the primary magnet for South Asian immigrants has been cities, as is the case for the other immigrant groups, the historically distinct ethnic enclaves that characterized most other immigrant groups have not existed until recently for Indians, Pakistanis, Bangladeshis, and others from the Indian subcontinent, with exception of such areas as Devon Avenue in Chicago and Jackson Heights in Flushing, New York. Anti-Asian immigrant restrictions in the 1920s through 1940s forced earlier twentieth-century immigrants from the Punjab region who had settled on the West Coast either to return to their home countries or to integrate themselves into Mexican American and other marginalized communities of color. While the story of an immigrant from India or another Asian country arriving in such small communities as Muncie wasn't unheard of, it was not widely documented because such arrivals tended to occur in a more haphazard and accidental manner, with one new family arriving every two or three years, rather than several all at once.[12]

The relative isolation of South Asian individuals in the United States also might be seen as characteristic of the South Asian diaspora, a word that traces its derivation to Greek words suggesting scattering or dispersal. Prior to the mid-twentieth century, the term was used primarily to speak of Jews and the banishments and persecutions that those of Jewish affiliation experienced in one part of the world after another. Jews were regarded as a people without a permanent home, a land they could call their own. With the post–World War II acceleration of global migration among more varied groups of people, diaspora came into wide use as a way of referring to social groupings of peoples who were not so much outsiders to the nations they left as what Jigna Desai has referred to as "insiders removed," allowing peoples without any one firm affiliation to a place to create a sense of ownership to a settled space through the establishment of common community structures and through consumption of such popular cultural products as Bollywood films.[13] In this sense, South Asians in Muncie—like South Asians elsewhere in the United States—could find the contentment described earlier without a need to claim the space as home in a permanent sense.

Immigrants to the United States historically created homelike community spaces through the formation of such neighborhoods as a city's Chinatown or Little Italy. In areas that are larger and more metropolitan than Muncie, South Asian Americans have followed this practice with the establishment of grocery stores, clothing and jewelry shops, travel agencies, restaurants, temples, and community centers. These institutions, often regarded as vital to the sustenance of a diaspora community, have not been a part of Muncie even into the second decade of the twenty-first century.[14] Yet a community of South Asians did form in Muncie and has grown in size and resilience from the mid-1960s. What enabled that community to form? How did the immigrants find each other and come together? The experiences of Muncie's elder South Asians in the sections that follow offer a few examples of how such immigrant communities might come together.

Being Indian Abroad

It is Thanksgiving Day in 2003. My parents and I have just finished dinner. My mother has prepared her traditional Thanksgiving meal, a vegetarian feast with many all-American favorites: green beans, sweet potatoes, a cranberry relish. On the table also are Indian foods: *karhi*, a hearty soup made thick with chickpea flour and yogurt; and *pulao*, a rice dish with vegetables and nuts. Complementing all these dishes are "cheesy onion rolls," my mother's classic: brown-and-serve rolls filled with a mixture of sautéed onions, grated cheddar cheese, and crushed red peppers, and baked until the rolls are brown and the cheese sizzling. My mother created them when I was a teenager, partly to appease my demands for a Thanksgiving meal that was more "American." I make them in my home every year, as do my sisters. Thanksgiving would not be the same without them.

My father came to the United States by what he describes as "a matter of circumstance." Born in 1932, he grew up in a small village located off a dirt road west of Gurgaon, India, that winds toward the main artery connecting New Delhi to Jaipur. Gurgaon has grown into an industrial center and prosperous suburb of New Delhi. In my father's childhood in British India, however, the village was quite far removed from city life. Men and women would perform morning ablutions in designated fields and would bathe in a nearby river. Children attended a local school until eighth grade and then, if they were boys, joined their family's primary economic occupation.

My father went to a high school in a neighboring village because his best friend was doing so and because his elder brother urged him to continue his studies in the hope that work outside the village would help support the family. When his best friend began signing his last name as "Gupta" instead of "Aggarwal," my father, who also had gone by Aggarwal, adopted Gupta. His grades were quite good, and one of his teachers recommended he go to college. He finished college in the early years of India's independence and began teaching in a small city known as Bhiwani. He was presented with numerous marriage proposals, beginning in his early twenties, and in 1959, at age twenty-six, he married Shailla, a college-educated young woman from New Delhi, as the result of an arrangement initiated by a friend of both their families. He continued to teach in Bhiwani until one day a friend told him of an opportunity to study in America.

My mother, born in 1936, grew up in the middle-class urban society that served the British colonial apparatus. Her father was a bureaucrat within the British administration; she was born in the hill resort of Simla, where the British authority would relocate their administration during New Delhi's hot summers. From the British influence that surrounded her childhood, my mother grew up with a fondness for English literature and a yearning to travel to the places in Europe described in books she read. While her elder brother and male cousins in her joint family household joined the anticolonial movement and engaged in acts of civil disobedience, she read novels by Jane Austen and the Brontë sisters and dreamed of seeing London, Paris, and Rome. She also embraced the values of a self-sufficient India that Mahatma Gandhi's campaigns for independence espoused. For years, she displayed photographs of Gandhi and of independent India's first prime minister, Jawaharlal Nehru, on our living-room walls.

Shailla refers to Naim as "a self-made man." My father, however, insists that what occurred in his life was not crafted by him. "I am a product of circumstances," he insists. "I had no real goals or aspirations. I only accepted what life offered to me."

They did not expect their emigration from India to be permanent.

"I wanted adventure," my mother says. "I wanted to see the world. My brother would laugh at me. He thought I was a dreamer, and that being a dreamer would never bring me anything but pain. Then I met your father and we were married. I had to go and live all by myself, not even with a mother-in-law, because he was teaching in Bhiwani, and I had to learn how to do everything myself. I was very young and very inexperienced. And then he started to talk about wanting to further his studies by going to America."

We talked about their early years in the United States as our Thanksgiving dinner digested. Next to the electric fireplace where my father was sitting was a magazine rack. On top was the latest edition of *India Abroad*. The newspaper began circulating in New York City in 1970 as "a handful of smudgy black and white pages" aimed at "linking Indians settled in the US and Canada with a thoughtful roundup of news from home."[15] That newspaper made its debut at a time when Indian media was touting the highly successful profile of the burgeoning diaspora community in the United States. Sandhya Shukla points, for instance, to a 1973 issue of the India-published magazine *Illustrated Weekly of India* that stated, "There are 50,000 Indians and Pakistanis in New York. Unlike their compatriots in Europe who do menial jobs and live in congested lodging houses, those in the States are educated, affluent and believe in gracious living."[16]

Even though *India Abroad* is now read predominantly online, a paper copy would arrive fortnightly in my parents' mailbox well into the twenty-first

The author's parents, Naim and Shailla Gupta, at the Delhi Railway Station, garlanded and surrounded by family members as they prepared to leave India in August 1961. A relative took this photo and later presented it to the author's parents when the family made their first return visit to India in December 1967. (Courtesy Shailla Gupta)

century. My mother and father each would read the current issue and then give it to one of the other Indian families in Muncie. These individuals, after reading it, passed it on as well.

This reading and sharing practice was one way the elder immigrants sustained community life among themselves in Muncie. The habit of reading and sharing *India Abroad* was one way of creating a structure of permanence. It gave them a way of locating themselves as persons from India and residents of the United States who found commonality with others who held these shared links. Reading a newspaper dedicated to news of Indians residing abroad that was published in English also created a vehicle for the community to transcend the many diverse ethnic, religious, and linguistic differences among them and to imagine themselves as being of Indian origin in both a culturally and nationally unifying sense. The linkage of *India Abroad* with the success-story portrayal of Indians in the United States that the *Illustrated Weekly of India* quote highlights offered further reinforcement to these Indians that their placement in the United

States had made them special. They might be far away from their home countries and their families, but they were representing India positively in America. In this sense, they recreated a version of what Benedict Anderson has called the "nation as imagined community."[17]

A favorable impression of Indians in America formed the narrative core of another elder immigrant couples' memories of their early years in America, that of Tilak and Subhadhra. It also highlighted how migration away from India did not have to mean permanent displacement. It could instead be of a circular nature with movement between multiple locales. By 2003, Tilak and Subhadhra were maintaining two residences—one in Muncie and one in Bangalore, India. They also were spending considerable time in Indianapolis in the homes of their adult daughters.

"What made you decide to leave India?" I asked Tilak and Subadhra in early October. The three of us were sitting and talking in their family room in Muncie, the tape recorder on an arm of a sofa, next to Tilak's elbow. The house smelled faintly of incense and jasmine that Subhadhra had used during a puja, marking the rising of the full moon three days earlier.

Tilak had begun teaching at age eighteen and was at a university in southern India when an opportunity to go abroad came. "What happened here . . . was this," Tilak began. "A professor with whom I studied, he was a famous man in India." Tilak thought that if he did any further study he would do so in India, but his professor urged him to set his sights higher. "He always thought I had the knowledge to go further—'Don't be satisfied with just a master's,' he said."

"He told me, 'You'd better go to America. There, you'll do well.'"

A generous scholarship made the promise of America even harder to refuse. Still, Tilak hesitated. Born in 1932, he was just twenty-seven years old in 1959, the year he boarded a ship bound for New York. Subhadhra was barely eighteen, and he would be leaving her and their three-month-old daughter behind.

"After he got all his invitations, I told him not to go," says Subhadhra, picking up the story from her husband. "Our baby was born, and she was so small. He was going there, and I didn't know when I would be going. I didn't want him to go. Then someone said, 'Oh you are stopping him; this is a good opportunity for him. You can go later. Why are you stopping him?'"

"But well, we had heard these things in our village," she went on. "We had heard that when people go there, to study, they get married and they won't come back. Indian people have done that."

"But," Tilak says, picking up the narrative, "we thought I would go back. Because this scholarship that I got, they made me sign two things. One was that I would promise not to get married in the United States. The other thing was that once I went back, that I would stay a minimum of three years."

Tilak and Subhadhra's daughters were living in Indianapolis in 2003, and Tilak and Subhardra would spend much of their time with them. Typically, they would stay a few days each week at their home in Muncie, then go to Indianapolis for long weekends with their daughters and their two grandchildren. They also would live outside the United States for about three months each year in a condominium they had purchased in Bangalore.

"I love Muncie," said Subhadhra. "We have always liked it here. We are not here all the time, of course, but when we are here, we enjoy it very much."

"This is our family house now," she added, gesturing toward the furniture and bookcases filling their Muncie home. "It is our home, when we are here."

Both the experiences of my parents and of Tilak and Subhadhra call attention to how "home" had come to acquire a multilocale meaning. For my parents, India remained a place to which they might someday return. For Tilak and Subhadhra, India and Muncie—along with Indianapolis—had become geographic points on a circuit of places in which they resided on a frequent but never completely permanent basis. Home became not just a word that immigrants could not define but also a term that did not necessarily need to be a part of their way of life. At the same time, the stories evoked a sense of how the experiences of living first under European colonialism and later within the rubric of American racism might code such South Asian immigrants' behaviors, even if the immigrants were not immediately aware of the impacts themselves. The lack of fixity in understanding home brought them together as strangers who found each other and were able to transcend ethnic, linguistic, and religious differences as a result of economic and occupational compatibility to form communities of friends. Most of the immigrants I interviewed said coming to Muncie had exposed them to a multicultured India they might not have experienced so intimately if they had remained in India. Not only was there diversity in the number of languages that their new friends spoke, there also were multitudes of different ways in which food was prepared and eaten, and religious beliefs were articulated and practiced. Tilak, as the grandson of an orthodox Brahman priest, for instance, maintained his dietary obligations so dutifully that when he was traveling to another city for a conference or workshop, Subhadhra would send him special foods by overnight mail.

Even those who were not from what is present-day India cited this diversity as a characteristic of the Muncie South Asians. Mushtaq was born in what was known as Bengal under British colonialism but became a part of East Pakistan after independence and the bloody partition of the subcontinent that accompanied the British departure. He arrived in Muncie via migrations from Bengal to Karachi in what was West Pakistan, and then to Toronto. One memory he shared during a group discussion I had organized for the older émigrés was his first encounter with Tilak and my father. He recalls the encounter as two separate meetings that occurred on the same day while he was in Muncie for his interview for his Ball State faculty position. A professor was driving him around Halteman Village and took him to the two Indian professors' homes. At the first house, Mushtaq recalled, Tilak was weeding the garden in his dhoti; at the second house, Naim was mowing the lawn in his shorts.

How friendships and community formed among the group had much to do with a commonality of class. While practices of social differentiation such as caste had informed many of these immigrants' ways of interacting with others in India, their pursuit of education abroad had placed them into a common social class in the United States, and because they did not know any other Indians, this shared class affiliation overrode caste distinctions. Some of my interviewees alluded to caste as informing their practices of religious rituals and of shaping beliefs about diet and marriage that they sometimes passed on to their children. However, none regarded it as a factor in how they established friendships with other South Asians in diaspora. For most, it was the shared affiliation with Ball State and familiarity with the flavors of foods and forms of cooking associated with their home countries that brought them together. Just as a logic of multiculturalism in the United States could flatten ethnic diversities into broader, more homogenized categories, distinctions of caste, religion, and regional affiliation among South Asians were lost within their placement in U.S. society as part of an upwardly mobile, educated middle class. The immigrants also had grown up learning a common language—English, the language of the British Empire, taught in their schools. Though many could converse a little in Hindi, the ability to speak English in addition to whatever ancestral languages might have been used in their families or home towns or villages helped firm up the friendships among the new immigrants.

As these stories show, these immigrants also did not have permanent settlement in the United States on their minds. My parents, Tilak and Subhadhra, and Mushtaq and Haina all saw America as a place where they would sojourn, and their nations of departure as the countries to which they would eventually return. Ultimately, however, the intention to go back diminished. As the next section shows, each couple had an opportunity to return to India—or, in the case of Mushtaq and Haina, Bangladesh. But when the opportunities arose, they stayed in the United States. What caused this change of heart? The next section offers a re-reading of a family tale as one way of understanding the tension between the intention of return and reality of remaining abroad.

A Lost Container of the Past

My mother called me one morning in Honolulu in 2000. She and my father had decided to move out of Halteman Village and were having a home built for them on the west side of the city closer to Ball Memorial Hospital. Her two knee-replacement surgeries and a couple of medical emergencies involving my father had prompted them to design the new home so that their bedroom could be on the first floor, and larger, more private rooms could be established for their daughters and their spouses and children during family visits. She had been in the attic sorting through clutter, looking for things to discard, and had found what we have come to call the lost suitcase. It was a blue vinyl suitcase that was lost in their journey to America from India, found a few months later, and then seemingly lost again in the decades of life in Muncie.

Listening to my mother talk about the suitcase took my mind back to the story they used to tell about their journey: the train trip from New Delhi to Bombay and the promises to come home soon; the ship from Bombay to London, with the stops in Egypt, Greece, and Italy; the plane trip from London to New York; the Greyhound bus from New York to Cedar Falls, Iowa, where she accidentally bit into a hamburger and nearly vomited when she tasted beef for the first time.

Somewhere on the journey, after the ship docked, the suitcase was lost. It held pictures of their families, along with almost all my mother's clothing as well as the gold jewelry her father had insisted he give her instead of money because money would be easily spent. When my parents arrived in Cedar Falls in 1961, all she had in the way of clothing was the sari she was wearing and one other saffron-colored sari packed at the last minute in a bag that held my father's belongings. All she could feel was panic. She and her husband were in the middle of America, marooned, knowing nobody or nothing. Even as my father philosophically told her not to worry, that things would work out somehow, my mother remembered feeling alone and wanting to go home. At the bus depot in Iowa, she sensed for the first time that this might not happen.

My parents and I have talked about the suitcase several times, my parents retelling the story, I analyzing and pondering what it meant. My mother insists frequently that it is best not to dwell on the past. In America, she felt she had learned the value of living in the present. It helped her create a thriving small business and made her into a respected community leader. She took pride in knowing that when civic organizations need a helping hand, she was among those trusted enough to be called. She had learned to appreciate Muncie and to give back to the community as much as she could. She, like my father, has expressed a desire to write her life story, but the task of beginning has been daunting for her. My father penned a draft history in longhand during a winter the two of them spent in 2012 in Florida, capturing his memories with the same level of neatness and concision that was schooled into him in India. My mother, however, found it difficult to sit down and organize her thoughts. When her mind traveled into the past, she would find herself caught in a flow of memory. One story would unfold into another. And another. She would lose track of time. Her life, which seemed organized, would fly out of order.

Much more talkative and emotionally expressive than my father, my mother described her new-to-America self as young and idealistic, so different, she said, from the person she had become. She remembered feeling completely empty in Iowa when she first arrived, as empty as the land appeared beyond the road that stretched along the bus depot. Later, she would come to love the haunting emptiness of rolling fields in early summer, corn stalks appearing to cover every inch of soil, the last rose-brown rays of a summer sunset lighting the horizon beyond. But when she first arrived, the fields only brought the strangeness of America into sharper focus, making her feel as if all that once had felt familiar was slipping from her grasp. Even the suitcase that held the accoutrements of her familiar home life had been lost.

For immigrants, the journey from a home country to a new abode is frequently a narrative of displacement. That sense of displacement often generates such emotions as loneliness and a longing to return. My mother's memory of losing her suitcase fits this portrait. For her, losing the suitcase was akin to losing her past—her home—through migration. She attained her desire for adventure. But, as her elder brother prophesied, adventure brought pain. The suitcase—a container—held home. When it was lost, the past was lost. Only the present remained.

Yet as the stories of adjustment to America that my parents shared suggest, narratives on immigrant success can end happily, if one is well-educated, upwardly mobile, and positioned as the post-1965 South Asian immigrants were to do well in the United States. As representatives of the material success of Indians abroad, the post-1965 immigrants found each other and formed communities that also celebrated their success. They held dinner and dance events in honor of such festivals as Diwali and created cultural events organized around the August 15 anniversary of India's independence from British rule. Newspaper clippings and photographs in my parents' collection of albums feature our family celebrating Diwali, my mother demonstrating for schoolchildren and

Naim and Shailla Gupta, rejoicing over the discovery of a suitcase containing Shailla's saris in this October 27, 1961, image from the *Waterloo Daily Courier* newspaper in Iowa. The suitcase, among the belongings the couple brought with them from India, had been lost during the journey from India to the United States. (*Waterloo–Cedar Falls Courier*)

church groups how to put on a sari, and articles on preparing an Indian meal. Later clippings feature accomplishments by my two sisters and me in school and our careers. The lost suitcase story became a way my parents could speak of their success in the United States as a balancing of their past in India with a present and beckoning future in America. That balance became possible in the story when the suitcase was found.

During one of our conversations about the lost suitcase, my father left the room and returned a few minutes later with one of the photo albums. He showed me a newspaper clipping from 1961 about them, an immigrant couple from India who lost their suitcase, then found it. A news bulletin, my father recalled, went out: "Can anyone help this couple?" A month or so later, good news arrived. The suitcase was found in a Chicago storage room, marked lost and unclaimed. My parents had settled into a boardinghouse in Cedar Falls, Iowa, where they had stayed until my father secured a graduate assistantship position at the University of Iowa. He took a bus to Chicago to get the suitcase—and nearly lost it again when a luggage handler accidentally placed it on a bus bound for New York City. A newspaper in the area ran a story about the reuniting of the suitcase with the Indian couple. An accompanying photo showed the suitcase opened, my mother's saris revealed, and my mother kissing my father shyly.

"She was embarrassed about that," my father remarked, pointing to the photo in the yellowed newspaper clip.

"I didn't want to do that," my mother recalled. "But they insisted. 'Come on, just give your hero a kiss,' the reporter said. I told her that if my father saw such a photo, he would kill me."

"It was what people do in America," my father said.

. . .

The recovery of the suitcase and the shy kiss marked a figurative turning point in my parents' narrative about whether to return to India or stay in the United States. My mother made the decision to give up her Indian citizenship in 1974. She called it "one of the hardest things I have ever done."

My father waited twenty years longer.

"I would think about it," he said. "I would order the papers, and then they would come and I would tear them up."

The difficulty of the decision was tied to a slow sense of acceptance acquired over a passing of time that they were not going to return to India to live. For them, as for many immigrants, there was a period first of denial, then of helpless resignation, and then a coming of terms that led to acceptance of the adopted country as the nation of citizenship. Neither my mother nor my father felt convinced that the United States was home when they applied for citizenship. But U.S. citizenship opened a new opportunity. They could sponsor other members of her family to emigrate. My father's nephew came in 1974 as a student. After settling into a career, he married and raised two daughters to adult age. One of my mother's sisters came as the result of an arranged marriage in 1975 and had two children, as did her brother who came in 1976. Another sister and another brother, his wife, and their child all came long enough to obtain permanent residency cards that allowed them to reside in the United States as well as India. Another niece came in 2000, and a nephew in 2013. This was what their story of their lost suitcase was ultimately about. Losing the suitcase helped my parents find a new home.

For my mother, memories of the journey from the heartland of India to the midwestern United States were rekindled in 2000 when the suitcase—once lost, then found, and then lost again in the residue of material items that she accumulated over the years—was "found" once more, this time in tatters, in the attic. The rediscovery came at a time when my parents were preparing to move out of a house they had lived in for twenty-six years. The suitcase was in such poor condition that she was not sure whether it would be able to be moved to their new home. She was calling me in Honolulu to ask what I thought she should do. I told her to try and keep as much of the suitcase as she could and that we would find some use for it. The reality was that there was no functional use. But I could not bear the loss of such a material artifact of my parent's story. My mother managed to save a piece of the suitcase panel, which had a seal bearing the insignia of their ship stamped on it. She saved it, even as she wondered why anyone would care about keeping it or why anyone would want to know the story of her past journey. Her puzzlement about my obsession with her past deepened when I went to Iowa City in 2003, two months before coming to Muncie. I walked through the streets surrounding the University of Iowa campus with a cell phone in hand, talking to my parents and trying to locate the boardinghouses, student rooms, and Quonset huts where they as young immigrants had lived and where I as their daughter had been born.

One remnant of Naim and Shailla's immigrant journey from India to the United States is a piece of a vinyl suitcase bearing the name of the ship on which they traveled from Bombay (now known as Mumbai) to London. The suitcase, initially lost in transit, was found a few months after the couple's arrival in Cedar Falls, Iowa. (Courtesy Shailla Gupta)

My urgency to know about their past paralleled the sense of invisibility I felt permeated their lives in Muncie. Against the backdrop of Middletown studies and against the perceptions that there was no such thing as a South Asian community in Muncie, I felt I needed tangible evidence of their traces to their American past. Unlike them, the experience of being born and brought up in the United States made dismissal of the self as foreign or invisible in the American landscape more difficult to bear.

At the same time, I felt the dilapidation of the suitcase symbolized a sense of weakness my parents might have felt as they were planning their lives as an elderly couple in America. I remembered how we came to realize as a family that we would not ever live in India. We made one effort to do so in 1973, when my father received a one-year sabbatical. My parents sold the Plymouth Valiant that had brought them to Muncie as well as a station wagon they had more recently purchased, rented out their home, and arranged for their children to not attend school for a year. They purchased one-way tickets to India.

The experiment failed. "It was hard, very hard." my father recalled. "The girls kept getting sick, and, well, I think we had just gotten used to a more comfortable life. Even getting gas for our stove so we could cook, even that was something we found out we didn't know how to do. Everyone [in India] kept telling me, 'Why do you want to come back? There's nothing for you here. Go back.'"

My father explained these circumstances to the group of younger immigrants who had spoken during the discussion group described earlier about the inaccessibility of home. The India the younger immigrants left was not the impoverished ex-colony of the 1960s; it was the emergent Asian economic powerhouse. It was a place to which immigrants could return. For him, it was not. Our family was back in Muncie by July 1974, ten months after we had left. My parents' savings were depleted. America, it seemed, not only had taken away their capability to live in India as Indians would but also had chained them to lifelong employment in the United States in order to learn to live prosperously in America—as Americans.

Tilak and Subhadhra tried to go back, too.

"I wanted to go back," Tilak replied. "In fact, I used to fight with a lot of Indians . . . I used to argue with them and say, 'You are not helpful if you stay. With the God-given knowledge you have, you can help so many people.'

"They used to tell me, 'You can go back, but believe me I am not going back. You will get so frustrated you will want to return here.'"

He went back to India and was able to secure a position as the head of a mathematics department at an engineering college. And, he recalled, "To be honest, I got frustrated."

Teachers at the college were not focused on helping students understand concepts. They just tried to make sure students memorized lessons so they would pass exams. Tilak tried to correct the situation: "I told them, 'This is not how it is done in America. We should make sure the students understand the concepts so that they can apply it to practical problems.' But the board would not allow me . . . they said, 'Just because you have come from America, you want to change everything?' I would say, 'You people are living in the dark ages.' And like that, I got frustrated. Nobody would listen to me."

In this sense, return might have meant surrendering a sense of self as a success, a position that the immigrant narrative circulating in both Indian and overseas Indian media had popularized. Coming back to India might have meant acceptance of the self as just any other Indian. Permanent return under such conditions was not ideal.

Coming to Terms

It was late August 2003 and the summer sun had just set. I walked with my parents up a curving walkway toward Mushtaq and Haina's home, less than a mile from where my parents lived in Muncie. Mushtaq answered the door with a beaming smile and hearty handshake. Haina quickly prepared tea and samosas, folding a mixture of peas and potato from an earlier meal into Pillsbury dough and frying up the rolls.

While my father retired from the university in the mid-1990s, Mushtaq continued to teach into his seventies, retiring in 2007.

"If I retire, I don't know what I would do in Muncie," he mused in 2003. "Muncie, it's too small. I would like to live in an environment where things are nice, a community where . . ." His voice trailed off.

A telephone ring interrupted the silence. Haina hastened to answer it.

No response. A minute or so later, the phone rang again.

For a second, she seemed puzzled. Then she smiled.

"It must be Bangladesh." She picked up the phone. No response. "Yes, Bangladesh." She explained: "Sometimes, the line doesn't go through."

My mother smiled and started remembering how difficult it used to be to receive an international phone call from India. First, our family would receive a telegram that a phone call would come on a certain day. We would wait at home. Wait and wait. Finally, the phone would ring. It would be the operator, saying the call was being put through. More waiting would follow.

And then the call would come. Over static, my parents would strain to hear the caller, asking if all was okay. The message that had to be communicated by voice—the message that was too important to be transmitted by mail—would be made quickly. Relatives would get on the line. My sisters and I would pick up the phone extensions located around the house for a quick word with relatives, these phantom figures I knew only from meeting most of them twice: once as a five-year-old in 1967 and once as an eleven-year-old in 1973.

Hello, hello . . .

Namaste, ji.

Kase he? Tikh. Tikh.

Good-bye. Good-bye. Good-bye. Be well.

And the call would end.

Mushtaq picked up the conversational thread he had left off. "My coming here, to this country, was not entirely voluntary," he said. "I was in Canada, working for the deputy secretary of Pakistan. I got a call from Ball State—I wasn't interested. But my brother . . . we had this saying and he repeated it . . . 'If you're served a full plate of food, don't turn it down.' So, well, I put in the request and got my leave from Pakistan extended. I thought I'd be here for one year. In the meantime, the war started and well then . . ."

His voice trailed off again.

"My mind is still back home, but I am now here."

Although Mushtaq met my parents during his initial visit to Muncie, it was a momentary crisis that made them friends. My father had gone to a grocery store on a weekend afternoon and saw Mushtaq and Haina. They had just arrived in Muncie with their three daughters and an infant son. The house they rented did not have its electricity or water turned on, and a bottle that Haina had packed for her son needed cleaning.

"Follow me," my father told Mushtaq. "Come to my house."

My mother found a sterilizer she had last used for her youngest daughter's baby bottles some eighteen months before in the back shelf of one of her cupboards. Our families had dinner together, and my father helped Mushtaq arrange to get the electricity and water in the rental home running. Mushtaq's family settled into Muncie and decades later, he and Haina were among my parents' oldest friends.

Fifty Years in America

Four decades later, Mushtaq continued to live quietly in Muncie, enjoying retirement with Haina. His youngest child, a heart surgeon, became the first of the American-raised generation of Muncie South Asians to return to the town, taking a position at Ball Memorial Hospital in 2010. It was only after the son relocated to a suburb of Indianapolis in 2013 that Mushtaq and Haina decided that it was time for them, too, to move with them.

Tilak enjoyed a long career at Ball State and lived to see a lifelong dream realized before he passed away in 2013 at the age of eighty-one: the publication of a book on the achievements of mathematicians in early India. Although he and Subhadra spent much of their time as retirees with their two daughters and at their condominium in Bangalore, they kept their home in Muncie. Staying in Indiana never quite became a conscious decision. More, it was that going back to India became something they talked less about.

My mother said that she came to realize that she was not ever going to return to India, except as a visitor, after her elder sister and brother died in the mid-1980s. She saw her father for the last time in 1992 when she traveled to India with me; he passed away in late 1993. I saw my grandmother for the last time when I traveled to India alone in 1996 and was joined there by my father; my grandmother died in 1997. I, too, found my trips to India occurring less often.

One of my last trips to India was in 1999 as part of a study-abroad trip that included learning Hindi while traveling to Gangotri, high in the Himalayas and trekking to Gaumukh, the glacier that is the source of the holy Hindu river, the Ganges (or Ganga). My mother had long hoped to visit Gaumukh. By 1999, she had reconciled herself to realizing that this was one more dream that would not materialize. Before I left for India, she asked me to make a blessing at Gaumukh for her, and to bring back pictures. She felt she no longer had the strength to make such a journey. Her daughter would have to make it on her behalf. Her own body was exhausted, dilapidated, much as the suitcase was in its rediscovered state. Just as it might not have the strength to travel to a new home, she might not travel again to India, once their home, now a rather foreign abode.

"I still dream of adventure," my mother said. "I still think of India as my spiritual home. It is where I hope to go someday, after this life. But I have had to make myself realize that we were not going to go back. After my father died, I had to ask myself—what is there for me?"

My parents shifted their focus from India to the United States, putting the family name on the hobby shop. As the elder Indians in the Muncie community in the first part of the twenty-first century, they often encouraged new arrivals to involve themselves not just with South Asians but with Muncie's social and civic events as well. Often, my mother observed, new South Asian arrivals did not understand why it was important to involve themselves in Muncie's public community affairs. "I want them to feel that it is important to get involved," she said, "to know what is happening here and to be ready to contribute as they can."

Throughout his seventies my father went to weekly meetings of the Kiwanis Club. At one Kiwanis meeting, a Christian evangelical preacher, the Reverend William Keller, was invited to give a talk. During it, he said that only those people who read the Bible could go to heaven.

The Kiwanians have a practice, where a member can donate a dollar to a charitable pot and then share a thought. So the next week, my father gave $1 and stood up. "I'm a Hindu, not a Christian," he said. "I don't read the Bible; I read the Gita. But I don't think God will deny me heaven." When he finished, he noted somewhat proudly that quite a few people applauded.

My father said Keller resigned in a huff from the Kiwanians in the late 1990s after they denied him the money he sought for a pet project. Keller later reapplied. The bid was rejected. My father pointed to this incident as an example of how Muncie residents respond to bigoted behavior by refusing to tolerate it, at least in public. He saw such examples as ways also that Muncie had changed from the days when he was told that as a noncitizen he could not apply for tenure. But he admitted that at the same time he, too, had changed. When he left India, he had promised his mother two things: he would never eat meat and he would not become a Christian. His mother died in 1971, three years after his father passed away. My father did keep his first promise, but he chose with my mother to join the Unitarian Universalist Church of Muncie in the early 1990s. He called the church a space where he can continue to worship as a Hindu and still be a part of a community in Muncie.

In the second decade of the twenty-first century, South Asian names appeared on marquees outside health clinics and medical offices around Muncie. It would not be surprising to meet a young South Asian woman behind the sales desk at a shopping center kiosk or to notice the Indian kebob restaurant tucked into a shopping center that a Nepali immigrant opened in 2010. If one mentioned the name Gupta to a Muncie resident who had been in the city more than ten years, it is likely that they would associate the name with my father's work at the university, my mother's activities at the Unitarian church, my father's weekly attendance at the Kiwanis Club, or the Indian couple who used to run the hobby shop. These indicators suggest that the presence of Indians and other nonwhite, non-Protestant peoples are transforming what it means to be typical in Muncie. The immigrant narratives in this chapter are a part of that experience. They suggest that change and adaptation are more likely to define how one conceptualizes home than continuity. As my mother put it in the closing moments of one of my discussion groups, "How can there be a root without a route?"

CHAPTER 3

Fitting In

Muncie South Asians and Childhood

> Finally, I suppose, the most difficult (and most rewarding)
> thing in my life has been the fact that I was born a Negro and
> was forced, therefore, to effect some kind of truce with this
> reality. (Truce, by the way, is the best one can hope for.)
> —James Baldwin, "Autobiographical Notes"

October 20, 2003
Carmel, Indiana

HG: One of the protocols of academic research is that of protecting the confidentiality of research participants as much as possible. To that end, everyone who participates in this study will be identified with a pseudonym.

Would you like to choose your pseudonym?

RESEARCH PARTICIPANT: I'd like to be called "Priscilla."

HG: Priscilla . . . ? Well . . . okay, you can be Priscilla. But . . . why? Why do you want to be associated with a name like that?

(Research participant, hereafter known as Priscilla, laughs.)

PRISCILLA: That was always my name when we did Pioneer Days back in elementary school, either Patricia or Priscilla. Because there were no Indians here back then. I needed to have a different name, a name, you know, that someone on the Mayflower might have had.

HG: So . . . This is kind of a strange question, but you couldn't be yourself, [go by your own name] on Pioneer Day? You had to be Priscilla or Patricia? Tell me about that a little bit. Does that strike you as odd, or did it strike you as odd, growing up?

PRISCILLA: No . . . because I knew at that time in the pioneer times there probably were no Indians—Indians from India, you know—and we were just trying, I guess, trying to make me fit in with all the other kids in the class and make it so that I didn't stand out with a totally different name. And so we always tried to find something as close to [her name] as possible.

Building America

The Puritan outcasts traveling across the Atlantic Ocean via the *Mayflower* in 1621 have long been credited for building not only the political and economic infrastructure of the United States but also in creating its cultural soul. Immigrants from northern and western Europe followed the Mayflower pilgrims to North America. The early French settler J. Herbert St. John de Crèvecoeur wrote in "What Is an American?" that this movement created "a mixture of English, Scotch, Irish, French, Dutch, Germans, and Swedes" from which "that race now called Americans" arose. "Here," Crèvecoeur wrote, "individuals of all nations are melted into a new race of men."[1]

The evolution of Europeans into Americans was hardly pristine, of course. The European settlers displaced the indigenous Americans from their traditional lands and undermined their cultural traditions, despite celebrating their first encounters in school events like Pioneer Days. Slave ships from the late 1400s through the late 1800s carried an estimated 12.4 million individuals out of Africa to plantations established by European imperialist powers throughout the world, with about 10 percent of those individuals arriving as slaves to help build the future United States.[2] Their descendants continue to live in America through truces fraught with hardship and racial animosity.

Immigrants from China, Japan, the Philippines, and the Indian subcontinent also arrived in the United States by ship, beginning in the nineteenth century and continuing well into the twentieth century before air travel became a more efficient mode of transport. Muslim peddlers from Bengal, for instance, traveled to the United States beginning in the 1880s to sell such "Oriental goods" as embroidered cotton and silk, small rugs, and perfumes. These merchants established a trading network through the East Coast and Deep South that relied on kinship ties in their home villages and new relationships among communities of color in the United States.[3] Even as their presence is not recorded as part of America's history, later generations of South Asian immigrants followed their path. When Priscilla's father left India in 1959 for the United States, he did so by ship, as did my parents in 1961.

A riddle one of my uncles told me in 1967 when my parents took my sisters and me to India for the first time links their late-twentieth-century experience of ship travel to those of the earlier Asian and African travelers. The riddle teller notes that a ship left Bombay for the United States and says to the listener, "*What* was the name of the captain." If the riddle teller inflects the end of the sentence correctly, the phrase sounds like a sentence rather than a question and prompts the listener to ask "What?" The teller then says, "'What' was the name of the captain," revealing the word play.

I listened to the riddle as a five-year-old who knew that her parents had left India by ship. Later, I saw in it a story of an emerging relationship between upper-caste, well-educated Indians who were born in the waning years of the British Empire and the labor needs of the post–World War II U.S. economy. Young men and women who aspired to further their education and professional experience in ways unavailable in an India slowly recovering from a century of direct British rule used ships as the most affordable means to emigrate. They traveled through the Suez Canal and Mediterranean before docking in London. In London, brokers who also were products of the British Empire–influenced relationship between Bombay and London would help the immigrants obtain affordable air passage to the United States.

Like my parents, Tilak and his wife, Subhadhra, were marked as foreign, and as such, the history of migration into the United States not only traveled with them but also categorized where they would fit into an America defined by the European Mayflower arrivals intersecting with those of the slave ships. Foreignness differentiated them from the dominant white and considerably more subordinate African American cultures.[4] By not being able to fit the prototype of the ideal American, these immigrants came to be defined as other to the dominant norm. But what about their children who spent the better part of their youth and adolescent years growing up on American soil? This chapter concerns the daughters of Tilak and Subhadhra, and my sisters and me. Priscilla, two years younger than I, was the younger daughter of Tilak. Her elder sister, whom I will call Cheryl, was about four years older than I. The two of them, my sister Nisha (who was three years younger than I), my sister Anju (four years younger than I), and I were the only Hindu Indian children in Muncie for many years. Foreignness played differing roles in marking each of our bodies. These stories show myriad and often contradictory ways in which certain experiences led each of us to gain consciousness of our selves as individuals of a South Asian ancestry and an American upbringing. This consciousness served at times as a source of pride, at other times a matter of shame, in some cases a protective shield, and in others a burdensome confusion that had to be tangled out. In this sense, pride, shame, protection, and confusion have coexisted, overlapping and intersecting in ways that might disrupt or at least surprise the self, offering perhaps a different understanding of the uneasy truces with reality to which the epigraph from James Baldwin refers.

Ways of Knowing

In 1974 a Christmas celebration took place in my school gym. I was in the sixth grade and had just returned to the United States after spending the previous school year in India. I loved Christmas caroling and had missed not being able to take part in this annual American holiday in the previous year. The principal made an announcement over the school's public address system for the classes to begin assembling in the gym. As my class entered the gym, I saw the kinder-gartners seated on the floor cross-legged just beneath the school's stage and my two sisters, who were in the second and third grades, seated with their classes on chairs behind them. I joined the older students at the back. The school choir performed and the music teacher led us through several songs. Then, it was time for the final song. The principal went to the front and asked the students who were not from America to come forward and lead the school in the last song.

Sitting near the back of the gym with the other sixth graders, I saw some children from the lower grades go forward. I presumed that they were the children of foreign students who had come to Ball State University. More of these children were entering our school as Ball State's international profile grew, but these children, I was sure, were not in the same category as me. I was born in the United States and my father was a professor, not a student. Then, my class-mates began nudging me.

"Go, Himanee."

"He's talking about you."

"You have to go to the front."

I stayed in my chair, shaking my head.

"Not me," I said. "I'm from the United States."

"He said 'not from America originally.' Aren't you from India? Go. Hurry up. They're waiting for you."

I looked around, wondering where my teacher was and whether I would get into trouble if I didn't go forward. Finally, I gave in. I walked to the front of the gym, joining perhaps a dozen other children. Facing the rest of the school, I felt awkward and foreign as the music teacher began playing the opening chords to "Joy to the World." In the year that Richard M. Nixon resigned from the presi-dency, India exploded its first atomic bomb, and U.S. troops began their pullout from Vietnam, the bodies of the "foreigners" faced "Americans" in an unsettling tribute to the world. I, in the meantime, was left with feelings of confusion: Was I an American? Or an Indian? Why did it seem so troubling, in that moment at least, to be both?

. . .

When Priscilla told me her Pioneer Days story nearly thirty years later, I remembered this experience in the gym. I thought her story held an ironic undertone that might offer one way of understanding how in the black-white racial hierarchy of America's life, children of non-European immigrants who are born or grow up in the United States craft their lives in ways that might allow them to protect their senses of self while also giving them empathy with both the white and African American other. I saw the use of Priscilla as a shield, much as I later saw the anger that welled up inside me during my wedding sangeet as a means of fighting back the kind of embarrassment that had filled me when my school branded me a foreigner during our Christmas celebration.

When I shared my thoughts with Priscilla, however, she offered a different interpretation. She understood her story as a story of pride in herself and her ability to be a girl of Indian ancestry taking part in a joyful American school activity. She remembered how she and the other students in her elementary-school classes would dress up in clothes in the style of seventeenth-century America and take part in daily activities associated with the period, such as making soap. The television series *Little House on the Prairie* was airing during those years, and provided one more role model for playing pioneer. When I shared with Priscilla my reading of her choice of name, she was surprised. She explained to me that she had made the choice based on her fond memories of her childhood in Muncie.

Pondering Priscilla's choice of name again after our follow-up conversation caused me to think through the historic processes of how the Indian body came to be marked in the United States not just as foreign but also in a homogenizing way as simply Indian (or South Asian) without any attention paid broadly to the many ethnic, religious, regional, and linguistic differences that exist among this group of people. These markings call attention to the dualities of choice within societal relationships that affect Asian Americans. Yen Le Espiritu long has argued, for instance, that while individuals might believe they are seizing control of a particular set of circumstances in carrying out such acts as naming the self, the knowledge-producing processes of the dominant society's discourses strive to retain an upper hand by insisting on naming the self against the will of the individual in question.[5] Similarly, Dina G. Okamoto has pointed to how processes of racialization code these naming practices, pushing diverse ethnic groups to assume a panethnic identity such as Indian American, South Asian American, or even more broadly Asian American.[6]

As my mind swept from Priscilla's memory of her name to my memory of feeling humiliated for being called out as a foreigner, I saw the results of an affect—a felt but not necessarily easy-to-articulate way of knowing—that results from being a party to hegemony-making practices at the everyday level. Affective ways of knowing might provoke memories of pain, discomfort, sadness, self-doubt, and questioning of one's place in society. When subject to critical analysis, however, they become new ways of understanding how historic constructions of the citizen-self are placed within frameworks of national and cultural belonging, and the effect that such placements might have on the individual herself. The meanings read into such experiences, however, can be highly personal and not necessarily representative of what others with whom the individual interacts might think.

I draw on stories shared by interviewees, discourse analysis, and my own memories to develop the analysis this chapter offers. Within that frame, let us look first at how my conversation with Priscilla came about. Institutional review-board protocols for academic research required me to carry out my work in a way that would not harm the physicality or reputation of my participants. While harm was the last thing that I wished to create, I was uncomfortable with the protocol standards of keeping participants' identities anonymous. In my mind, names held meaning and defined particular life worlds and should not be treated as mere labels attached to individuals for convenience. However, I did want to protect the privacy of my interviewees and decided that rather than giving them names myself, I would ask them each to choose a pseudonym, ideally one that would be relevant to their lives in Muncie.

I fully expected my interviewees to choose names of a recognizable South Asian origin; I was not expecting choices such as Priscilla. Initially I resisted these choices. When other interviewees asked for "American" names, I tried to convince them to choose names that aligned with their ethnic heritage or the part of South Asia from where they had come. Many then politely declined my offer to choose their own name and asked me to assign them a name that I felt would be appropriate, gestures that essentially caused me to cohere with the academic practice of assigning identities in a manner that I had deemed dehumanizing. I did not think about the fact that my own assumptions about names were being challenged until Priscilla expressed her choice. From that choice emerged part of her story. It is a story of relationality, based on how she and I understood our abilities to name and identify with our selves.

Priscilla remembered herself as Priscilla with merriment. As she observed in our follow-up conversation, "I really had a lot of fun playing Priscilla. It was fun to immerse yourself in the character. It was play-acting." Whereas I read her choice of name as evoking a space where one either had to accept being categorized as foreign or had to give up any individualized distinctiveness in order to assimilate to a white and Christian defined norm, she played out a role she enjoyed. Much as the fictional character in Bich Minh Nguyen's 2014 book *Pioneer Girl* recollects Laura Ingalls Wilder's pioneer family book series on which the *Little House on the Prairie* television series was based, Priscilla immersed herself in the persona of a character whom she was not but who could represent a part of what she loved about her childhood in Muncie.[7]

As members of the only two families in Muncie whose parents had come from India, Priscilla and I, along with our sisters, attended the same schools and took part in many similar activities: playing the piano, learning to swim, participating in French Club, and going to basketball games. We knew our parents had come from the same country; that also gave us something in common. Our parents, however, also had come from different parts of that country and had brought with them differing values regarding religion, acculturation, and childrearing. Tilak and Subhadhra asked their children to remain vegetarian and structured their family life around the daily Hindu religious practices that had been associated with their family for generations. They spoke their ancestral language of Kannada with their children at home, did not allow them to date, and required them to come home from school events by 9 P.M.

My parents took a different approach. They chose not to teach my sisters and me their first language of Hindi, and while they discouraged our desires to date, they were more relaxed with rules about curfews than Tilak and Subhadhra. My parents remained vegetarian but took my sisters and me to McDonald's regularly with the idea that the children could acculturate to American life through eating hamburgers. We celebrated the fall festival Diwali by decorating our house with Christmas lights. Both my parents and Tilak and Subhadhra often invited non–South Asians to their homes for Diwali celebrations, and after joining the Unitarian Universalist church in the 1980s, my parents helped organize more public celebrations of the holiday. However, my sisters and I received little religious education from my parents beyond my father telling us stories from the epics *Mahabharata* and *Ramayana* (from which Diwali is said to originate) at bedtime. Our participation in religious rituals also was occasional, whereas it was part of the daily rhythm of life in Priscilla's family.

We four children were friendly but never close for reasons that might have had to do with the differing ways in which we were brought up as well as the divergent manners in which we had come to articulate our selves and our places in the world. These differences help underscore the demographic diversity of South Asian Americans and further call attention to the racializing ways governmental policies homogenize identities of peoples on the basis of ethnic and/or national origins. While we each saw much affinity between ourselves as children of Indian parents in Muncie, upon reaching adulthood we went separate ways. My sister Anju, who was born and brought up in Muncie, graduated from Ball State University with a degree in actuarial science and married a Wisconsin-born man of European ancestry. She lived outside St. Paul, Minnesota. My other sister, Nisha, was born in Cleveland a few months before my parents came to Muncie. She went to Purdue University to study engineering before transferring to Indiana University, where she switched her major to psychology and met her future husband, an Indiana-born man of Belgian and German ancestry. She was living in Syracuse, New York, with her husband and two daughters, where she was completing a doctorate in Cultural Foundations of Education, counseling minority students, and teaching women's studies. Cheryl had become a physician. Priscilla had completed a degree in pharmacology, married a man who had come from the same part of India as her family, had two children, lived in several parts of the United States, and was working in 1995 near the Alfred P. Murrah Federal Building in Oklahoma City when the bombing staged by Timothy McVeigh occurred.

These paths through the contemporary history, geography, and social conditions of the various parts of the United States heightened my curiosity about how each of us looked back on our years of growing up as the children of immigrants. I wanted to know how our varied lives might nuance the portrayal of America's typicality. The stories that follow suggest we might look at Muncie as a locality where American typicality resides neither in the predominantly white, nonimmigrant, Christian portrayal inherited from the legacy of *Middletown*'s popularity nor in the more recent scholarly efforts to bring the groups of peoples the Lynd team researchers excluded into the story but rather as in the sometimes-tense and sometimes-vibrant differences in perception that emerge out of these processes. Those differences in perception speak to divergences in meaning that reside within any locality's communities and highlight the futility of governmental and other institutional processes to establish categories of meaning with any finality.

Solace in Faith

"Growing up, we were two Indian families," observed Cheryl. "We adopted what we could to be American, but we were in a situation where you feel like you're always going against the grain, against the crowd."

Cheryl shared these words as I interviewed her at her parents' home. At age forty-four in 2003, she was the eldest of the American-raised South Asian children from Muncie. When she began high school in 1971, there were about five thousand immigrants from India residing in the United States, only a fraction of whom had settled in Indiana. No designated census category existed for Indians at the time, although a 1960 estimate put the number of Asian Indians in the state at 361. Most of those individuals resided in Indianapolis, although other cities such as Kokomo, Fort Wayne, and Terre Haute had a few Indian and South Asian families.[8]

"We were the statistically insignificant," says Cheryl, referring to how those African American and foreign-born individuals left out of *Middletown* were characterized. "All we had was the Americanism and what we were taught at home."

Cheryl's understanding of "Americanism"—what it meant to be American—was coded perhaps by her childhood and adolescent years, which were characteristic of the 1.5 generation of South Asian Americans. She was born in 1959 in the town where her father Tilak was raised, about forty miles from Bangalore. She and her mother joined her father in Minneapolis in 1960. She returned with her parents to India in 1964, where Priscilla was born in 1965. Soon after, an opportunity to join the Ball State University faculty opened up for her father. He came to Muncie for a year in 1967, and she joined him with her mother and sister a year later. Following his initial appointment, Tilak received a two-year fellowship at the University of Buffalo–State University of New York to complete his doctorate, so the family moved to western New York before returning to Muncie in 1971. By age twelve, Cheryl had lived in India and in several cities in the United States. Her main source of rootedness came from being part of a family that had defined itself in terms of how it carried out religious rituals and cultural traditions of its ancestral past.

Cheryl was a particularly fast learner, and by the time her family arrived in Muncie, her studies had advanced well beyond her age. She skipped the fifth grade, then the seventh grade, and began high school at Northside at age twelve. "At Muncie North, for the longest time, I was the only Indian," she recalled. "It bothered me in the beginning. . . . Then, I started to think through who I was and where my roots were, and over time, my identity started to evolve."

Unlike the communities of Indian and other Asian Americans that had begun to form along the West Coast and in larger, more metropolitan East Coast cities, few ethnic neighborhoods or South Asian–oriented businesses existed in Indiana before 1980. Indians who did live in Indiana would arrange trips with each other to Chicago to obtain spices and Indian foods, or would try to maintain vegetarian diets with salads, cheese sandwiches, and vegetarian pizzas.[9]

Our family, for instance, would eat pizza at least once a week, made from a Chef Boyardee packaged mix that my mother would enhance with canned olives and mushrooms and other vegetables and spices. Pizza became an important staple among the handful of Indians we knew in Indiana, with some adding green chili peppers, carrots, ginger, and even radishes to the list of available toppings.

The moves among various parts of the United States and her parents' hometown in India helped create an understanding for Cheryl that her small immediate nuclear family included her parents and sister who resided in the United States. However, regardless of where she lived, she also understood that she belonged to a much larger transnational family whose members passed on religious and cultural traditions from one generation to the next. She attributes this connectivity with her extended family to giving her the strength to withstand the peer pressure she started to face when she was enrolled in Muncie schools. As part of a family with a great-grandfather who was a priest, Cheryl described her family's practice of Hindu rituals as more ceremonial and more religious than that of most other Asian Indians she knew, in childhood as well as adulthood. Her family would begin each morning with a half-hour of puja, celebrate auspicious days together, maintain a vegetarian and alcohol-free diet, and would conclude the day with a shorter evening puja. Before each round of prayer, each member of the family would ready themselves by taking a bath.

"We did things that way because that's the way it was handed down over the generations," Cheryl says.

Cheryl's family lived first in Muncie in a duplex maintained by Ball State and then in a house near the campus. Her parents bought a home in the Halteman Village neighborhood in the early 1970s. Cheryl's mother, Subhadhra, described the street on which the family lived as being "mostly Catholic." One day soon after they moved into the neighborhood, Subhadhra recalled, Cheryl's younger sister Priscilla came in from playing outside and was crying. "I asked her, 'Why are you crying?'" Subhadhra said. "She said, 'All my friends go to church. Why can we not go to church? Does that mean we don't believe in God?' I told her, 'We have a temple at home. See? That is our church. Tomorrow, you call your friends and show them our temple. Tell them in Indian custom the temple is at home and that we go every day.'"

A fear about what it might mean if one did not go to church calls attention to the power that social institutions bring to bear in racially marking immigrant children of non-European and non-Christian ancestries as different and foreign. Like my fears of upsetting my devoutly Christian in-laws on the night before my wedding, the worry that a Hindu family living in a Christian-dominant America might not believe in God resonated with experiences of

South Asian children elsewhere in the United States being taunted as "Hindus" or "dot heads" and told to "get out of our country." These derogatory remarks call up the racist violence that Indians and others who were deemed undesirable in the United States faced amid the anti-immigrant hostility of the early twentieth century and can force such children to see themselves, often negatively, as unable to be American. That confusion pushes them into a position of having to choose at times whether to accept the values of their parental and home communities or those of their school peers and the mainstream society.[10]

Subhadhra sensed the repercussion her children might face and chose what she felt was a proactive stance. "I realized at that time that I must keep up all of my traditions, my puja, my practices for my children," she said. "I could either do that or send them to church. Otherwise, they would not know how to belong. They would have conflicts." Priscilla, in recalling this incident, also remembered that after she invited her friends over, they saw that she prayed, too, just differently from how they did. They accepted her for who she was and would look forward to how her family would decorate their house as part of the rituals associated with specific religious holidays.

The steadiness of the home ritual also became a source of strength for Cheryl, allowing her to establish herself as different in a way that she felt was positive. She described herself as being a Hindu "in the truest sense," which defined all her values, actions, and understanding of herself. "I think the first test of finding out who I was came through being around my friends and realizing that I didn't have to be anyone different from who I was. Once I understood that, they accepted me for who I was."

Cheryl began taking classes at Ball State while completing her four years of high school. By the time she was twenty-two years old, she had completed her bachelor's and master's degrees. She then enrolled in medical school, completing a specialization in internal medicine. She began practicing medicine in Danville, Illinois. After her father suffered a series of heart attacks, she moved to Indianapolis to be closer to him. She described her work in 2003 as a private practice that was "straight 9-to-5 with weekends off," which gave her time for her daily prayers, to see her parents, who usually would stay for two or three days a week in her home, and to spend at least one of her weekend days with her sisters' two children. In her free time, she would read and practice singing some favorite songs. She also took advantage of the much larger South Asian community that had grown in Indianapolis to attend social functions and to worship at the city's first Hindu temple.

"My nephew [Priscilla's elder child] goes to a Bhagavad Gita class where he learns Hindi," said Cheryl in 2003. "We spoke Kannada at home, but I don't know how to read or write it. He got a book with the alphabet and learned the whole thing in three weeks. My sister and I took French—that was our other language."

Still, she said, "I am happy. I have peace of mind and good health. I'm happy with what I'm doing. I appreciate what I have and I don't take it for granted. I'm happy that I have my faith."

Cheryl and I spoke a few days after the full moon in October, which she and her family had observed with a lengthy puja. I attended the closing hours of the prayer, joining several elder members of Muncie's South Asian community who were seated either cross-legged on a white sheet spread over the living room floor or on the sofas pushed back against the walls. It was the first time I had visited their house since I had left Muncie for college in 1981, and as I greeted Tilak with my hands folded in namaste and smiled and waved at Priscilla and Cheryl, I felt myself back in a familiar place. Although I could not understand the language or the intricacies of the ritual, Subadhra's quiet, rhythmic chants helped create a meditative space that reminded me of pujas I had attended over the years.

When I returned the next afternoon to visit more informally, the house still smelled of the fresh flowers and herbs from the puja. But in the family room, relics of Cheryl and Priscilla's childhood suggested elements of a more typical middle-class Muncie life. Plastic busts of Beethoven, Bach, Haydn, and Brahms lined a piano, awards for taking part in recitals. Miniatures of the Washington Monument and White House that the girls assembled during a family trip to the capitol sat on a shelf.

"They wanted to see everything," said Tilak, remembering the trip. "We had to extend the vacation because they kept asking to do more."

"Our parents, they were our total support" said Cheryl. "There was no social support, no community of Indians like there is now. So whatever they gave us, we kids became that."

Not an Indian Indian

"What made our family different is that we spread our wings," said Anju. "Mom and Dad taught us to be independent, and we are."

My sister and I spoke in a room filled with her favorite childhood books, books that she would read and reread regularly for relaxation—the pioneer family series by Laura Ingalls Wilder, the Anne of Green Gables series by Lucy Maud Montgomery, and a variety of books by the British author Enid Blyton. I laughed when I saw her copy of *The Hobbit* by J. R. R. Tolkien on the shelf. That copy of the book had been given to me in 1973 when our family lived in India. I never read it.

"I'll get you another copy of the book if you want to read it," Anju said. "But you can't have that one. That book is very special to me."

Born in 1966, Anju celebrated her seventh birthday during the year we lived in India. While I was old enough to study from the textbooks our school had provided, she had just begun to learn how to read. Bored and unable to speak the Indian languages that were being used around us, Anju would read.

Anju's kitchen also was filled with books, cookbooks she collected over the years. Like our mother who managed to make processed Midwest foods palatable through such combinations as grilled cheese sandwiches with syrup, Anju's creative passions were tied up with cooking. She rarely cooked what she called "Indian food," however, and when we spoke of a friend who had come to her house in hopes of getting a great Indian meal only to be served risotto, she rolled her eyes and laughed.

"Yeah, I get that a lot," said Anju. "I'm not a very Indian Indian."

"Do I want to be more Indian? Maybe. Maybe not. I don't think so. I'm pretty happy with the life I have. I'm pretty happy with who I am."

Like Cheryl and Priscilla, we lived in Halteman Village. Our parents bought a house in the neighborhood in 1967, a few months after Anju was born. I entered elementary school in 1968. The elementary school was at the end of my street. I would walk to school with a friend who lived across the street. After school, we would play at her house or mine, or we would join other children outside for kickball or foursquare.

Until the third grade, when my other sister Nisha entered kindergarten, I was the only child of South Asian ancestry in the school. There was one African American boy in my class; he later became a successful musician. There were three other African American children in the school, one of whom was my classmate's younger sister. The other two African Americans also were brother and sister and were the children of the first African American faculty member hired by Ball State. The family lived two blocks from my home, near the neighborhood swimming pool. I knew the children as friendly. Years later, I learned that the family had had to move into the neighborhood at night so that their white neighbors would not see them arriving. Racial slurs were hurled at them and a cross was burned in their front yard. The parents sent their children to the neighborhood school anyway, putting their faith in a hope that the other students would treat them fairly.[11]

I never knew about this incident growing up. I learned of it while doing the research for this book and wondered why it had been kept such a secret. Silence about it seemed to resonate with my mother's reluctance to dwell on the past, a silence she only broke after attending the funeral of the children's mother in 2014. At the funeral, she met other university professors and their spouses who were of color and had been in Muncie in those years. "It was hard for all of us," she told me. "It was better in some ways not to talk." That decision not to talk about racism was a way of dealing with the present in a manner that would not call up Muncie's history of Ku Klux Klan control and the organization's downtown parades.

But history is not seamlessly silent, as the following story from Anju emphasizes: "When I was nine years old and I was on the swim team—I don't know where we were, maybe in Marion, for a swim meet and . . . I had never had this happen to me before, and this kid walks by and says, 'When did they let niggers onto swim teams?' And then he refused to swim in the pool because I was in the pool. And then, well, I was just shocked. I was not a black person. I was just me."

Anju remembered Muncie as a place that was pleasant and safe for children. But looking back, she said she realized that Muncie was a hard place in which to grow up. She remembered swimming, playing tennis, taking part in the local 4-H club, and being able to get on her bicycle and ride anywhere. "From the time I was nine years old, I'd ride to the library, get a pile of books, and bring them back. You can't do that here. Muncie is a small enough community that a kid can be safe there, a little freer." At the same time, she said, "I think we couldn't figure out how to be Indian, or where we were supposed to fit. We didn't have anything, anyone to go by."

Anju's comment calls attention to an inability to find a fit within Muncie's public culture as a person who was neither white, black, nor foreign-born. Social messages like the offensive statement she had received at the swimming pool might have prompted her to try and disassociate herself from African Americans in a racial sense. But being of dark skin and of parents of a non–European Christian category put whiteness out of reach for her, too. Foreignness was also elusive because she was not an Indian Indian; she was born and brought up in Muncie. By the time Anju was six years old, there were a half-dozen Indian families in Muncie. When the families came together for a social gathering, they usually spoke a common language, which was English. If the parents chose to teach their children another language, it was the language spoken in the part of India they had come from. Our parents, who were Hindi speakers, had a fondness for Hindi movies, and occasionally a screening of a film from India would be arranged at a college or community auditorium in a nearby town. Through the university networks, our parents would learn of these screenings. We would climb into the car, and my father would drive us one or two hours to attend these films. Not knowing the language or understanding the religious, caste, class, and other cultural conflicts in the films, we would fall asleep.

"The Indians today, they're just amazed that we didn't learn Hindi," Anju said. "I say, 'Don't you understand? There wasn't anybody to speak Hindi with.'"

For Anju, my other sister, and me, not learning Hindi was the result of our parents choosing to speak only English with us. They rationalized their choice in terms of wanting their children to acculturate without the confusion of having to learn two separate languages and on a belief that the children could pick up Hindi later as adults. Our parents supported our taking French and Latin in high school for that reason. In their minds, we as older children had gained the skills needed for formal language study. Tilak and Subhadhra spoke Kannada to their daughters at home, but all reported that they lacked written materials to study the language formally. As a result, Cheryl and Priscilla also studied French in high school, and Cheryl continued to speak French into adulthood.

These decisions, while grounded in a parental sense of doing what was best for children, also put Indian-ness out of reach for Anju. As I thought about her statement about not knowing how to be an Indian, I recalled the year our family lived in India. I celebrated my eleventh birthday there and had begun to assert a sense of myself that had been grounded in an understanding of what a normative American was supposed to be like. The reaction from members of our extended family, perhaps predictably, was to joke about how American I was. To then return to the United States and to Muncie and be singled out as a non-American deepened a sense of confusion in terms of where to fit. The options were being black or being white, and neither worked. The fact that both choices carried a history of racial violence and exclusiveness was not something a child of the early 1970s could know in an intellectual sense. It could only be felt, affectively as a consciousness of self fluttered across a spectrum of self-respect and gratification on one end and embarrassment and unease on the other.

The sense of cultural isolation Anju recalled resonated with the lonely sense of growing up as a child in one of only two Indian families Cheryl described. For Cheryl, that loneliness was resolved through a relationship with an India she had known through lived experience. Born in the town where her father grew up and living some of her formative years in India and some in the United States also gave her a more grounded sense of self that could be tied to the life she experienced in India as well as the feeling of coming into her own that she described as being part of her adolescence in Muncie. Speaking Kannada with her parents at home also created a connectivity, which Anju lacked because her parents chose not to speak in Hindi.

Like many children of university-educated parents, Anju found solace in books. One of her memories of living in India was learning to read. The copy of *The Hobbit* that she treated as special has been part of a collection of books she's held onto for her entire life. Her love for reading stayed with her as closely as the memories of family who petted and loved her as a young child in the year that our family spent in India. How she articulated those family ties shaped her memories of Muncie as being unpleasant and racist on one hand but nurturing and caring of her on the other.

Anju was one of the top students in her senior class and received scholarships to several different schools. She decided to stay in Muncie and go to Ball State because it had a strong actuarial program. Going to Ball State also was what she described as a "safe choice" because "the professors were all like uncles and aunties to me. Not just the Indians, but others, too. Their kids were my friends. We all grew up together." At the same time, she thinks of Muncie as a place where she lived for twenty-two years, which "is a long time to be in a place that you don't really love."

As I considered Anju's ambivalence toward Muncie, I remembered being eight years old and sitting on the concrete pavement near the diving boards at our neighborhood pool. A boy who was a couple of years younger than I approached me and asked if my family "were black people." The question confused me. I knew my parents were Indian, but I wasn't sure what my sisters and I were. A friend who was white overheard his question and said, "She is not black. She's Indian. Her parents came from India." The next time I saw the boy he told me that Indians were not allowed at the pool. I knew that he was wrong because both African American and Indian families swam at the pool, but I did not like his comments and tried after that to avoid him. That memory, like the memory of the sixth-grade Christmas celebration in which I felt singled out as foreign, calls attention to how certain spaces in Muncie, like swimming pools and schools, remained segregated in a de facto sense. Even if these spaces were technically open to all persons regardless of race or ethnicity, the idea of which individuals were normative to those spaces remained white.

Stories of racial hostility permeate the margins of Muncie's official history and echo histories of racial hostilities that document how Indians, Chinese, Japanese, Filipinos, and scores of other dark-skinned immigrants were, like the African American descendants of slaves, subject to the restrictions of the Jim Crow laws as well as the fear of racially motivated violence. These stories have remained largely untold, at least in part because of the lack of a comprehensible framework for understanding racism as it has affected persons of South Asian ancestry. Historically, the social powers of categorization have placed South

Asian and other Asian Americans in a space of being neither white nor black. The result of that categorization has been a sense of isolation: as Cheryl and Anju describe in differing ways, growing up as a child of Indian immigrants in a predominantly white town like Muncie meant living an existence of being all alone. That racist experiences were remembered as occasional events occurring against another set of generally fond memories might obscure their significance. Yet the stories illustrate how efforts just to be one's self are constrained by societal efforts to categorize bodies in ways that slide between foreignness, blackness, and whiteness disguised as Americanness, and what the implications of that categorizing are. The American-born South Asian body cannot be coded as black, white, or even unequivocally foreign. As much as Anju might have tried to define her fit into Muncie, she could not be classified and made known within *Middletown*'s common denominator of the Midwest American as a mix of "Yankees from New England and New York" alongside "a foreign-born stock largely from Great Britain, Ireland, and Germany."[12] She also could not be understood as what was coded as the opposite of that: the black, American-born descendent of slaves. Anju could wish for an assimilation that would let her ignore her otherness. Or she could try to be "just me," simply herself.

Anju was in elementary school from 1972 to 1978. During these years, changes in federal immigration policies enabled immigrants from India who had settled in the United States to sponsor individuals in their more extended family networks to enter the United States. In those years, our parents sponsored several relatives, including one of my cousins, an uncle, and an aunt. Many of these relatives initially lived in our home. Anju remembered those new arrivals with fondness. While the time spent alternating between living in India and the United States helped Cheryl see her family as large and transnational, our newly arriving relatives expanded Anju's definition of family, bringing it closer to an Americanized norm. A lack of an extended family in the United States can penalize American-raised South Asian children by denying them the opportunity to participate in such school events as grandparents' days, widening the gap between these children and their counterparts who have relatives living close by.[13] For Anju, this penalty was eased when our elder cousin "who's like a brother to me" moved into our house, and uncles and aunts who also lived with us for weeks or months gave her familial love. These experiences, she said, helped her see what it meant to be part of a family in ways she considered "somewhat Indian" but not really American.

"I find it odd that people think that once their kids are eighteen, they should move out the house, or that you're not responsible for your parents once you move out on your own," she said. "I'm totally prepared to have mom and dad come live with us as they get older, if they ever wanted to make that choice. I don't have that same feeling with [her husband's] parents."

"I don't know . . . the family thing, it's important."

As a child, Anju would sometimes attend swim team practices at Tuhey Pool, a public facility in Muncie. The pool underwent a series of renovations in the early twenty-first century and reopened in 2011 during a time that I happened to be in Muncie. I went there to swim, remembering swim team practices in 1972 when my neighbor competed in the U.S. team trials for the Olympics. The glamor of a Muncie woman competing with the best got many of the girls in our neighborhood excited about swimming. We would carpool to Tuhey for practices in the evenings, not knowing that such accomplishments were occurring alongside the federal government's Title IX ruling that required schools to make participation in sports accessible to girls or that my neighbor's father had argued with our elementary school principal about the value of letting girls participate in sports. We also did not know that Tuhey had been a whites-only swimming pool until 1956, when two African American community activists took three young African American boys to the facility, an act that had forced city officials into closing the pool until an agreement could be brokered to make the public place available to all. Local civil-rights activist Hurley Goodall called the desegregation of Tuhey Pool one of the most important stories of Muncie.[14] It never was taught in our classes on local history.

Respecting Parental Norms

My mother and I were attending a groundbreaking ceremony in Indianapolis for east-central Indiana's first Hindu temple when I reconnected with Priscilla. She had been married twelve years and had just moved with her husband and two children to Indianapolis to live. Through her sister and parents, she had gotten involved with the Hindu Indian community that had spearheaded the fundraising campaign for building the temple to which Hindus throughout Indiana contributed. The ceremony included a lunch, and Priscilla was among the women helping with the serving. She did not look at all like the girl with braids and wire-rimmed glasses I had remembered from Muncie, and I would not have recognized her if my mother had not pointed her out. Her hair was tied back, the glasses and braids were gone, and, instead of the blue jeans and blouses that I had remembered her wearing, she was in a salwar kameez. Most of her attention was directed toward making sure her four-year-old daughter didn't get lost in the crowd. As she greeted me, amid the murmurs of Hindi, Marathi, Kannada, and other languages being spoken in the crowd, I could hear in her voice a familiar Indiana twang.

She was interested in my project and invited me a few weeks later to have lunch at her home in Carmel, an Indianapolis suburb. She asked me to arrive after 11 A.M., after her husband had left for work, her eleven-year-old son had gone to school, and she had gotten her daughter ready for nursery school. We would have a few hours to talk before her family came home. Her home life followed much of the structure that had shaped her childhood, with a small puja room in the house and the saying of prayers guiding the rhythm of each day.

"I didn't rebel because I knew that whatever my parents were doing or saying was for the best," recalled Priscilla. "I pretty much had faith in what they said. And as I was growing up I realized that for me it was best to listen just because of the type of person I am." Priscilla grew up in Muncie, as did her sister, my two sisters, and I, in a protected family environment. She described her childhood through memories: losing a shoe while outside playing, eating a bowl of hard candy that felt enormously big, and coming over to our house and spilling powder all over the floor. "I was so small," she said, laughing at the memories. "I see my own kids doing similar things now and I remember how I once did them, too."

She also remembered a teacher who told her parents when she was in the sixth grade that she needed to take her schoolwork more seriously because her report card contained a couple of Bs. That teacher gave her the incentive to work hard, which Priscilla said gave her the drive to do well in high school. This helped her earn scholarships to attend college and graduate school. "He helped me see what I could achieve," she remembered. Her memory of this teacher paralleled a memory shared by her sister Cheryl, who spoke of a mentor in medical school who helped her grow from a "young sapling" into "a strong oak tree."

Like her sister, Priscilla grew up in Muncie following the behavioral norms her parents had established, norms that she said protected her from peer pressure at school and helped establish for her a positive sense of how she was different. "I'm the type of person who can get pushed around pretty easily. Doing what my parents wanted me to do helped me get out of situations where I didn't have control." The norms also were easy to follow when she was a child because "everyone knew I was Indian and accepted me for who I was. I never had anyone make fun of me for being a vegetarian, and back in those days, girls didn't go dating until they were sixteen, seventeen. None of my friends really went dating, so the fact that I didn't date wasn't an issue."

Priscilla's parents used to take the family back to their hometown in India every three or four years, often for three months at a time. Those visits, she said, "created some of the old-fashioned me, but living in America also made me believe in rights for all people. Like the caste system is something I don't agree with." Priscilla compared exclusivist practices of her extended family in

India at temples to the more inclusive norms at many Hindu temples built since the 1980s in the United States. In India, her family practiced such rules as not touching persons of a low caste and of restricting entry into certain parts of Hindu temples to those of the highest castes. In the United States, Priscilla said, "Everybody goes to temple. If someone asks me what caste I am, I kind of give them a funny look because to me it's just a question you don't ask. It doesn't make a difference; it has nothing to do with who the person is. When I go to India and I see it, I have to adhere to it to a certain extent. But I've never agreed with it."

After finishing high school, Priscilla went to college at Purdue University. There she lived in a dorm for four years and had to make decisions for herself for the first time. She had difficulties finding vegetarian food in the school cafeteria and often got sick after trying to do things like eat spaghetti with ketchup in order to avoid meat sauces. Also challenging was the behavior of other students. Because college felt like a less-secure environment than home, Priscilla avoided dorm parties and dances in college, telling others that she had studying to do. "I was afraid the peer pressure would make me do something I didn't want to," she recalled. "Every human has temptations, and I didn't know how strong I would be to resist the temptations." Also hard to resist was an expectation that if one Indian student participated in such activities as dances, others should, too. "In the past, it was, 'Oh, she's Indian. She doesn't do those kinds of things because she's Indian,'" Priscilla said. But when other Indian students would participate in such activities, the idea that it was being Indian that solely accounted for her nonparticipation was harder perhaps for her non-Indian peers to believe. Priscilla remembered that when other Indian females began going to dances and parties, other students would say, "'She's Indian and she does that. If she can do it, why can't you?'"

After finishing college, Priscilla began a doctoral program in pharmacology. While she was doing her coursework, her father learned of a young man from his region and caste from India who was in medical school in New York. Her parents thought he might be a suitable match for their daughter. Priscilla had been in the tenth grade when a relative had gotten married, and she recalled the process of arranging the marriage and the wedding ceremonies as beautiful. She had decided then that she might want a similar kind of marriage for herself, and so when her parents proposed a trip to New York to meet the young man, she agreed. After she became engaged, Priscilla decided to shift her studies to a master's degree so she could finish her degree before getting married.

Priscilla said that as a child she practiced the Hindu religious rituals of her family's tradition, not understanding more than the idea that there was a God.

What she learned, she says, came from her parents because few, if any, publications on Hinduism were available in English. Even though she could speak Kannada but could not read it, materials printed in Kannada were nevertheless inaccessible to her. Over time, her knowledge of Hinduism deepened as more books and other materials became available in English.

"Every time I go to India I grab books," she says. "I've come to understand more about God, and religion is the way I get through difficult times. I try to do puja every morning to tell God how much I care about him and thank him for taking such good care of us," she says. "At the same time, I really like that saying that Christians have about footsteps in the sand." In that story, there are two sets of footsteps in easy times, indicating that God is walking behind a man, and one set in harder times, when God carries the man. "That's how I feel about God."

By the time Priscilla finished high school in 1983, the number of Indian and other South Asian families in Muncie had increased to a couple of dozen. The ages of the children in these families varied considerably. Those age differences, along with different upbringings, made it more difficult for the children of the immigrants to come together into a community like their parents had been able to, leaving the first generation of Muncie-raised South Asian children without a significant peer group of ethnic familiars. The presence of ethnic peers was significant for children born after 1975 who grew up in Muncie. In my interviews with those individuals, many attributed the presence of such peers in Muncie and its surrounding communities as helping them understand their identities as South Asian Americans in a positive sense, whereas the older Muncie-raised South Asians all alluded to the lack of such a group. For the elder group, however, the lack of South Asians was not necessarily a liability. In Priscilla's case, it created a sort of safety net, allowing her to develop her personal values and beliefs in her own way. She could comply with caste rules while in India without really agreeing with them. At the same time, she could play-act a role in elementary school as Mayflower ship traveler. In doing so, Priscilla wove a life that let her inhabit more than one identity category at a time.

Undesirable Indians

From the recorded presence of a man from Madras in a New England port in the late eighteenth century, Indians have been perceived in the United States as either exotic or inferior. Beliefs that Indians are exotic are derived partly from the representations of the Orient that were generated through late-eighteenth- and early-nineteenth-century European scholarly texts that helped inform Ralph

Waldo Emerson's development of early American transcendentalist thought. They gained further solidity in the American mindset with the appearance of the Hindu monk Swami Vivekananda at the 1893 World Parliament of Religions and his subsequent tour of the United States, through which he introduced the American public to Hinduism as his Vedanta and yoga-inspired approach interpreted it. Circulation of Vivekananda's views established a homogenized understanding of Indians as Hindus and of Hinduism being composed of specific tenets and rituals when the religion was in reality practiced in myriad ways.[15]

As perceptions of Vivekananda's Hinduism inspired imaginings of Indians as exotic, Punjabi laborers in California faced racist attacks. These men had begun entering the United States in the mid-nineteenth century and worked as railroad builders, lumberjacks, and farm laborers. They went first to British Columbia and Washington state until anti-Indian hostility led them to migrate into California's emergent corporate agricultural industry.[16] Government documents have described these men as East Indians, differentiating them from the indigenous Americans whom Columbus misnamed Indians. Newspaper articles and common parlance often used such terms as "Hindoo" or "rag heads," referring to the turbans that many wore, even as most of them were not Hindu but rather Muslim or Sikh.

Like many immigrants, the Punjabis were hard-working men who, despite being unable to read or write, established relationships with bankers, lawyers, and other professionals in the towns where they resided. Over time, these relationships allowed them to move from being hired labor to owning farms. Outside their individualized networks, however, these men were perceived as backward and dirty, with one Federal Immigration Commission investigator commenting in 1909 that "the Hindus are regarded as the least desirable, or, better, the most undesirable, of all the eastern Asiatic races which have come to share our soil." As anti-immigrant sentiments swept through the United States in the early twentieth century, government officials denied entry to some seventeen hundred Punjabis between 1911 and 1917.[17] The anti-immigration sentiment led to a series of early-twentieth-century court rulings that sought to establish a definition of white, which had been the criteria for obtaining citizenship since 1790. These cases culminated with the U.S. Supreme Court ruling in the 1923 *United States v. Bhagat Singh Thind* case that persons of Indian ancestry who had been able to acquire citizenship on basis of having descended from a Caucasian race could not be eligible for citizenship because white was not understood to be Caucasian but rather what was commonly understood as white. A year later, the restrictive Johnson-Reed Act barred Indians and other non-northern and western Europeans from entering the United States.

The perception that Indians were nonwhite and hence undesirable foreigners dominated popular understandings for the next several decades. Then, with the passage of the 1965 Immigration Act and the advent of a new stereotyped term "model minority," the understanding of the Indian body underwent a change from one of being a scourge in America to that of being a hard-working immigrant endowed (perhaps genetically) with the smartness to overcome racial and social marginalization to succeed in America economically and culturally in ways that outpaced even the dominant whites.[18]

Defining the Foreigner

"When I was growing up in Muncie, I didn't really think of myself as a child of immigrants," says Nisha. "I kind of grew up learning about immigrants and the meaning of immigration as associated much more with Ellis Island and the waves of immigrants that were coming from Europe, the Irish."

"My understanding of immigrants was that they were people that came who had no money. They didn't come here to go to school; they came here because they had no money. That made a big difference because my parents, they came for an education. They came here with a lot of support."

Nisha outlined this understanding in 2003 as we sat on the carpeted floor of an upstairs room in her home in Syracuse, New York. The room was filled with her five-year-old daughter's toys, her and her husband's books, a computer monitor, and stacks of notebooks. Nisha was completing a doctoral degree at the time, and her husband was teaching history at area community colleges and high schools. Nisha's other daughter, a four-month-old, slept in her lap as we talked. In 2010 Nisha's family moved to Louisville, Kentucky, where she had taken a position as a curriculum specialist and an instructor of women and gender studies at the University of Louisville. One of the attractions for the family in making the move was that Louisville was closer to Muncie and Fort Wayne, Indiana (where her husband's parents lived). The move also helps contextualize how Nisha discussed her childhood in Muncie as critical to shaping both her parenting and her professional work. That move highlights the importance of family connections in sustaining a sense of identity that Priscilla, Cheryl, and Anju discuss as well as the impacts of being disconnected from an immigrant experience that Nisha felt.

"If I'd grown up in a Chicago or a D.C., I wouldn't have come to this critical stage," said Nisha in 2003. "It's because my identity was called into question that I got there. Living in Muncie allowed me that experience. If I grew up in an Indian enclave, I wouldn't have known I was being othered."

Nisha was born in February 1966, one year after passage of the 1965 Immigration Act, which led in part to establishment of the metropolitan area Indian enclaves that she references. Those communities gave the younger South Asian Americans who grew up in Muncie an experience of being part of a strong ethnic community that several of our younger cousins who were born in Chicago and Washington, D.C., in the early 1980s had shared. One of our cousins, born in 1980 in a suburb of Washington, D.C., had a best friend from the start of elementary school who was Indian. Another one of our cousins, who emigrated from India in 2001, was living in a community also outside Washington, D.C., that was more than 50 percent South Asian. These younger generations of South Asian Americans, like Cheryl's nephew, grew up attending classical dance classes, taking Hindi lessons at community centers, participating with their parents in community temple activities, and consuming contemporary Indian culture via film videos, jewelry and sari shops, and restaurants. "There was never any question that we were Indian," one of my cousins told me. "We were around other Indians all the time."

For Nisha, the experience was different. Her awareness of other South Asians was limited to knowing two other families until students from India, Pakistan, Bangladesh, and other countries began to come in larger numbers to Ball State and to reside in the low-cost housing complex Scheidler Apartments behind our house. She dated her memories of feeling othered to the year our family returned to Muncie after living for one year in India. Before the trip, Nisha said, "I was with the white kids. I was one of them." After that, "They just cut me off. I wasn't a part of them anymore."

When we returned from India, we moved into a new house closer to our elementary school and directly adjacent to Scheidler Apartments, which the university had constructed to help accommodate its fast-growing married- and foreign-student population. The apartments opened in 1971 and by 1974 the presence of foreign university students had grown quite apparent, as more of their children were entering our school. I entered the sixth grade the year we returned and went to junior high school the year after, so I didn't notice the change much. Nisha, however, was in the third grade in 1974, and felt the impact keenly.

"So every year there would be maybe one or two kids who would be in our classes, who were from other countries," she says. "These kids would come to school . . . sometimes they wouldn't speak English very well. They would be really shy. They would be dressed in very traditional ethnic, cultural dress."

"At least until fourth grade, a distinction was made. These other kids who didn't speak English very well and lived in Scheidler were different from us."

Then, she added, "Once I started getting into adolescence, I sort of started getting grouped with those kids. And I didn't want to be. I wanted to assimilate."

Nisha narrated her childhood in terms of coming to understand that there was a theoretical distinction between ethnicity, which she felt she understood as a child, and race, which she said she came to understand through her graduate studies and professional work. She distinguished ethnicity from race by relating the former to a nonjudgmental ethnic or cultural difference and the latter to a more judgmental practice of defining within a social hierarchy constructed by others. Our school peers would refer to the children of students residing in Scheidler Apartments as "Scheidler rats," a derogatory phrase that called up racist connotations from the early twentieth century of nonwhite Anglo-Saxon Protestant immigrants as an infestation. "When I look back now, I realize that what I experienced [in childhood] was race. Our skin was different, our names were different, and some of our practices were different. But [what racialized the experience] had to do with how we were treated."

"How do you feel you were treated?" I asked.

"Well, I don't think I was treated very well," she replied. "I don't have very fond memories . . . I was always treated as if I was different, other, lesser."

Nisha's story points to a disjuncture in many historical studies of South Asian immigrants to the United States that separate the immigrants from Punjab who came in the early twentieth century from those who came after World War II and in increasingly large numbers after 1965. The changes in immigration laws that spurred the post-1965 growth of the South Asian American community were in part the result of political activism by the Punjabi immigrants who had settled on the West Coast as well as some immigrants who had integrated into some industrial cities and Spanish-speaking areas of Harlem in New York City in the 1920s through 1940s. Following the 1923 Bhagat Singh Thind ruling, nearly three thousand Indian immigrants either were returned to their home countries or left voluntarily, out of fear for their own safety. Many of those who remained married Mexican American women and had children who grew up speaking Spanish and English. While some of these immigrants sought to not call attention to practices that would mark them as Indian out of fears for personal safety, others formed organizations affiliated with their Sikh and Muslim faiths. These organizations also had a political agenda and began lobbying the U.S. Congress to restore the right to naturalized citizenship rights that the Thind case had stripped. While the white-dominant culture continued to racialize these immigrants and their descendants by referring to them derogatorily as "Hindoos," the immigrants themselves accepted the label as a way of defining their ethnicity on the basis of their country of origin and then translating their collective identity into a political commitment to fight the racist criteria for citizenship. The immigrants celebrated India's independence from British rule on August 15, 1947, one year following another victory: passage of the Luce-Cellar Act, which allowed nonwhite immigrants residing in the United States the opportunity to gain citizenship. The Luce-Cellar Act also lifted the barriers against Indian immigration and allowed 105 Indians to emigrate annually.[19]

By 1965, the children of the early-twentieth-century immigrants were adults. Like their fathers who had married into Mexican families, many of the children also had married non-Indian or mixed-race partners. While subject to the same segregation laws that prohibited African Americans from entering restaurants, barbershops, movie theaters, and swimming pools, these individuals also were aware of their ancestral ties to India and saw the 1965 change in law as an opportunity to welcome newcomers from India to the United States. For these earlier immigrants, there was no distinction between ethnicity and race. Indians and other South Asians coming into the United States would be defined as such in an ethnic and nationalist sense but would also be classified in racialized terms in accordance with the logic of race that defined American life. However, the newer post-1965 immigrants did not particularly understand their position in a manner defined by race. They also did not see affinity between their place in America and that of the South Asian immigrants before them. As some of the earlier histories of South Asian Americans have shown, many of the newer South Asian immigrants who arrived in the United States in the 1960s reacted to the mixed-race, multiethnic Indians with amusement. When the descendants of the earlier immigrants suggested they shared a homeland and common ethnic roots with the newer migrants, the newer arrivals often laughed, seeing themselves as ethnically distinct and racially higher in the American hierarchy.[20]

More recent works on South Asian Americans have sought connectivity between the earlier and later groups of immigrants.[21] Still, the earlier historiography reinforced these hierarchical distinctions by referring to the earlier immigrants as discrete and separate from the post-1965 immigrants and as less fortunate individuals who by intermarrying with Mexican Americans and other non-Indians had lost their ethnic Indian culture. The newer, post-1965 immigrants, by contrast, were portrayed as nationally distinct and as eager to re-create in the United States an ethnic culture that emphasized India's diversity and its urban, cosmopolitan culture.[22] The newer immigrants, as Karen Leonard observed, "have had no compelling reason to recognize the rural, less well-educated, half-Indian descendants of Punjabi peasants and they have not done so."[23]

As the Punjabi immigrants of the early twentieth century fought for civil rights, popular perceptions of southern and eastern European immigrants also underwent a shift. Previously subject to the same racially discriminatory treatment that the Punjabi laborers endured, the darker-complexioned European immigrants began in the 1930s to be perceived less as "unwanted aliens" who had been barred by the 1924 Immigration Act and more as white ethnic Europeans who, like their northern and western European predecessors, had become American by choice. This shift came as ethnic antagonisms between varying European immigrant groups began breaking down through desires to forge a common identity of being American, reinforcing the racialization of the American as white and allowing for the segregation and antimiscegenation laws that divided U.S. society by race to remain in place.[24] Nisha's childhood understanding of immigrants as individuals who did not have money and as coming from Europe resonated with the historic reclamation of the European immigrant identity as redemptive. This reclamation led to the viewing of the non-European immigrant identity as immutably foreign.

Racialized as an immigrant from about fourth grade on, Nisha recalls trying to understand herself better as an Indian who might share the same cultural practices with other Indians. Our father's family had had a practice of not eating eggs on Tuesdays, which our parents continued in Muncie. Nisha decided that she would add a variation to this practice by not eating meat. "You and the rest of the family, I remember you making fun of me when I said that," she told me. "That, and then trying to speak Hindi . . . people would make fun of it, and say, 'You're saying it wrong' . . . and then try to correct me."

"That's fine, but it doesn't encourage one to try to pursue ways to be Indian."

Entering college, Nisha began her studies at Purdue University with the intention of becoming an engineer. She transferred after her first year, however, to Indiana University and began taking classes in psychology and other social sciences. She also became politically involved with the antiapartheid movement and joined efforts on her campus to pressure the university to divest its assets in South Africa. "I started understanding race because of the antiapartheid movements, and as I read up on it, I started to understand how race operated in this country, too." That understanding moved her to switch her undergraduate major to psychology and to do graduate work in education with an emphasis on multicultural counseling. "[While] being in such a small town restricted my ability to interact with other Indians," Nisha said, "in my professional career, Indian students find me. I like to think it's because I'm competent and I can help them." She recalled being invited to the home of an Indian couple as a graduate student and showing up in shorts and a t-shirt only to discover that they had prepared an elaborate formal meal. "I felt so awkward that I could hardly eat anything," she remembered, "but now that I understand that these things happen to everyone, I try to be friendly to everyone and help others understand these experiences."

Nisha said remembering her childhood in Muncie provokes anger. "When I think about it, I can't stand Muncie anymore. It's such a white town. It doesn't allow me to be authentic, to be me." Yet that anger over her inability—like Anju's—to just "be me" also gives her a source of strength, sustaining her willingness to fight her feelings about the past. Nisha has wanted her children, who are biracial, to spend time with their maternal grandparents in Muncie and to understand that some of their ancestry is Indian. She wears salwar kameez from time to time and has organized her household so that she cooks Indian food a couple days a week. One of her family's regular activities is to create "the roti assembly line" to prepare the flat bread. Two people roll the dough into circles, one person cooks the flat bread on a curved griddle known as a *tawa*, and the fourth butters the final product. Still, she worried in 2003 about how her daughters understood themselves. Her eldest daughter would describe visiting Fort Wayne, where Nisha's husband is from, as "going to see Grandpa and Grandma" while talking about visiting Muncie to see our parents as "going to India."

"Studies indicate that by age five kids are consciously aware of race and its hierarchy," said Nisha. "I don't want her to grow up like Nelly Wong, scrubbing her skin every night to make it whiter. I had those feelings growing up. I don't want her to."

Truces with Reality

FEMALE VOICE: Did I tell you about the employer who posted a job opening on the Internet and got so many applications he didn't know what to do.

MALE VOICE: No, tell me about it.

FEMALE VOICE: He even got one from Sri Lanka.

MALE VOICE: Sri Lanka? He'd hire someone from Sri Lanka instead of someone locally?

FEMALE VOICE: No, of course not. But that's just the point. . . .

[*She goes on to explain how coming to the job service center would have helped the employer find a suitable match for his job opening locally.*]

But, he didn't do that. And the pile of resumes got so high that one day it tottered over and they fell on him.

MALE VOICE: Oh no.

FEMALE VOICE: Crushing him, burying him underneath all the debris, and the worst thing was, the human resources director got caught under them with him.

This droll dialogue aired in a public service announcement for the east-central Indiana Job Service Center on WERK radio in Muncie in 2003. I heard it several times as I drove around Muncie. I often had the radio tuned to WERK because it was the Top 40s station of the 1970s, playing my favorite hit songs as a teen. The depiction of the Sri Lankan job applicant came as a growing number of South Asian immigrants began dominating entries to the United States via temporary H-1B visas or as international students, both of which provided little assurance that the individuals in question could remain in the country if their technical skills or intellectual talents were not useful to the nation's economy.[25] In doing so, it points to how racial discourses in the Heartland continued to position white, Muncie-raised individuals as superior to others. If employers knew what they were doing, the dialogue implied, they would not have to look overseas to Sri Lanka for help. The dialogue also evokes the riddle of the ship captain that my uncle told me as a five-year-old, especially when both were placed into the narratives of migration of slaves, indentured laborers, early-twentieth-century Indian workers, post-1965 success stories, and the contingency of life that residing in the United States as a temporary resident connoted. All these groups endured much hardship and hostility in both Britain and the United States in an effort to create better lives for themselves and their families.

The narratives of the riddle, the radio ad, and the ship in this sense hold within them stories about the relationship between South Asian immigrants and the labor needs of the U.S. economy. Implicitly, they reveal stories of how the racial hierarchies of American society force one of nonwhite ancestry into truces with their own realities, truces that, as Baldwin suggests, might be the most one can expect. These stories stretch over nearly two centuries and complicate the perception that the presence of South Asians in the United States is relatively new. The stories also offer examples of how popular perceptions of the nonwhite, non-European immigrant body have quickly slid through history from industrious and useful to unworthy, and how that slippage is part of a daily reality that affects South Asian Americans and others of color. The stories that Cheryl, Anju, Priscilla, and Nisha each share are filled with instances of such realities.

James Baldwin wrote the words that opened this chapter in a letter to his son. Published in an autobiographical essay, the idea of being born a Negro and trying "to effect some kind of truce with this reality" reads a little like an advice manual on how one might cope with an unwelcoming America. Baldwin, like many African American writers, deserves credit for helping us to imagine a more multiracial America. But a truce is merely an agreement, and not necessarily a peaceful one. It leaves one asking questions about what histories are silenced. It does not provide a means of creating an antiracist society in Muncie or in the United States that would promote inclusion. Could there be a way to think of America differently?

One photograph might offer a clue. In the late 1990s as the South Asian population in the United States approached 2 million, Indian-born writer Bharati Mukherjee evoked her own immigrant journey from an orthodox Brahmanical household in Calcutta to Iowa City, Iowa, by posing for a *Mother Jones* magazine photo in cornfields with an American flag draped over her body like a sari. "I am an American, not an Asian-American," Mukherjee declared in an opening pull quote that accompanied the photo and her essay "American Dreamer," which berates India-born immigrants who wished to remain insulated from the racialized realities of American life.[26] Mukherjee's declaration of herself as a nonhyphenated American reinforces a myth that all immigrants can "melt" into the "new breed of Americans" that Hector St. Jean de Crèvecoeur lauded, regardless of their nation of origin and/or religious identity. That assimilationist ethos erases the history of hostilities that Asian, African, and Eastern and Southern European immigrants have faced. The fact that Mukherjee's body was draped with the U.S. flag further connotes a jingoistic message, calling up U.S. imperialism in the Persian Gulf and elsewhere.

However, using the framework of James Baldwin's "truce with reality" and the insights on naming and identity choices that emerged in the stories of four of the first South Asian American children to grow up in Muncie, one might look at the photograph differently. In it, Mukherjee is standing in cornfields that resembled those that had abutted our backyard in Muncie before being cleared to make way for Ball State's Scheidler apartments. Her time and place of arrival in the United States was 1961 and Iowa City. Thus, her presence in the photograph represents an Indian immigrant in small-town Middle America at a time when no Indian community was believed to exist. The cornfields, too, might symbolize labor and land, lands first snatched by Europeans from Indigenous American cultivators and then labored in by tens of thousands of non-European worker bodies to build an America that refused to see itself as being represented by the bodies of its others. In a sense, the photograph brings to visibility the bodies and stories of nonwhites that the truce with reality evokes. The truce then is revealed as acknowledging how nonwhites must bury their racially coded experiences of pain, suffering, and dehumanization to live in a white America.

Yet the stories of the past never disappear entirely. Coming to the United States, observes Sridevi Menon, forces one to "confront other histories" that mark the American landscape.[27] My goal in interviewing Muncie South Asian Americans was to make visible a community I had grown up in that I felt had been rendered invisible. My "Middletown" would have been peopled with individuals who had names of Indian, Pakistani, and Bangladeshi origin. Yet the institutional review-board protocols forced a protection of confidentiality that made it harder to create a portrait of a community of diverse names, faces, ethnicities, races, religions, and voices. I had tried to attain my goal by establishing a practice in which individual interviewees could choose names that would protect their confidentiality but still speak to their personal genealogy. If the names could not be actual names of the interviewees themselves, they at least could be names that connoted a South Asian American identity.

Nevertheless, Priscilla's choice—like Mukherjee's body and the history of the cornfields in the photograph—suggests that it is not so much the name that matters or the way that one chooses to identify one's self as it is the historic experience within those labels and the narratives that emerge out of that experience. Like a symbol of American pride distorted into the folds of an Indian sari, choosing non–South Asian names creates a space where one can affirm a place in the United States on terms of one's choice. In this sense, we are left once again with a truce that is neither ideal nor easy but remains a contingency from which new articulations of what it means to be American can emerge.

CHAPTER 4

Navigating Rebellion and Respect

South Asian Teenagers and High School Life

> The small community tends to be a place of usual personalities,
> usual jobs, usual recreations. Many of the odd personalities—the
> political or economic radical, the artistic individual, the person
> with a flair for the unusual—migrate to larger cities where
> the cultural pattern is less rigid. . . . Those unsatisfied souls
> who remain in Middletown tend often to carry on difficult lives
> of outward conformity and unhappy underlying rebellion.
>
> —Robert S. Lynd and Helen Merrell Lynd,
> *Middletown in Transition*, 1937

Muncie, Indiana
1981

Filmmakers Joel DeMott and Jeff Kreines trained their small, handheld cameras on a group of friends who had congregated at Lynn Massie's home on the south side of Muncie, gathering footage for what was to become their award-winning documentary, *Seventeen*. In this scene, the central character, Lynn, a young white woman attending Southside High School, is upset because friends of her African American boyfriend John Vance were harassing her and her family. Lynn's mother, Shari, also is angry. She complains that she had woken up at 3 A.M. a few nights earlier to find a cross burning in the yard. She declared that whoever burned the cross didn't know the family because "if they did, they'd know we're not like that."

Drinking a beer in her kitchen with her husband, Jim, Shari remarks that some blacks are "niggers" and some are "black people" just as some people are "white trash" and some are "white." The telephone rings. Another harasser. Lynn warns the caller that her mother carries a gun and isn't afraid to use it. Shari advises her daughter and the young men grouped around her not to go out "in certain neighborhoods" alone.

Seventeen, filmed in 1981 as part of a public-television series titled *Middletown*, captures both the allure and risk of the nonconformity that Robert Lynd had found lacking among residents when he revisited Muncie in 1935 to research *Middletown in Transition*. The film reinforces belief in the geographic line that the book featured as dividing residents by race and by class, as well as the dangers of not honoring those lines. The *Middletown* film series' curators envisioned *Seventeen* as an honest but upbeat portrayal of students in their last year of high school preparing to make the transition to adulthood. The film became a target of derision because, in part, of what it actually showed: teenagers at Muncie Southside High School drinking excessively, smoking marijuana, cutting class, talking back to teachers, and dating across racial lines; teachers trying to nudge the students toward understanding their last year of high school as being a transition to adulthood, and urging them to consider activities like cooking as practices of responsible living and studies of the family as messages of the values of good citizenship and great parenting. In the film, one young woman drops out of school after becoming pregnant, while the presumed father vacillates between denial of responsibility and an embrace of delight over the baby's eventual birth. At the Massie home, Shari and Jim parent in their own ways: they drink beer with the teens as they dole out advice on coexisting in an interracial world. "You're safe if you're all together," Shari tells her daughter and her friends. "But if someone catches you alone in a place where they don't think you belong, you might find yourself in a lot of trouble without any protection."

The filmmakers Kreines and DeMott all but lived with Lynn and her family and friends for a year, shadowing them as their constant companions, filming and remaining within a few feet of them at all times. The pair edited their footage with a goal of re-creating a "real world" that viewers could imagine themselves experiencing in a manner that was not voyeuristic but co-participatory. What DeMott and Kreines produced, however, did not sit well with Muncie parents, PBS executives, or school authorities. As rumors of what the pair was filming began to circulate, these parties individually and collectively started to ask questions about whether the content would portray high-school life in Muncie as they wanted it to appear. Questions escalated into protests, and protests into threats of lawsuits and warnings of physical harm. When faced with the Muncie outcry, series director Peter Davis, who also had directed the heavily protested anti–Vietnam War film *Hearts and Minds*, withdrew *Seventeen* from the series.

DeMott and Kreines released their film independently in 1985, and it won the Sundance Film Award for Best Documentary. It then disappeared from public view until 2010, when the *Middletown* series became available for purchase via DVD.

Like Lynn Massie, I was a high school senior in 1981. I attended Northside High School on the other side of town and was part of a more middle-class, college-bound student body in contrast to the more working-class demographic of Southside. I learned about *Seventeen* in a scholarly article published in 2004 that contained a footnote referencing the protests. Curious about this film that had been made but never screened publicly in Muncie, I found a copy and watched it several times. I found its story both sickening and provocative. The main characters, the dialogue, and scenes of high-school life brought back repulsive memories of growing up in Muncie, evoking experiences like the one of being spat on at my school playground. Yet many of the scenes also seemed to resonate with stories I had gathered from the South Asian American adults I interviewed. Like Lynn Massie and myself, these individuals—nine women and two men—also had memories of attending schools where drinking, smoking, using marijuana, swearing, and dating within and across racial lines were among the unofficial activities. Like me, all of the Muncie-raised South Asians left the city soon after finishing high school or college to pursue professional careers. Like the individuals in *Seventeen*, these Muncie-raised South Asians also seemed almost forgotten, footnotes in the histories not only of the city but perhaps of South Asian America, too. I decided to try and retrieve those footnotes of history by telling their stories and mine alongside the story of what had happened with the film *Seventeen.*

What emerges from this effort at retrieval is a strange but resilient understanding of rebellion against societal norms. Rebellion is understood in this sense as an act that results in understandings, intimacies, and alliances among peoples who breach racial, heteronormative, and economic lines. This chapter explores how the term "rebellion" came up in stories that Muncie-raised South Asians shared with me and places those discussions within the context of Muncie's reputation for representing American typicality as well as the racial and economic dynamics of the city. This view of rebellion also adds to envisionings of a more multiply voiced Muncie and America.

Being Ourselves

"I was the most rebellious [of my siblings]," recalled Lynsi, a Muncie-raised South Asian who graduated from high school in the same year I did.

"How were you rebellious?" I asked.

"I didn't go to the Bengali parties," she replied. "I didn't wear the Bengali, you know, the sari. I never have. I really didn't spend any time with anyone in the culture. I dated, did things that were definitely not part of the culture."

"I never drank. I never smoked . . . in the American measurement that would be rebellion. I think I was just not following the expectations of the culture."

"What do you mean by the culture?" I asked.

"Bengali, decidedly Muslim," she said. "Very tightly knit, you know that. Everybody knows everybody. A clique."

Lynsi shared these observations with me when I visited her home outside Chicago. Forty years old at the time, she identified herself as an American who was Bengali by ethnicity and Muslim by religion. She was born in Karachi, Pakistan, and grew up in Muncie from the fourth grade on; she completed high school at the Burris Laboratory School and her undergraduate degree at Ball State. She moved first to Florida and later to Chicago, where she completed master's and doctoral degrees, specializing in criminal justice. When we reconnected, she was a professor of sociology and was completing work on a scholarly encyclopedia.

Lynsi remembered Muncie much as my sister Anju did, as a place she loved growing up in but after leaving did not want to return to live. Lynsi also remembered it as the place where she asserted herself as an individual in ways that were like her non–South Asian school peers. She characterized that self-assertion as setting her apart from her parents' Bengali culture, and she saw that setting apart as making her appear rebellious.

Lynsi's stories of her teenage years called up memories of my life in those years as well. My parents discouraged dating, drinking, and drug use without expressly forbidding it. They spoke of the value of their Indian culture and encouraged me to adhere to its norms of obedience to parents, particularly when it came to marriages, which they felt should be arranged. Those norms made little sense to me, so I responded by talking to boys on the phone and going over to friends' houses to drink beer. I did not want to "get into trouble." I just wanted to feel like I could take part in something my friends were doing, regardless of whether my parents approved. Like Lynsi, I wouldn't wear the ethnic attire associated with my family's heritage, and I was not interested in getting to know anyone of Indian or other South Asian ancestry. And, like Lynsi, I went against my parents' expectations that I study medicine or engineering and instead pursued a passion to write.

"Did your parents know about the dating?" I asked Lynsi.

"No. God no," she replied with a laugh. "Well, my mom probably did. My dad may have, but I doubt it."

"Did you date?" she asked, after a pause.

"No, I would have if I could have," I said. "I drank."

Lynsi told me that she did not feel she was being purposefully rebellious. This description resonated with my own feelings that my actions, too, were not so much about rebellion as much as they were about fitting in with mostly white Muncie peers. While our friends might have been rebelling against parental expectations, I, as an Indian girl, did not consider them rebels as much as a peer group of which I wanted to be a part.

Other Muncie-raised South Asians who grew up in this period also brought up the word "rebellion" as they spoke about their childhood and adolescent years. They remembered their rebellions as consisting of working part-time jobs outside the home, going out for walks late at night, and adopting styles of dress that differed from their parents' preferences. They, too, differentiated their rebellions from what they called an "American" idea of rebellion, which they tended to regard as the less respectable behaviors of getting so drunk or so stoned as to lose control of one's ability to control actions, or of engaging in premarital sex—an act that could lead, of course, to an unwanted pregnancy. All of us were children of either university professors or medical doctors, and were regarded as bright children among both Muncie adults and our peers. Perhaps because we were born to parents who were highly educated professionals working in socially prestigious positions, we understood that our actions as teenagers were in harmony with a discursively defined framework of American upward mobility because in so many ways we were responding to the same racialized and gender-based cues of our mostly white, middle-class peers. The only things that we felt we were questioning were the parameters of middle-class respectability. We did not understand how or why our immigrant parents viewed part-time jobs, dressing in stylish teen clothes, wearing makeup, and going out for dates as harmful or disrespectful to them. Our rebellions were about bridging perceived gaps between the values that were imparted in our homes and the behaviors which our mostly white peers indulged at school and elsewhere. We did not want to upset or hurt our parents. Instead, as my sister Anju put it in the previous chapter, we just wanted to be ourselves.

"I had my rebellion stage in medical school," recalled Vinod. "I let my hair grow out; it was down to my shoulders. Boy, my dad was irritated."

Vinod's description of rebellion made us both laugh. Dictionary definitions for the term "rebellion" associate it with "opposition to a named authority," "defiance," and "revolt, sometimes military." I had remembered Vinod mainly as a quiet boy, and in his professional and personal adult roles as a doctor in central Michigan, he did not seem like one who would revolt in the least.

He was born in Muncie in 1969. Both of us remembered playing together as children when there would be dinner parties and Diwali celebrations in our different families' homes. But as he spoke of his years of coming to terms with a South Asian American identity that he characterized as "Indian and American, half and half," his depiction of his rebellion became a vehicle for becoming an individual who was a part of an Indian culture he appreciated but did not feel he understood as well as he would have liked, and of an American culture that, in Muncie particularly, had trapped him in a cage he felt he needed to escape.

For adolescents in America in the late twentieth century, rebellion was an accepted, sometimes heralded rite of passage. Within the westernized framework, rebellion was regarded as a part of teenage life, which involved self-exploration, engagement with creative expression, assertion of independence, and willingness to question societal norms.[1] The opposite of rebellion in this scenario would be conforming to expectations for upwardly mobile success, such as going to school, working a part-time job, and testing the social acceptance of certain hairstyles or dress. While Vinod was rebelling against the wishes of his parents, he was doing so in a respectful way that perhaps adults and their aging parents might laugh together about later. He was conforming to the expectations of the social class that his parents had moved into after his father had attained the status of university professor.

A desire to remain respectable helps explain a dilemma that emerged as I shared my analyses of the stories of rebellion with the interviewees themselves: many of them asked me—in a respectful, almost apologetic way—not to use their stories in this book. The reasons varied. Some worried their stories would identify them to others in the South Asian community as well as other people from Muncie. Others questioned my readings of their stories, noting that while they respected my viewpoint as a researcher, they did not think my analyses represented their experiences. Many feared that divulging their memories would hurt the feelings of their parents or be disrespectful of them. For many of them, respect for parents overwrote any memory of adolescent behavior—rebellious or otherwise—that my questions might have called up. The following anonymous quotes, which I did choose to use, illuminate these feelings well:

> We were quite isolated when we were growing up. So we spoke our parents' language at home, but we never could learn to read it or write it. Because there was no place to learn it. . . . To this day, I can speak my parents' language, but I don't know any more than that.

> The most important thing for me growing up was not to hurt my parents.

There . . . were odd things, things that were never explained. Like I had a lot of facial hair when I was growing up, but was not allowed to shave.

My mother and father wanted the best for me, but I am not sure they knew how to give it to me.

We were supposed to send our grandparents a Valentine's Day card; that was a school assignment. I couldn't do that, because I couldn't speak or write in my grandparents' language. I had to ask my parents to do it for me.

Vinod's rebellion, like Lynsi's and like mine, occurred in the early to mid-1980s, before a vibrant South Asian youth culture existed in the United States. Studies of youth culture published since then have noted that the teenage years had become accepted as a distinct era in the lives of American and European individuals soon after World War II. However, the notion was relatively nonexistent among South Asians until the late 1990s. South Asian parents both in their home countries and diaspora viewed the teenage years as either an extension of childhood or as a precursor to college and/or marriage.[2]

The children of the South Asian immigrants who came to Muncie in the 1960s and early 1970s grew up, of course, within both the South Asian and European American frameworks of adolescence. For this reason, it is not surprising that when I asked them what they remembered about their lives in Muncie, many brought up the word "rebellion" first, then proceeded to describe how they were rebellious, and then, after giving their statements some thought, asked that I not include their stories in this book. Perhaps, too, it also is not surprising that their parents did not mention rebellion at all when they discussed their children. The parents, as immigrants, were operating out of a different framework of expectations for teenagers. Their framework was based on what they had understood adolescence to be when they were teenagers and young adults in pre-Partition India. They came of age as their countries shook themselves free of British rule and were immediately divided on the basis of religious differences that had become painfully politicized. Their teenage years, in many cases, were more about family and community survival and less about finding and asserting senses of self.

The requests that the Muncie-raised interviewees made to excise their stories led me to theorize more deeply on the reasons for such reluctance. In doing so, I came to realize that the requests themselves were challenging a conventional view within Asian American studies scholarship on relationships between Asian American immigrant parents and American-raised children. The conventional view saw these relationships as fraught with intergenerational conflict.[3] The interviewees, on the other hand, were reinforcing intergenerational bonds. My own willingness to remove their stories also challenged the presumption of intergenerational conflict. Such examples revealed that while adult children might disagree with their parents, the levels of respect between members of differing South Asian American generations tend to deepen with time. It was painful to delete what I felt were poignant and deeply illuminative stories of our generation's experience in Muncie as the first generation of American-raised South Asians. Yet I was willing to comply with the requests because of the relationships I had rekindled with members of Muncie's South Asian community. I, too, did not want to cause pain to their immigrant parents.

My interviewees' requests for privacy also resonated with the experiences captured on film in *Seventeen*. My decision to protect their stories from public disclosure stands in contrast to the scrutiny to which the teenagers and family members congregated at the Massie home and around Southside High School were subjected when the film was produced and when the outcry over its portrayals erupted. Very few individuals whose lives were featured in that documentary have ever spoken positively of what the film portrayed or of their roles in it, even decades after the film's release. If they have spoken publicly at all, it has usually been to express anger at how they were portrayed.[4] In this sense, the silencing of stories from the South Asian Americans who came of age as adolescents and young adults in Muncie helps to establish a deeper understanding of what it means to be publicly portrayed as a rebel.

The protests against *Seventeen* and suppression of the film also underscored a struggle to define the differences between rebellion and respect. Because DeMott and Kreines chose to portray rebellion against societal norms instead of conformity to them, the film evoked wrath. For instance, Southside High School principal James Hedge complained that while the filmmakers had told the school that they planned "to include athletics, homecoming, prom, commencement and everything in between" in order "to make a film which former students could be proud of," "none of the positive aspects are shown." Others criticized the film for showing teenagers engaging in acts that either were illegal, such as marijuana smoking and underage drinking, or violated such entrenched norms such as dating across racial lines.[5] These statements gain added currency when one looks at how they speak within the context of how Muncie's reputation of representing American typicality was also being rearticulated in the period during which *Seventeen* was filmed. Let us turn now to a look at that context.

Perpetuating Conformity

When Robert S. Lynd returned to Muncie to research *Middletown in Transition*, he did so with a smaller research budget, a shorter time frame, and a more cynical mindset than he had possessed in 1924. By the 1930s, as the United States had slid into the Great Depression, Lynd had read the works of Karl Marx and had expressed a growing disillusionment with the consumerist aspects of American society.[6] *Middletown in Transition* reflects Lynd's disenchantment with the typical American. He and his co-author and wife, Helen Merrell Lynd, reported that Middletown residents disliked "unhappy, 'abnormal' things"; preferred "to think and talk about the normal"; believed "'the family' means 'a nice marriage with children,'"; and did not tolerate children who acted as if they might have more wisdom than adults.[7] Such characteristics of complacent Muncie residents resonate with the remarks of those who criticized *Seventeen*.

Some Middletown scholars characterized *Middletown in Transition* as the Lynds' epitaph for Muncie. However, Muncie's reputation for typicality continued to remain a site of scholarly curiosity through the 1940s into the 1960s, and interest began to surface in the 1970s for a third Middletown study, particularly among sociologists who were curious as to how the Great Depression, the post–World War II prosperity, and the decade of protest and civil rights struggles on the 1960s had affected the Middletown citizens' outlooks on the world. This interest resulted in two undertakings: a $500,000 surveying and sampling study led by three esteemed sociologists, one of whom had been a student of Robert Lynd's; and the $3 million Middletown Film Project developed by three Ball State University professors and film director Davis. The National Science Foundation funded the sociological study, and the National Endowment for the Humanities and Xerox Corporation funded the film series.[8] This governmental and corporate support highlighted the importance placed on the projects.

The sociological study, titled Middletown III, was envisioned as a set of interrelated projects that would examine each of the six themes that had organized the earlier Lynd studies and was to be published in a set of half-dozen scholarly books. It involved three lead researchers—Theodore Caplow, Bruce Chadwick, and Howard Bahr—and about twenty-five graduate students, postdoctoral researchers, interviewers, secretaries, and others to assemble a sophisticated statistical sampling. The lead researchers had considerably more professional expertise in the field than Robert S. Lynd and Helen Merrell Lynd had possessed but respected the practices that the researchers who had worked with the couple had set and adopted the Lynd team's methods of researching newspaper archives, attending community gatherings, and interviewing community leaders. They also relied heavily on surveying and statistical analysis to develop their conclusions.[9]

The scholarly teams published several journal articles and two books based on the data they gathered. The published work reflected the heavy academic expertise of the researchers but failed to convey the folksy narrative tone that had made *Middletown* so enticing to popular commentators and the general public. As a result, the profile of American culture in the late 1970s conveyed in the books seemed stale and as if there was little new to report. The first book, *Middletown Families: Fifty Years of Change and Continuity*, for instance, reports that one-third of the city's high school students were grandchildren of the students who filled out the Lynd team's high school questionnaires in 1924. It suggests that this fact represented a stable, little-changed community demographic and concludes that the traditional family in Muncie was not breaking apart. The second book, *All Faithful People: Change and Continuity in Middletown's Religion*, portrays a religious environment where Christianity flourished, with Sunday mornings in Muncie characterized by cars crowding the streets as they carried families to church, followed by afternoon visits to restaurants and the city's mall. The authors of both texts concluded that their findings were not different from what the Lynds had uncovered, and that Muncie had not significantly changed. "The most striking feature of Middletown is that it contains nothing extraordinary," wrote co-authors Caplow, Chadwick, and Bahr in *All Faithful People*. "Its population [in the 1920s] was mostly white, native born, mostly Protestant." *Middletown Families* stated: "Middletown does not make its own history but patiently suffers the history made outside."[10]

Despite these assertions, both books did document several important statistical details that, when delved into, showed signs of significant change. Among these details were the growth in the African American population; the presence of four high schools in the city by 1977, compared with just one in 1929; and a debilitating shift in the economic base that had accompanied the beginnings of deindustrialization in the 1970s from primarily industrial and commercial to increasingly lower-wage services. The statistical documentation also found that the city had a large number of adult bookstores and massage parlors and that more than one-third of the female teenage population were clients of the local Planned Parenthood.[11] However, the authors included little analysis of these statistics. They reported them and allowed meaning to emerge from the discursive frame established by the earlier Middletown studies. From their standpoint, Muncie remained much as *Middletown in Transition* had portrayed it: a predominantly white Christian city locked into generations of religious and cultural patterns of conformity. Not much had changed.

Troubling Conformity

"People ask me, 'Did you hang out with blacks or whites?'" recalled Lynsi. "I say, 'With whites.' I totally integrated with [whites]. I never had any black friends."

"That's really frightening," Lynsi said. "Think about that. Muncie is very much a white community, at least the part of Muncie where we were raised. The south side of Muncie is very different. I didn't even know how to get to the south side of Muncie; I still don't know how. That's kind of scary."

Many of the Muncie-raised South Asians I interviewed were children or teenagers during the years Middletown III took place. While they were not deliberately screened out as the foreign-born and African Americans were in the first Middletown projects of the 1920s and 1930s, the follow-up projects offered little acknowledgement of their families' presence. Many of my Muncie-raised interviewees remembered the public environments of their teen years in ways that matched the Middletown III data: as feeling "too white," "too small," "too hick," and too lacking in the kind of social and cultural diversity they sought. They remembered their home environments differently, as characterized by parents who were loving but strict. Even as they expressed love for their parents and a need to be respectful of them, they sensed a dissonance between the lessons of life absorbed through family members in their homes and the values to which the children were exposed in more public spaces, such as schools.

Many of their sentiments mirrored mine. I had left Muncie as soon as I completed high school and had had little desire to return. Reflecting on these parallels decades later, I wondered if we had been exposed as children and teens to a Muncie that was truly Muncie, or if we, like *Middletown* readers, had received through our childhoods an incomplete experience. Was Muncie as "white" and "as lacking in diversity" as many of us remembered it to be? Did we experience Muncie in a way that made it seem, like the Middletown legacy, whiter and more homogenous than it was? What led us to experience Muncie as we did—to not know about cross burnings in our neighborhoods and in neighborhoods like those of the Massie family? To feel as if the mainly white peer group at school was the only standard by which we could measure ourselves?

Lynsi entered Ball State University in the early 1980s and took her first course in criminal justice. She began volunteering at a shelter for battered women in Muncie and realized she loved the work of bringing justice to people via punishments for offenders and assistance for victims. "Everything I've done in my life to date has been about this," she said. "I've worked with couples in violent relationships. I've worked with children, inmates, with police departments on training programs."

I learned about this work only when I spoke with Lynsi. I was somewhat surprised that I had not heard about it from my parents, who had continued to be close to her parents, but I also realized that while Lynsi and I had known each other growing up, we had been more like acquaintances than friends. When I asked her why she thought this might have been the case, she speculated on a variety of reasons, including the fact that her family was Muslim, while my family was Hindu. Then she alluded again to rebellion:

"I wasn't around a lot," she said. "I was with a certain set of friends; I was with them all the time. I didn't do a lot with my parents."

What was she rebelling against? "The culture," was her response. "The way that I was expected to do something like become a scientist or work in a field where there were a lot of Asians. The way I was expected to marry into the culture."

"You know, when I was in graduate school, I was going to do a study on this very same thing that you're doing now," Lynsi added.

"On Muncie South Asians, on us?" I asked.

"Looking at first generation children growing up in the United States and how our lives are different from our parents'."

"What happened?"

"My parents discouraged me," Lynsi said. "'What you don't know can't hurt' was what they told me."

Lynsi's story called up my experience of being asked what Indian community existed in Muncie. It also paralleled the Middletown III projects characterization of the city as unchanged. Putting these together suggests some common threads. It is expected that people conform to a certain set of cultural or societal expectations of who they are in an America that remains defined in a particular way. People who do not conform are seen as rebellious, and rebellion is something that needs to be contained.

Gregory Williams's memoir, *Life on the Color Line: The True Story of a White Boy Who Discovered He Was Black*, further highlights the resilience of such expectations. The son of a white mother and a fairer-skinned African American father, Williams spent his early childhood in the 1940s in Virginia, believing he was white. After his mother left his father, the father took him and his younger brother to Muncie to live. On the bus ride between Virginia and Indiana, the father gave the boys some news. In Muncie, the father would be black. The boys might be regarded as black, or there was a chance that they could continue to pass as white. The father suggested the boys consider their choices: If they could pass as white, their future paths through society might be much smoother. If they remained black, they were in for a life of trouble.

Williams made his choice on his first day of high school at Muncie Central. He writes: "I climbed the marble steps to the auditorium. The smell of musty wood filled the air as I scanned the cavernous room . . . [which was] divided into three distinct sections, north, south, and a broad vacant middle. Black students huddled together on the south side. Whites filled the north. The middle section flowed between them like a deep unnavigable river."[12] He asked himself whether to join his friends who were African American or whether to try migrating toward the whites and the promise of upward mobility. He chose his friends.

Williams's choice reinforces historic perceptions of Muncie being not one city but rather two, divided on the basis of race, as do Lynsi's questions about how to get to the south side. *Seventeen* also reinforces this split, characterizing the division as being based, however, not just on race but also class, as both the content and vernacular in dialogue from the following scene illustrate: Lynn and her white female friend Tink are at the Delaware County Fair's Midway with their African American male dates. Tink is upset because she feels like her boyfriend is ignoring her "because all of his black friends are around." Lynn and Tink confront the males with this issue as the group leave the fairgrounds together in a car.

"You figure this," declares Lynn. "You guys ain't the ones getting a bad name. We are. White girls just don't mess with no black guys, but we swallow our pride for you guys because we care for you."

"After we're seen with one of you ain't no white dude ever gonna touch us again," adds Tink. "But after you guys are seen with a white girl ain't nobody cares."

It might seem clear that the young women, by virtue of being white, held a certain level of racialized privilege that allowed them the kinds of opportunities that Gregory Williams might have been able to enjoy, had he chosen to join the whites. From the girls' perspective, however, no consciousness of that privilege existed—at least in terms of how the scene was documented in the film. To them, the thaw in race relations that separated Williams's era of high-school life from theirs created an opportunity for African Americans, but nothing for whites of working-class backgrounds. Such a sentiment reflects the defensiveness expressed by racially or religiously dominant groups who fear that a loss of social privileges will result from more equitable distributions of resources and power among diverse groups.

Seventeen is difficult to watch, partly because the film documents a particular historical timeframe in Muncie in a way that forces the viewer to relive that past as if it were the present and partly because one sees how privileges of race and class play out. For me, watching the film brought back memories of an inter-racial but racially and economically tense environment that had been hard to comprehend without knowing much about the history of the racial relation-ships in the city where I was living. Experiencing Muncie's racial climate via the film made me wonder what my parents and the parents of my other South Asian American interviewees might have known of the racism prevalent in the community and what they chose to conceal. Were their concerns about generally accepted teenage behaviors such as dating, getting part-time jobs, going out late at night, growing hair long, and sampling alcohol rooted at least partially in concerns about the Muncie environment? Perhaps our parents were using rules about driving, coming home at night, and dating as a way to shield us from these racial tensions that they might not have understood but affec-tively sensed. If this were the case, the rules might be seen as also presenting the Muncie-raised teenagers with a subtle message about the socioeconomic capital of race: Whites represented the successful aspects of America that one ought to seek. Blacks signified the opposite.

But the shield could only be partial if one were growing up with an under-standing of one's parents that was perhaps stronger than the parents had of themselves. As I watched *Seventeen*, I thought of Lynsi's words, "What you don't know can't hurt." *Seventeen* revealed many details of Muncie life that I didn't know at the time. It also reminded me of many aspects of that life that I had known but had chosen to forget. I perhaps had deployed this forgetting as a result of my socialization toward white, upwardly mobile societal norms.

South Asian Americans growing up in Muncie in the 1970s did have to decide how to place themselves in relation to the whites and blacks with whom we interacted. As descendants of South Asian immigrants, they could not fit into a clearly defined category within the rubric of Americanness. At least part of the reason for this lack of clarity was due to the historic use of federal-census designations to establish one's identity within governmentally defined groups. In the mid-1970s, Indian American interest groups in larger cities began lob-bying the federal government to create the census designation Asian Indian within a racially defined Asian category that would allow individuals of such an affiliation to claim minority status. The pages of *India Abroad* and other pub-lications aimed at South Asian diaspora communities that many immigrants avidly read were full of reports on these lobbying efforts. However, there was little awareness of the impact that these efforts might have on South Asian Americans in smaller communities like Muncie. Until the Asian Indian des-ignation was placed on census forms for the first time in 1980, those who lived in the 1970s in middle-American small towns like Muncie had no way to define themselves in a way that would be institutionally comprehensible as anything besides other.[13]

Many Muncie-raised South Asians found the position of invisible other to be safe in the racially tense atmosphere of the 1970s and 1980s. Vinod recalled being in the Boy Scouts. His father had encouraged him and his two brothers to excel in the Boy Scouts because he appreciated the values of self-reliance, discipline, and moral fortitude the organization represented. While Vinod might have agreed internally with those values, outwardly, he said, "At my school, the Boy Scouts were for wusses." Vinod already had experienced ridicule; among other things, he had been called a cow worshipper. So when he attained the status of Eagle Scout, he begged his mother not to call the Muncie newspaper to report the achievement because he knew it would be announced over the school's public address system. "When I was a freshman, a few kids, Caucasian kids, made it to Eagle Scout," he recalled. "The school made a big deal out of it, and those boys were just ridiculed. I didn't need any more of that than I was already getting."

Economic Shifts

Muncie's economy had been primarily industrial and small-scale commercial through the first two-thirds of the twentieth century. By the mid-1970s, the city had begun to rely increasingly on Ball State University and the services and healthcare sectors for economic activity. These new economic bases were on the city's north side. By the late 1970s, this shift had led to what *Middletown Families* authors Caplow, Chadwick, and Bahr characterized as a "sharp segregation of college students and professors in the quarter of the city where the university is located, in contrast to . . . the families who drew their living from manufacturing, construction, and retail trade."[14] The north side neighborhoods were filled with wide tree-shaded streets, newly built two-story homes, large front and back yards, and screened patios. Meanwhile, much of the African American population lived at or near the poverty level in slums near the center of the city, and the lower-middle-class and working-class white population was concentrated in modest homes and trailer-park communities on the city's south side.[15]

The changes in the city's economy further reinforced Muncie's geographic divisions at a time in the post–civil rights era of the 1970s when there appeared to be more opportunity for amicable relationships between persons of different races. As the *Middletown Families* co-authors reported: "The darkie jokes, the anti-Semitic jokes, and the racial and religious epithets that used to be a large part of the local folklore are now uttered furtively" and "the freedom of action of Middletown's black citizens in all relationships with whites has been vastly increased by the eradication of the whole body of formal and informal regulations that . . . subordinated all blacks to all whites as recently as 1935."[16] An opportunity to further promote racial intermixing, however, was lost with decisions that the city's school board made in the late 1960s on building new schools.

By the late 1950s, Muncie's growing population had resulted in such a massive overcrowding at Central High School that the city and school board began planning to build new schools. African Americans fought these projects, arguing that new schools would further polarize the city. African American community leaders and other Muncie civil-rights activists advocated instead that the city modernize and expand Central so it could accommodate all the city's students, creating an integrated public environment in which teenagers of all different racial, ethnic, and economic backgrounds would interact. The white, middle-class power elite that dominated city politics overruled this proposal, and two new high schools opened: Southside in 1962 and Northside in 1970.[17]

The new schools divided the student population by race and class. By the time Lynsi and I entered high school, Muncie was almost like three separate cities, defined by its economic and racial geographic lines and the cultures of its schools. Northside was predominantly white and upper middle class, with a scattering of African American and working-class whites, while Burris, the laboratory school on the Ball State campus, was even more heavily white and middle class. Central was more racially and economically mixed than Northside but more white than it had been in Gregory Williams's time. Southside was economically working class and lower class, with a student body that was about 40 percent African American and 60 percent white. Racial tensions at Southside boiled into a citywide riot in 1967 when the white-majority students voted to call themselves the Rebels and to make their school mascot the Confederate flag.[18]

The geographic configuration of the high schools also separated Muncie students, who had first attended neighborhood elementary schools and then larger, less geographically specific middle schools before all going to the single high school, Central. After 1970, students from all over the city went to one of four middle schools and were then funneled to Northside High School if they lived in the northern or northeastern parts of the city, to Southside if they resided in the south, to Central if they lived in the western and east-central areas, or to Burris, an option for those affiliated with Ball State. These changes often disrupted friendships and affected how Muncie's children and teens came to identify themselves racially and economically in relation to their citywide peers.

Lynsi and I both attended a middle school known as Storer before being funneled to different high schools. At Storer, Lynsi recalled, she met a girl from the south side of Muncie who became her best friend in middle school, and remained so despite the geographic delineations of who belonged where. Lynsi remembered meeting her "like it was just yesterday" on the first day of school in a home-economics class. "We were making lollipops," she recalled. "You had to find partners and she and I were looking for partners, and we found each other."

Lynsi described her best friend as "a girl from the wrong side of the tracks" who "got pregnant her senior year of high school, not somebody mom and dad would want me to hang out with, truly."

"She always had the coolest clothes," said Lynsi. "I always had to wear these ugly clothes that I hated; my parents think I'm neurotic when I say that, but they weren't the most fashionable clothes. So I'd have her bring clothes for me to school and I would change."

"She lived in a trailer park," Lynsi added. "In all the years that I knew her, I was never allowed to spend the night at her house. Not once. But every weekend, at our house, she was there, spending the night with me."

Lynsi's story highlights the economic segregation that had begun to define Muncie in the 1970s. In doing so, it also underscores how Muncie had become what she remembered as "very much a white community" where it would be hard to find the communities of the south side if one were not an African American or working class white. As the daughter of affluent, highly educated parents, she, like many other Muncie-raised South Asians, had no reason to visit that part of the city or to know that it existed. Where the new high schools were built helped facilitate these separations, unless teenagers and others breached them, as Lynsi and her friend did.

After leaving middle school, Lynsi's friend went to Southside. Lynsi would have gone to Central, but she chose instead to go to Burris, exercising the privilege she had of being a child of a Ball State faculty member. Lynsi's friend would come to Burris after her classes at Southside let out. The two also continued to spend weekends together at Lynsi's house.

I, too, had a friend who lived in a trailer park. Like Lynsi, I had met my friend in middle school, where we both played in the school's orchestra. My friend and I had the good luck of both going to Northside together. She would come to my house after school, and we would practice for the orchestra together. Afterward, I would pull out piano music for popular songs to play while she would sing. In the years I knew her, I never went to her home or her neighborhood. I never asked why. Many years later, it occurred to me that I could not recall her ever having invited me. Was this because she didn't want me to see how she lived?

Or was it because she didn't think I would want to know about the conditions of her family and community life outside of school? These questions, along with the memories Lynsi shared, resonate with the sense of danger related to such practices as interracial dating and going into neighborhoods where one "did not belong" that *Seventeen* portrayed. In doing so, they show a community where there was intermixing among races and classes, despite what might be seen as surveillance by the city and its school board to keep people in their proper places. Against this backdrop, Gregory Williams, the white Muncie boy who learned he was black, met in high school the woman who would eventually become his wife. She was white. Despite pressure from her family not to date an African American, their relationship found a way to flourish.

The Middletown Film Project

Middletown Film Project director Peter Davis had hoped that the six themes from the 1929 *Middletown* text—getting a living, making a home, training the young, using leisure, engaging in religious practice, and engaging in community activities—would capture both the spirit of the Middletown legacy and the changes taking place in the city. He hired separate directors for each film and left them each to develop their assigned theme as they saw fit. Each film was marked by its individual directors' personal style and point of view, and collectively the series offered vivid portrayals of the economic and social changes in Muncie.

The first film in the series, *The Campaign*, presented the Muncie mayoral race as a choice between Alan Wilson, a Republican lawyer from the north side, and Jim Carey, a boisterous, blue-collar Democrat from the south side, driving home the economic divisions of Muncie. The second film, *The Big Game*, highlighted racial divisions in positioning Rick Rowray, a white player from Central High, against Andre Morgan, an African American player from a high school in nearby Anderson. Rowray was shown as a quiet, highly disciplined player who was in demand by college recruiters. Morgan, by contrast, lived in a single-parent home, struggled to graduate, and hoped for a basketball scholarship to free him from Indiana. These films were followed by *Family Business*, about the economic struggles of maintaining a family-run Shakey's Pizza Parlor; *Community of Praise*, about a Pentecostal Christian community; and *Second Time Around*, a story of two divorced adults preparing to make a second try at marriage.

Seventeen was to be the series finale and was supposed to celebrate high school. What the film depicted instead was high-school life, crosscut by the economic and racial tensions that teenagers in high school were dealing with daily. On the south side, Lynn Massie and her friends piled into cars after school to cruise. With cigarettes lit, beer cans popped open, and hard rock and funk music thumping from stereos, they sang, laughed, and read out loud the love notes sent by their boyfriends as they accelerated their cars. The cars also wound through African American neighborhoods. Toilet paper and streamers decorated the trees and the porches of some of these houses, the houses of athletes decorated by Muncie cheerleaders before major sports events.

Seventeen opened with a scene in cooking class with Ms. Hartle, a home-economics teacher, instructing students to "take a half-cup of white sugar and a half-cup of brown, and mix it all together," hinting of the interracial themes of the film. As she berated students for inattention and cutting class, one young woman told the teacher to "go kiss my ass" while another, Lynn, warned that if the teacher gave her another "F," her mother would come to the school and kick the teacher's ass.

Intermixed with the teenagers' overt disrespect for authority were scenes of interracial collegiality: A white child sat on the bleachers behind two Southside High School African American basketball players during a pregame warmup, eating popcorn and talking with them about the rival team. Black and white students ate together in the school cafeteria. Lynn sat with an African American female friend in the Muncie Fieldhouse bleachers during the sectional final of the 1981 state high-school basketball tournament and ran joyously with her to the floor when the Southside team claimed the title after defeating Northside. When Ms. Hartle, who is white, learned that one of her male students, who is African American, had gotten a girl pregnant, she alternated between scolding the male student for allowing such a thing to happen and expressing delight and pleasure over the impending new child. The male student brought the mother-to-be, who had stopped attending regular classes, to see her. Ms. Hartle both chided the woman and offered advice on mothering.

Under this seeming harmony, several scenes drove home the lingering power of Muncie's segregated past. During lunch, an African American young woman remarked that prom "is for white people and you won't find blacks going." Lynn brought her African American boyfriend John home to meet her parents but confided while driving in a car with filmmaker DeMott that if she were to go to the prom with a black male, her mother would wear her out with a whipping. The cross-burning incident in the Massie backyard reinforced the danger of crossing boundaries, and when prom night arrived, the African American young woman's prophesy was realized: all of the couples shown on the dance floor were white.

Unlike the statistical detail and the ponderous narrative that characterized *Middletown Families* and *All Faithful People*, each of the one- to two-hour films in the series offered a visually dramatic insight into what a group of individuals who might be characterized as "ordinary Americans" were experiencing at the cusp of the civil-rights era and the swing toward the 1980s Reagan era of political and social conservatism. The owner of the Shakey's Pizza Parlor was heavily in debt but made a valiant effort to ensure that all his children received a college education. The bride-to-be in *Second Time Around* was in college but wanted, after marriage, to be a stay-at-home mom. She agreed, in the end, to get a job so that, at a time when mortgage rates were in the double digits, she and her fiancé could afford a home. In *Seventeen*, there was no talk of college or a future after high school at all because all the factories that employed blue-collar workers were outsourcing or cutting back, leaving few good jobs available for the new graduates. In playing up these themes, the Middletown films created a sobering portrait of a working-class America in decline that could offer its next generation little.

Davis said in a filmed interviewed that accompanied the 2010 DVD set that the series represented Muncie itself. "We were there for three years, filming. We were everywhere, and everybody knew us." Given this assertion, it is striking that the films focused so heavily on Muncie's south side. Only the films *The Campaign* and *Second Time Around* contained footage of the north side. This omission erased the presence of Ball State and its surrounding economically and culturally affluent neighborhoods. While one brief scene in *The Campaign* showed a candidate at Burris being quizzed by white civics students, none of the films makes any mention of Northside, beyond a few references to girls attending the school who date sons of the owner of the Shakey's franchise. The geographic and social divisions of Muncie, as a result, become a story between two high schools: Central, historically institutionalized as the white hometown school; and Southside, the lower-class, mixed-race upstart on the fringes.

These omissions gain significance as one realizes that the areas of the city the Middletown film series did not show housed a small but growing number of South Asian American families such as mine, whose children had grown into adolescence and were active participants in their schools. Just as the founding member of the Center for Middletown Studies whom I had met at the Ball State conference in 2003 had expressed amazed surprise at the presence of an Indian community in Muncie, it appeared that, based on what the Middletown Film Project depicts, no persons of this ancestry or of any other group that was not white or black existed in Muncie. This reinforced the institutional invisibility that South Asians and others experienced through a lack of such things before 1980 as a distinct census category.

In an era where the working class was dying, the new economic engines were on the north side. This side of Muncie was not shown at all. Instead, the death of middle America was reinforced. Near the end of *Seventeen*, an all-night keg party was underway at the Massie home. Rock-and-roll music blared from a stereo. Most of the teens were drunk or heavily stoned from a combination of beer and marijuana. Lynn's mother, Shari, was drinking and dancing with the teenagers. Later, she fried eggs and bacon in the kitchen for a young man from a nearby trailer park who was drinking nonstop and sobbing because his friend Timothy "Church Mouse" Parker was in critical condition at Ball Memorial Hospital following an automobile accident a couple of days earlier. (The sobbing young man later became Lynn's husband, as stated in the film notes accompanying the 2010 DVD release of the *Middletown* series.) Lynn's father came home from work just as police arrived to break up the party and, after promising to quiet the crowd, started to drink too.

As the party stretched into the night, Lynn retired to her bedroom with cigarettes. One of her female friends and two or three boys joined her. Word came that Church Mouse had died. A friend picked up the telephone receiver and dialed a local radio station to request the Bob Seger song "Against the Wind" in his memory.

The opening strains to the song began to fill the room. "There it is," Lynn cried out. "Crank it up. Crank it up."

The volume rose, and viewers of *Seventeen* could see the impact of Seger's song on the assembled group. The friend of Church Mouse dissolved into tears. Lynn's friend put her arms around him and started crying herself. Another young man shook his head and began to cry. Lynn's mother stood just outside the bedroom door, her head bowed, tears rolling down her face. Lynn stared straight ahead, her eyes full of pain.

By 1988, a precipitous decline in population that accompanied the city's deindustrialization during the 1980s prompted Muncie's school district to begin consolidating schools. Northside was closed and later became a middle school. Storer, the middle school that Lynsi and I attended with students from all over the city, was also closed and later became an elementary school. As student enrollments continued to fall into the early twenty-first century, city officials began considering plans to close Southside and send its students to Central. Consultants to the Middletown Film Project reported that Lynn was married briefly, had a child, and got divorced before marrying and then divorcing once again. Her first husband, the male friend of Church Mouse, was killed by a passing train as he made his way home one night, inebriated.

Muncie, India(na)

The eleven Muncie-raised South Asians I interviewed were between twenty and fifty years old when I first spoke with them. In the years since, all of them finished bachelor's degrees, and many held doctoral, medical, and other advanced degrees. All were working in professional careers of their choice, and many of their children had completed high school and college. It seemed that by most measurements these children had grown up to be successful adults. But ambivalence about their lives in Muncie and their relationships to the city lingered.

"I can remember certain Indian families in the Indiana area where the kids were totally western," said Vinod. "And I can remember other Indians' kids who were the exact opposite. I and my brothers, I think we fell somewhere in the middle."

"Was being in the middle a good place to be?" I asked.

"Well, I don't know. Learning Hindi, that would have been good. But going the other way, maybe we would have stood out more, been ridiculed more. Who knows?"

"The best thing that ever happened to me was losing a scholarship to go to medical school in Indiana," Vinod continued. That loss of an honor was his opportunity to leave the state and pursue his medical training in an area away from his family and the societal restrictions that had constrained him.

"Leaving Muncie," he said, "felt like being let out of a cage."

I thought of my own flight from Muncie in the fall of 1981. My parents and I were loading up our car to drive me to college at Northwestern University, five hours away, across the Indiana border into Illinois. As we were leaving, my mother gave me some advice: "Remember your Indian heritage," she told me. "Things will be much easier for you if you do." Decades later, I am still not sure what my mother's advice was meant to convey, and she herself does not recall the conversation. But I can't help wondering how it might relate to the economic and racial realities of Muncie at that time. As I was leaving for college, the Indian American interest groups who were lobbying for an Asian Indian census designation and minority status for those of South Asian ancestry had succeeded. For the first time since the formation of a South Asian American community in Muncie and in many other cities throughout America, persons of Indian and other South Asian ancestries had a name in America's racial hierarchy and a place that was not white, black, foreign, or other. Perhaps that designation meant something different to the immigrant South Asian generation who chose to stay in Muncie than it meant to their American-raised children who, after growing up within the black-and-white parameters of the city's culture, left. Like some of the other South Asian immigrants, my parents after 1980 became more committed to civic engagement in Muncie, and they participated through the early twenty-first century in community and political activist groups. I, like others who had grown up in Muncie, found a professional and/or political voice elsewhere.

Most of the Muncie South Asians of the immigrant generation I interviewed described their childhood and adolescent lives in the countries of their birth in terms of steps that led them to college, into marriages, and ultimately to immigrate to America and settle in Muncie. When I asked them to tell me about their children, they tended to focus on the successful and personally fulfilling lives that they perceived their children to be living outside of Muncie. The line that the Muncie-raised generation of South Asians drew between what they were exposed to at home and what they experienced in school seemed to be a division that their parents were unaware of, not troubled by, or, perhaps, were hesitant to discuss with me, as I was one of their children's peers.

Vinod described his parents' efforts to help him understand his Indian heritage "as wanting me and my brothers to understand that we were Indian without ramming it down our throats." He grew up watching Hindi movies, listening to Indian music, and eating Indian food for dinner at least two or three times a week. But he felt that his understanding of himself as an Indian was incomplete. He never learned to speak Hindi, and his family only traveled to India a few times.

"I think I lost touch with my Indian roots when I went away to college."

"Would you like to get back in touch with those roots?" I asked.

"I think so," Vinod replied. "I felt like we got gypped for some reason. I brought this up with my father some time back. A lot of Indian families would go back every two or three years. We only went back three times, twice in [his younger brother]'s lifetime, once in [his youngest brother]'s lifetime. I hold some resentment toward my parents for not taking us back more often. I know that I want to take my family back on a more regular basis. Hopefully, that will start to happen soon."

I shared some of the stories that the Muncie-raised South Asians told me in a talk hosted by Ball State's India Students Association and the Center for Middletown Studies, keeping the names of the interviewees anonymous. In doing so, I juxtaposed the South Asian American stories against the scenes of teenage drinking, drug use, and dating depicted in *Seventeen*. After I finished speaking, one man, who was an elder member of the South Asian community and a father of one of the children I interviewed, stood up. In a quiet tone, he asked: "In your findings, did the children have any advice for their parents? Anything that might prevent us from making the same mistakes again?"

That question—addressed to one "child" by one "adult" in a setting where we all had become adults—came with a trace of sadness. I felt an equal sadness as I wondered if both the immigrant and first American-raised generation had come to approach that question too late. Later that evening, I was at the Unitarian Universalist Church in Muncie for a second talk, this time for the South Asians of Muncie Association. A white woman who looked familiar approached me. "I'm not sure you remember me, but we were at Storer and Northside together," she said. "I know you're doing this presentation for the South Asians, but I was wondering if I could stay."

I remembered her as soon as she told me her name. She was in the same class with Lynsi and me, and she was one of the first girls at Storer who had been able to fight her way out of taking the home-economics classes that were required of young women in order to enroll in woodshop.

"Please stay," I said. "It's about the South Asian community, but . . . maybe it's also about all of us, all of us who grew up here in Muncie."

"Are you going to the reunion this summer," I added, "for Northside?"

A look of distaste crossed her face.

"Oh, I'm not sure. I'll have to think about it."

My presentation was ready, so we chatted for a few more minutes. She told me that she left Muncie after high school, earned graduate degrees, and came back when Ball State offered her a faculty position. She had joined the Unitarian church earlier that year, where she had met my mother.

"I hear that you got married," she said.

"I did," I said. "And you?"

"I live with a partner, but, uhh, we're not married."

"Not ready yet?"

She dropped her voice. "My partner . . . she's very patient with me."

The disclosure took me by surprise. I suddenly realized that the framework of race that I had been using to understand the South Asian American experiences in Muncie was far from being as clear-cut as I had analytically perceived it to be. The teenagers in *Seventeen* were no more normative of Middletown than I was, and I was no less normative than the former classmate standing beside me.

As South Asian community members started to arrive, I turned to greet a few people. She lingered by my side, however, so quickly I asked her if she had known in high school that she was gay.

"No. Oh no," she replied. "All I thought was that I was disturbed. It wasn't until I left Muncie that I started to realize I was okay, different, not heterosexual, but okay."

"There's a lot of pain in the past," she continued. "Even though I live in Muncie now, I don't like to think about those days. Like when you mentioned the reunion just now, I felt my back constrict viscerally. Just a flash, but it brought back a lot of pain."

What was this pain about? I wondered.

. . .

Lynn rushed out of a house with a bag of marijuana in the closing scene of *Seventeen*. She jumped into the driver's seat of a car as her friend seated next to her started rolling a joint. Driving past one of the factories that used to sustain the city, the girls took turns inhaling the smoke as their car radio played the Beatles' song "We Can Work It Out." And then, the moving screen froze. The music changed. Another Beatles' song, remixed into a 1970s medley, played. Lynn was freeze-framed smoking, staring into nowhere, as viewers heard "You're Gonna Lose That Girl."

In 2011 I was in Muncie visiting my parents when one of the elder members of the South Asian immigrant generation died. At the funeral, surrounded by many of my interviewees, I remembered the question I had been asked at the talk I had given several years earlier: Did the children have any advice for their parents? I wondered how the members of the immigrant generation and their children might be answering the question.

Vinod had expressed an interest in devoting a month or two each year to doing service work in India. Unbeknownst to Vinod, his father had expressed a similar desire when I had interviewed him at his home in Muncie.

Lynsi broke off two engagements before meeting her future husband, a medical doctor with a Catholic background. After the two of them decided they wanted to get married, they went to Muncie to see her parents. Lynsi's fiancé asked her father for her hand in marriage, and because her fiancé did not wish to convert to Islam, Lynsi says that her father never gave his formal consent. Still, at the wedding, her husband's father read from the Bible and Lynsi's father read from the Quran. As Lynsi danced with her father, she recalls him telling her that it was the happiest night of his life.

Other interviewees found through counseling and personal reflection that they could reconcile their dislike for Muncie through renewed respect for their parents in a variety of ways. When they spoke of Muncie as adults who were now older than Lynn Massie's parents were when Demott and Kreines captured the footage for *Seventeen*, they did so with affection and sometimes with hope. They remembered Muncie as Lynsi did, as a good place to grow up and a pleasant place to come back to as their parents aged.

The sobering scene that closes *Seventeen* suggests a future of no hope. But the strange history of the film and the strong but ultimately failed efforts to keep it from being screened present an opportunity for hope for Muncie and America, too. The Center for Middletown Studies' initial mission was to support the study of Muncie and Middletown that began with the studies by Robert and Helen Lynd. Filmmakers Joel DeMott and Jeff Kreines challenged the traditional viewing of Middletown when they portrayed not the Muncie represented in the archive but the Muncie they saw. Their refusal to surrender to the norm left behind a film that makes its viewers read their own interpretations into the images that they see, and search for their own connections between the experiences that the film portrays and their life worlds. The scenes in *Seventeen* scratched the veneer of Muncie's claim to a monoracial, heteronormative Christian community, and in doing so revealed a portrayal of the city that was perhaps unpleasant yet thought provoking. Like the Hearst Company's efforts to quell the success of Orson Welles's critically acclaimed *Citizen Kane*, city and school-district officials banded together vociferously against *Seventeen*, helping to keep it out of widespread public circulation for close to three decades. Like *Citizen Kane*, however, *Seventeen* ultimately received its fair view.

Seventeen and its odd history help illuminate what can be said and not said publicly about proper behavior, race relationships, and rebellion. The South Asian American experience in Muncie fits into that history by highlighting how the intricate relationships of race, religious affiliation, and cultural heritage are navigated differently among peoples who sometimes appear quite similar to one another. Being sensitive not only to what interviewees were willing to share in the moment of an interview but also to how they might respond years later to the handling of his or her words contributes to that understanding by showing both how much and how little I could actually know about what it meant to grow up as a child of immigrants in Muncie outside of my own experience. At the same time, the interviewee stories and their hesitations about having them shared publicly offer hints of how growing up in Muncie in the 1960s through 1980s influences how one must negotiate the parameters of what can and cannot be said in a post–civil-rights era America. What results is less a neatly packaged historical narrative and more a collection of voices, hesitations, and silences. It is in what these seemingly disconnected stories share with each other that a new understanding of Muncie and America might emerge.

CHAPTER 5

Cowpath Crossings

Postindustrial Work and Indian Doctors

> Historical fact: People stopped being human in 1913. That was the
> year Henry Ford put his cars on rollers and made his workers adopt
> the speed of the assembly line. At first, workers rebelled. They quit
> in droves, unable to accustom their bodies to the new pace of the
> age. Since then, however, the adaptation has been passed down:
> we've all inherited it to some degree, so that we plug right into
> joysticks and remotes, to repetitive motions of a hundred kinds.
> —Jeffrey Eugenides, *Middlesex*, 2002

September 2003
Muncie, Indiana

"America?" recalled Saleem, a fifty-three-year-old plastic surgeon in
Muncie.

"We lived in a very remote part of India, you know. Faizabad, that part of U.P.
was quite far removed from the world."

"Then one day my father came in and said, 'You know that vice principal's
son? He got a scholarship for 36,000 rupees—to go to America.' That was the
pinnacle of achievement, going abroad."

Saleem's life in a more rural part of north-central India contained from
an early age an imagined "abroad." This "abroad," as he recalled, was a cosmopolitan, sophisticated place where one could find one's self and succeed.
It evoked the images of an America that Abraham Verghese has described as
a place where medicine healed and doctors prospered, where doctors could
"train in a decent, ten-story hospital where the lifts are actually working";

"pass board-certification exams by [one's] own merit and not through pull or bribes;" "practice real medicine"; "drive a big car on decent roads, and eventually live in the Ansel Adams section of New Mexico and never come back" to their "wretched" hometowns.[1]

Saleem completed his initial medical training in India and left his hometown in 1977 to seek his imagined abroad. By then, he was traversing a well-worn path: tens of thousands of medical students, doctors, scientists, and engineers had left India to come to the United States between 1966 and 1977, taking advantage of a preferential immigration category that the U.S. government had established for skilled foreigners in the 1965 Immigration Act. Saleem landed in Boston, where he began his American medical training, which he subsequently continued in Easton, Pennsylvania, and Chattanooga, Tennessee. He arrived in Muncie in 1983 with his wife, Salina.

Malati, the forty-seven-year-old wife of Raj, also grew up with a dream of an abroad.

"When I was little, I would read all of my mom's British magazines and stuff. I would read *Reader's Digest*, and I would think about England. All I ever thought was, 'Hah, I need to grow up and go live in England.'"

Like Saleem, Malati left India for her abroad. She and Raj left their hometown of Kanpur, India, in 1984 with an infant son so that Raj could take up a medical residency at a hospital in Scarborough, England. Four years later, a second son was born, and opportunities for physicians, particularly foreign physicians, had dried up.

"The medical system in England was like a pyramid," explained Malati. "If that many people started at the bottom, only one person could reach the top level. The rest had to go back to their countries. So we were thinking, 'What shall we do? Once you're done with your residency, that's it.'"

"And then one day [Raj] hears from his sister in Detroit that there are residencies available at Henry Ford Hospital. So he goes there and gets interviewed, and gets selected. He comes back to Scarborough, and says, 'Hey, we're going to the U.S.'"

Late-Twentieth-Century Immigrants

Perhaps it was just a coincidence that the name of Henry Ford was attached to the hospital that brought Malati and her family to Detroit. However, Malati's invoking of such a well-known industrialist links the experiences of South Asian immigrants like herself who arrived in Muncie and other small cities in the United States in the 1980s and 1990s to those of earlier generations of immigrants, South Asian and otherwise. Early-twentieth-century foreigners from eastern, central, and southern Europe provided the Ford assembly lines their labor, and Ford in turn made them into Americans. Following the legacy of Ford, post–World War II immigrants from India and other parts of Asia took advantage of changes in the 1965 Immigration Act and provided the United States with scientific-research training, technological skills, and higher educational expertise to help build the Cold War economy of the 1960s and 1970s.

The closing decades of the twentieth century and early years of the twenty-first century brought a different generation of immigrants, a generation the stories of Saleem and Malati epitomize. Although the South Asians who began to arrive in the United States in the late 1970s and 1980s had a wider array of educational, occupational, and economic statuses, they often were even more highly educated, prosperous, and cosmopolitan than those of the 1960s and 1970s. These immigrants' stories, when placed against the transformation of the United States from the rigid, production- and assembly-line-oriented economy of the early twentieth century to the more free-flowing, services-oriented one of the early twenty-first century, illuminate continuities in larger historic narratives of immigration, industrialization, and the making of typical America. Such continuities also offer insights into how the archetype of typical Americanness continues to rely on a persistent flow of immigrant labor to power the U.S. economy and to meld quietly into the representation of that archetype as normatively white, of European ancestry, and Christian well into the twenty-first century.

The stories of Saleem and Malati also show the impact that their generation of South Asian immigrants has had in Muncie during a time of severe economic downturn for the city. That downturn—a result of the deindustrialization of the Rust Belt that hit small manufacturing-based cities like Muncie particularly hard—affected not only the personal psyches of these immigrants but also the lives of the Muncie residents who more closely resembled what the typical American was said to represent. The stories also reveal a sense of familial affection that runs through the South Asian American community in Muncie, which has been crucial through the 1980s into the early twenty-first century in sustaining that community. The affection not only bridges differences between generations of South Asians settling in Muncie but also serves as a protective armor for many individuals within the community, allowing them to sustain their lives in the predominantly white, Christian community and to fight back the isolation of being rendered invisible or foreign.

Saleem and Malati came to Muncie from the same geographic region of India. Both traversed the difficult but ultimately affluent path of medicine. Saleem arrived in Muncie in 1983, where his wife, Salina, gave birth to their two daughters. Malati and Raj arrived in 1994 with their two sons. By 2003, Saleem had built a successful surgery practice, and Malati's husband Raj was a well-established internist. Both couples described Muncie as a place that had brought them prosperity and happiness, and they proudly pointed to the accomplishments of their children. They channeled their prosperity into philanthropic and civic support for Muncie's economy, which had been devastated by scores of factory closings and massive job layoffs through the 1970s and 1980s. In doing so, they helped solidify the South Asian community that was established by my parents and their generation of immigrants two decades earlier.

For Saleem, coming to America was about freedom. It was a path away from intellectual frustration and social marginalization. Once he arrived, he never looked back. Returning to India, in his mind, would have meant becoming a doctor in a remote place and working in a clinic where the only medications available were vitamin pills and treatments for diarrhea. The journey away from India let Malati realize her childhood dream of living in England, but it also meant hardship: relocation first from her small community in India to the big city of Delhi, then overseas to England, and finally to America, where the family resided first in Detroit, then Lexington, Kentucky, and then in rural Appalachia before settling in Muncie. Her in-laws, who resided with her and Raj and their two teenage sons, praised the work that Malati and Raj did as marks of their children's worth. Malati said, "We did it the hard way," as she described the toll that medical residences took on family lives and remembered how Raj's around-the-clock residency requirements once prompted her three-year-old son to ask, "Mom, what does Dad look like?"

Saleem regarded India as his home country, but he did so with growing anxiety over how Hindu political and cultural dominance was marginalizing Muslims like himself. He spoke of his home country as a place he loved but no longer considered entirely safe. Malati—a Hindu—actively cultivated ties with Indian and other South Asian immigrant arrivals so she could find solace in a community of her own kind, even as she also sought to reach out to other women in Muncie whom she came to meet through her neighborhood and her children's acquaintances. She, too, loved India and expressed concern for the rise of Hindu-Muslim tensions. Yet the anxiety Saleem voiced about India was not a part of her story. In both cases, the differing emotions the two expressed have converged around a common experience of work. Exploring that theme led me to look at how work had shaped their lives and to consider their experiences against those of other nonwhite immigrants—and Asians in particular—who have continued into the twenty-first century to leave their home countries primarily for work. Such immigrants often have had little difficulty improving their lives economically in the United States. Yet, as Pawan Dhingra has observed, these individuals, by virtue of being "more wanted for their labor than for their lives," tend "to face rejection and isolation when they seek acceptance in both their employment and social lives." Dhingra's studies of how such immigrants create cultural identities, affiliations, and practices to compensate for this loneliness connect America's racist past to a multicultural present that runs just skin deep. Such immigrants, Dhingra concludes, "remain constructed by the state as both racial minorities and foreigners, apart from other races and immigrants."[2]

Neither Saleem nor Malati spoke of themselves as victims of discrimination against foreigners in the many conversations I held with each of them. Neither did their spouses or their children. As a result, I have sought to analyze their stories with care, to balance their individual words alongside my thoughts on how governmental policies, racially coded hierarchies, and the labor needs of a globalizing America inform the lives of immigrants affectively and cognitively long before they come to the United States. One can experience how such policies, hierarchies, and labor needs enact themselves in daily life within stories like the ones Saleem and Malati narrate. Such stories provide what Michel de Certeau has described as "the decorative container of a narrativity for everyday practices" that, in a sense, pay homage to private, noncelebrity individuals whose experiences otherwise would go unnoticed.[3] Bringing such stories to light helps us explore such larger questions as what it means to immigrate to an America that was once imagined as a land of opportunity but had become a place within a slimming globe of diminishing choices.

Henry Ford's America

The epigraph from novelist Jeffrey Eugenides that opens this chapter does not mention immigrants. Yet it un-silences a narrative of immigration when one recalls the intercrossing of immigrants and the industrial era of America's early twentieth century. The quote describes the urban factories of Detroit in the early twentieth century and captures a sense of how assembly-line work dehumanized labor and prompted rebellion until, as Eugenides notes, the workers learned to adapt. A preoccupation with the effects of industrialization on Americans' lives also comprises a theme of Robert S. Lynd and Helen Merrell Lynd's *Middletown*. The Lynds described the evolution of the American economy between 1890 and 1924 from agrarian to industrial as a painful transformation for American culture. Like Eugenides, the Lynds relegated the role of the foreign-born individual to the margins of that painful transformation in the effort to produce what came to be "typical America." Henry Ford's practices, however, bring those marginalized experiences to the center. They show the persistent yet hidden role of immigrants in transforming understandings of America domestically and abroad.

Ford was striving to transform America from a primarily agricultural- and artisanal-based economy into an industrial powerhouse that would drive the world. Like corporations of the early twenty-first century, he relied on the bodies of immigrants to construct this mighty America. Central to Ford's mission of building America was the creation of "Americans" out of the foreign laborers who worked in his plants. These workers represented fifty-three nationalities and spoke more than one hundred different languages. Ford assembled them all into required classes at his English Language School, where workers were taught not only English but also, via recitation, several lessons in what the industrial magnate described as practical American living. Plant supervisors routinely visited workers' homes in the evenings to see if they were engaging in what Ford defined as "un-American" behaviors: excessive drinking, out-of-wedlock sex, sending money to their home countries, or keeping boarders. Ford also required workers to take part in "The Pageant of the Ford Melting Pot." Workers would march to a large, makeshift pot, climb up a ladder into it, and disappear. Their teachers would stand on pedestals at the top of the pot stirring into it with giant spoons. Then the workers would come out dressed in straw hats and suits, waving American flags.[4]

While the Lynds chose a city without a large foreign-born population for their study of American culture, Ford actively recruited the foreign-born as workers and indoctrinated them into an American culture of his creation. Still, a similar logic united their efforts. Both were foregrounding an understanding of the American that presumed a surrender of past ethnic or national affiliations, and both were doing so in the early-twentieth-century era of anti-immigrant laws against nonwhite Europeans and Asians. This ideal American resonated with the archetype handed down through Hector St. Jean de Crèvecoeur's late-eighteenth-century writing of the American as a mixture of Europeans "melted" into a new race. It resurfaced in Ford's projects and in Saleem and Malati's stories. However, the realities Saleem and Malati encountered in trying to realize their dreams of going abroad differed from those of the earlier era, which also were a result of the discourses on Americanness that were built earlier.

Racing against Time

Saleem boarded a plane bound for Boston in early 1977. He recalled the date as being "either January 6 or 7." Every seat on the aircraft was filled—with Indian doctors.

All were bound for America. And all were racing against time. While changes in immigration laws in 1965 had made the United States more receptive to non-white, non-European immigrants, it also linked immigration more directly to the economic needs of the country. The 1965 change in law came as the U.S. economy was facing a shortfall of doctors, engineers, and other technically trained professionals. Amendments to the Social Security Act in 1966 established Medicare and Medicaid health-insurance systems. These changes led to an extension of private health-insurance plans, and, in turn, generated a demand for physicians, particularly in the rural areas and inner-city communities of the United States where white, American-born doctors were less inclined to want to practice. Faced with an impeding shortage of doctors, nurses, and other medical professionals, many medical schools and hospitals in the United States began searching for future American physicians abroad. As a result, an estimated seventy-five thousand foreign physicians entered the United States from 1966 to 1974, with the bulk of them arriving from India, China, Korea, and the Philippines.[5]

The plight of foreign doctors in American hospitals often was rife with racially coded labor abuses. Hospitals in poorer U.S. communities would offer incoming physicians limited training and often force them into doing the work of orderlies or other staff whose qualifications ranked well below theirs. In addition, licensing exams that U.S. hospitals imposed on foreign physicians often resulted in the doctors' being forced to return to their home countries if they failed the exams.[6] Abraham Verghese, who began his career as a "rookie doctor" in 1980, describes the hospitals that drew foreign medical trainees as embodying the "urban rot" debilitating America's industrial core: "The once grand county hospitals were sliding inexorably, like the cities themselves, into critical states.... Their patients had become the uninsured and indigent whose problems revolved around drug addiction and trauma. In the emergency rooms of these fading institutions, bodies were pressed together like so many sheep. Old people languished on stretchers shunted into hallways and corridors while beleaguered nurses attempted some form of triage." And, Verghese writes, "an inevitable accompaniment to this scene of a city hospital under siege was the sight of foreign physicians."[7]

What seemed abhorrent by U.S. standards was perceived as an abundance of opportunity in the imagination of young adults like Saleem who were studying or practicing medicine in remote localities of India. By the mid-1970s, individuals from India and the other nations of Asia dominated the U.S. immigration preferential category of professionals, of which doctors were a part. As Catherine Choy writes, 42,503 professionals migrated from Asia between 1970 and 1974, compared with 5,764 from other nations in North America, the second-largest category.[8] By 1976, as an era of martial law known in India's political history as the Emergency was in place, more and more medical students were looking for opportunities to emigrate. However, the high-category immigration preference that the United States had granted to foreign medical students was ending as the U.S. economy was slowing and the demand for doctors had diminished.

"[In early January 1977,] I went to Delhi, to the embassy," Saleem recalled. "I see all these big lines of doctors; they're all talking about some kind of law that has been passed in America. You have to get there by January 8 or 9; if you didn't, you wouldn't be admitted.

"I got the visa, but they told me, you must get there by January 7. I had to buy ticket, get income tax clearance; police clearance. This is January 2 or 3; I didn't have any money."

With his brother-in-law, Saleem rushed all over the Connaught Place section of Delhi, visiting one travel agent after another. Every flight out of India to America was booked. All with doctors.

Finally, he recalled, "I was just entering a travel agent's office; I see a long-lost friend walking into Connaught Circus. I tell him, no, I have no time to talk now. I have to go to America. With his help, I got one seat; he gave me some money, and I promised I would return it."

Before he could leave, however, Saleem had to receive security and tax clearances. He could not do that in Delhi; he had to return to Lucknow, the city where such matters were handled in his home district.

"We rushed to catch a train; we got the bus running; caught the train just as it was leaving. I had to pull my brother-in-law through the window. At least, because it was the Emergency, the trains were running on time. For once, that was good."

Saleem nevertheless felt enormous pressure. "I just kept thinking, 'If I don't get tax clearance, this will ruin my life. I won't be able to go to America.'"

He managed to get the clearances so he could return to Delhi and board his flight. During this time, he did not have a chance to tell his parents he was leaving. "They didn't have a telephone; I didn't have the courage to send a telegraph." So his wife, Salina, went to them. "They said to her, 'Where is our son?' She said, 'He's in America.'"

The drama didn't end with Saleem's departure. On the plane, an Alitalia jet, word came of a snowstorm. "We had a layover in Rome; they told us that the Boston airport was closed. I panicked."

Malati also recalled arriving in America amid a snowstorm. "We flew to Detroit. It was a horrible night. The plane wasn't given permission to land. We thought, 'Oh God, what are we letting ourselves in for?'"

· · ·

Saleem's vivid story of departure in a rush and Malati's brief recollection of an uncertain arrival offer insights into the political and economic framework of the global labor force of which they had become a part. The iconic Statue of Liberty's welcoming arms had some qualifications. Entry to America was framed less by an immigrant's desire and more by neo-imperialistic relationships between the wealthier "receiving" countries and the poorer "sending" ones. In the earlier decades of India's status as an independent nation, these policies were based on the British crown's relationship with its former colonies. By 1980, they were defined quite strongly by the economic needs of the United States' quest to maintain global political dominance through constant capitalist growth. There were jobs available in America, but where those positions would lead was an unanswered question.

Against these realities lay another one: the American economy that the Ford assembly line workers built and the Lynd team wrote about was breaking apart during the years Saleem and Malati arrived in the United States. Manufacturing plants, assembly-line factories, and other industrial employers in the Northeast and Midwest had begun relocating to the south and west and outside the United States in the 1970s, creating an era that has been described as postindustrial. Muncie suffered keenly from this change, as did numerous small cities whose economies had been based in manufacturing. In Muncie, the proportion of manufacturing jobs dropped by more than 50 percent between 1979 and 2009, and by the end of the first decade of the twenty-first century, all the town's large unionized employers had either gone out of business or had left the city. The changes forced residents who had pinned their hopes on future jobs manufacturing Ball jars, car batteries, and other industrial parts into either accepting a life on public assistance, working for lower wages in nonmanufacturing positions, or leaving the city. By 2000, Muncie's population had fallen nearly 12 percent from its peak in 1980, and 29 percent of the residents lived below the government-defined poverty line.[9]

"When I graduated from Muncie Central High School, you could go just about any place and get a job—a decent job," recalled Dennis Tyler, a longtime Muncie resident and one-time mayor. "You could go to BorgWarner, and if you didn't like BorgWarner you could leave and go to Chevrolet; if you didn't like Chevrolet you could leave and go to Delco; if you didn't like Delco you could leave and go to Acme-Lee, or dozens and dozens of other little places that were spinning off mom-and-pop tool-and-die shops." Workers could count on finding not only jobs but also homes. Max Fraser, who interviewed Tyler, described the Muncie of Tyler's past as a place where "work was plentiful and paid enough to afford one of the modest single-family homes crowded amid the small and large industrial plots that covered the city south of the White River."[10]

Most of the employers that longtime resident Tyler referred to had left the city by 2010. BorgWarner, which had opened its operations in Muncie in 1890, began downsizing its workforce in the 1980s and closed its plant in 2009. Chevrolet, which had operated a transmission-manufacturing plant in Muncie since 1935, grew rapidly through the 1950s and 1960s, and began reducing its workforce before closing altogether in 2006. Delco-Remy, which had begun operations in Muncie in 1928, left the city in 1998. The process of downsizing and closing these massive operations began in the late 1970s.[11] During these decades, another change occurred as Ball State University and Ball Memorial Hospital evolved into Muncie's two largest employers.

As corner stores and restaurants closed in the central city and on the south side, new restaurants and new subdivisions began appearing on the north side, where the university and hospital were based. The working class that remained in the city was employed largely in lower-wage service jobs in the retail outlets around the university and north-side shopping areas, or as gardeners, custodians, and home-maintenance workers for the newer middle-class families. Fraser captured the feeling of this change in a quote from a schoolteacher who described daily life as being marked by an instability and uncertainty that hovers "like a cloud" over people's lives all the time.[12]

I left Muncie for college in 1981 as that cloud of uncertainty was starting to form. When I returned over the years to visit my parents, I picked up indicators of life being drained from the city. The Amtrak train station that used to offer service between Muncie and Indianapolis as well as Muncie and Chicago closed in the mid-1980s. The airport that small carriers serviced with flights to Chicago, Cleveland, and Detroit ceased to allow commercial traffic by the late 1980s. Grocery-store chains and longstanding businesses closed or filed for bankruptcy, and year after year primary patrons of local restaurants I visited and the mall where I shopped seemed to look older and wearier. My high school— Muncie Northside—closed in 1988 as a result of declining enrollments, and on my visits back I would see fewer people I had known from my childhood. My mother would come home from a day of working at my parents' hobby-and-craft shop looking fatigued, talking of the aches in her knees as she prepared herself a cup of tea.

At least some of my mother's fatigue was due to the economic hardships she was witnessing. Even as my parents were relatively prosperous, regular customers of their small, family-run shop would drop in and tell her about applying for food stamps or of being laid off. Part-time workers she employed would not be able to afford a trip to the dentist, and she, as a small-business proprietor, could not afford to provide them with health insurance. Parents of children I grew up with would also visit the shop and relay news to my mother of their adult children experiencing illness, relocation for yet another new job, and, in a few cases, death.

My mother attributed the experiences of running a community-based business to a transformation of her sense of self. As she recollected her memories, she noted that she would not have gained an understanding of this dimension of Muncie life had she kept solely to her role as wife to a Ball State University professor. Working as a small-business owner in those difficult years gave her a sense of becoming more than a U.S. citizen. It made her an active civic participant in the city, and she began to identify Muncie more vocally as her adopted hometown. During the 1980s, she and my father took down a former family name—McKnight—that had been on the hobby shop since the 1920s and replaced it with their own: Gupta. They took a more active role in Muncie's chamber of commerce and began to support civic organizations and charitable causes. They also became more involved politically, supporting the Democratic Party nationally and, for local offices, nonpartisan candidates with whom they became acquainted through their work and their involvement with the Unitarian Universalist Church.

As my parents were remaking themselves, a new generation of South Asian immigrants started to arrive in Muncie, of whom Saleem and Malati were a part. Many of the members of this generation came to Muncie like my parents did, with good educations and a determination to succeed. Unlike my parents' generation, however, the newer arrivals to Muncie were more mixed demographically. They included some who were less well educated than the previous immigrants. These individuals' immigrant paths often led to retail work or into vocational training programs. Accompanying them were more medical doctors, engineers, computer and information specialists, and others who found work in corporate professions. The diminishing prospects of work for lower-wage retail and manufacturing workers caused many of these individuals to leave Muncie to pursue opportunities in larger cities. However, the more highly educated professionals who were able to secure jobs in well-paying professions stayed. Muncie, for them, remained a place of opportunity, at least partly because their work skills allowed them to offer services the community needed.

These highly educated immigrants helped create a group of South Asians in Muncie that was larger, more prosperous, and more organized as a diaspora community than my generation of American-raised children of immigrants could have possibly known. An organization called South Asians of Muncie

Association (SAMA) formed in these years, and public events involving the South Asian community grew more common. More South Asian names began to appear on billboards and medical-clinic marquees in the city, and, following national patterns of Asian American success, children of South Asian ancestry by the early twenty-first century began to secure winning spots in the area's spelling bees, science fairs, and high-school academics.

The stories these younger immigrants shared with me revealed a socially vibrant, philanthropically active community. The group, with its economic affluence, also was quite global in scope. These younger families traveled back and forth between India and the United States much more often than the immigrants of my parent's generation had, sometimes making two trips a year. Their children were more multilingual and better attuned to the more traditional as well as popular patterns of South Asian cultural life than the children of our generation had been, relying on an influx of cheap videos and, later, internet and social media sites to keep in touch with the latest films and fashions coming out of Mumbai's Bollywood film industry and other trendsetting spots in India.

At the same time, however, my conversations with these immigrants and their children conveyed a hint of a latent frustration with the dominant Muncie society. Few would speak of this frustration directly but nevertheless seemed to communicate in their close interactions with each other and in their relationships their behaviors conveyed with their work. Work, it seemed, dominated their lives. On the surface, this characteristic did not seem unusual for working professionals of the late twentieth and early twenty-first centuries; in fact, it seemed to resemble the growing disenchantment I had felt with my labor in newsrooms prior to entering graduate school. What surprised me was the pervasiveness of work and how it bled into their social lives. Doctors and technicians often arrived at my parents' house or at the homes of other South Asians for social events with pagers attached to their belts. If the pager went off, the individual would leave the room and handle the matter. Turning the pager off was not considered an option. Others would cancel a scheduled appointment with me at the last minute, apologizing because they had been called into work. And some declined to participate in the project altogether, basing their decisions apologetically on serving their employers. One gentleman, for instance, worried that divulging too much personal information would imperil his relationship with his company, which, he explained, was engaged in security work of a confidential nature. These behaviors embodied a feeling that they were living in America to work, and that while many were content with the personal successes they had achieved, they felt lonely, out of place, and somewhat insecure about their long-term social standing outside the South Asian community.

Placing these behaviors in the framework of the changing Muncie and U.S. economy offers some context. While the decline of Muncie's industrial base and the emergence of a services-oriented economy had created a space where newer immigrants particularly could profit, the quality of life for all had changed. With the end of a factory-regulated workday had come an expectation that the worker would be on duty not just during an eight-hour shift but all the time, twenty-four hours a day, seven days a week. Accompanying that expectation was an implicit loyalty patterned perhaps after Ford's investigations of workers' after-hours activities in which was inculcated an almost domineering bond between the corporate employer and the worker. A good worker was skilled as well as loyal. Being part of a team, having a sense of humor, and exhibiting an engaging personality were critical components of this loyalty. Workers who could not achieve a proper cultural fit in the workplace might struggle for acceptance and promotions. In an environment where job security was no longer a given, the cloud of uncertainty had permeated everyone.[13]

That state of uncertainty can be detected in the stories Saleem and Malati shared. For Saleem, every crisis became an opportunity. The last-minute approval of his visa got him into America, just in time. Catching the train running enabled him to make it to Lucknow to secure his clearance, just in time. Saleem described his experience as one of individual success, success that was enabled under uncertain conditions by luck.

While Malati ended her story with a satisfactory conclusion, the narrative tone of what it took to get to that end resounded with strains of difficulty that also capture the uncertainty of the postindustrial era. In her childhood, going abroad was a magazine-glossed thing to dream of. Immigrating first to England and then to the United States revealed the realities that undergirded the dream. In England, only a few foreign physicians could remain after three years of practice, and they were forced at that point to seek an alternative path. America offered that path. Yet it was a difficult path. In Detroit, Raj completed a fourth residency—following years of service he had previously completed, first in India and then in England. From there, it was several more years of service in Appalachia before the lure of secure employment beckoned in Muncie. Malati, however, also found blessings in her life of struggle and emphasized the importance that difficulty played in molding her character. "We really struggled," she recalled. "We reached this stage in life the hard way. It probably gave us better values. Not to take anything for granted is one of them."

Their stories of living with uncertainty stand in direct contrast with the memories of arrival in Muncie that the elder South Asian immigrants shared: Tilak and Subhadhra, Mushtaq and Haina, and my parents, among others, had every intention to return to India, and many tried to do so in the 1970s. None of them succeeded. Twenty years later, individuals like Saleem and Malati had had the experience of seeing Indians who left India and then tried to come back. For them, as a result, there was a sense of no going back, a feeling captured in an observation from Raj that "once you take that path of leaving your own country, a lot of things are no longer under your control."

Finding Your Own Kind

Saleem completed his general-surgery training in Easton, Pennsylvania. From there he went to Chattanooga for a special residency in plastic surgery. He arrived in Muncie in 1983 as part of a carefully thought-out plan.

"I wanted to practice in a medium-sized town, a place with good opportunity," he says. "I bought a *Reader's Digest* almanac to find out the population of various places. I found out there was a university here; a hospital. I compared values, and Muncie came out as the best place to practice plastic surgery. University, medium-sized town, large single hospital, so many surgeons but no plastic surgeons. I decided, 'That's the place I'm going to go.' But I had not seen Muncie."

He drove from Chattanooga and took an exit off Interstate 69 to Highway 32. The road was narrow; all rural, nothing. "I'm driving," he recalled. "It's barren. It's April, the leaves haven't yet started coming. It looked very depressing."

Saleem also recalled his initial encounters with doctors affiliated with Ball Memorial Hospital as being less than warm. Yet the quality of the hospital, the presence of a four-year research university, and the willingness—albeit a skeptical willingness—to grant a foreign plastic surgeon hospital privileges convinced Saleem to follow through with his plan. He moved to the city with Salina and opened an office. Salina sat in the front, and he filled the file cabinets with folders, empty folders, in order to appear professional. He advertised his services and began offering educational seminars that focused on what he could offer residents of Muncie. As he established the need his services could fill, his practice began to grow.

"I didn't know a single soul," he said. "I just opened my shop. Indian community? I didn't even think of it. I didn't have family. I didn't even think that much about money. I just wanted to do surgery on my own; to be my own boss."

Malati also remembered driving with Raj into the city. They were going down McGalliard Avenue and spotted a billboard.

"Suddenly, we saw, 'Gupta Hobby Center,'" reminisced Malati. "And I said, 'Gupta-ji is here?' And we were both like, 'Yes! There's someone called Gupta. Must be an Indian.'"

The existence of a "Gupta-ji" made Malati feel as if she could make Muncie her home. She explained: "It's a fact of the human race that you do need some-one of your own background eventually. Trust me; that's how it goes."

"We were like, 'Oh, so there's at least one; someone called Gupta here.' And then we were staying at a hotel. It was like so derelict. No one arranged big gatherings. The hospital didn't know that we would want to . . . now, it is so different. The moment [Raj] hears in the hospital that there's someone with Indian roots, he goes all out to call up the community and say, 'Come. Come to our house; we'll all eat together. There's a new person.' Just to make them feel at home, to give them a real taste of the Indian part of the community. Otherwise, why do you pick Muncie, if you don't know that there's anyone of your own kind here? Trust me, that's how it goes."

Both Saleem and Raj worked hard to achieve success in America, and their wives, Salina and Malati, worked hard alongside them. The hard work was punc-tuated by a realization that they were in the United States for good, that there was not going to be any permanent return to India. That loss of control underscores the reconciling of dreams with reality that Malati described. From childhood, she had imagined Abroad as being an England of "fine clothes, nice dishes, books." When she actually lived in England, she started to realize that "abroad" was not as glamorous as she had pictured it. By that point, going back to India in her mind was out of the question. When Raj interviewed for his position at Henry Ford Hospital, two of his sisters already had immigrated to the United States. His parents were weighing the option of joining them. It made sense for him and Malati to follow.

Both Malati and Raj told me they valued their lives in America and the oppor-tunities they have had to raise their children in ways that allowed them exposure to their parents' upbringings as well as the educational and economic oppor-tunities that working in prosperous positions in America opened up. But when they reminisced about their lives, I sensed some sadness. Malati had a desire for some sense of permanence. She wanted a home, her own home, she said. After finding that permanence, Raj expressed a sense of feeling chronic loneli-ness. He described the worth of an immigrant as being measured in terms of use value: "The worth of an immigrant is based on what one can do to improve the life of a local person. That's what we're worth."

Against Raj's assessment of the worth of an immigrant lay the economic realities of the Muncie they entered. As the industrial base decayed, the health-services and educational sectors based on Ball State University and Ball Memorial Hospital began to grow, contributing to a slight rebound in growth in the first decade of the twenty-first century and bringing the population as of the 2010 census to 70,085. Just as Ball State University had needed to look outward and start hiring foreign professors in the 1960s, so did the healthcare and educational sectors rely on the new immigrants to help the city survive. The worth of the immigrant in a sense was defined by the capabilities of those individuals to save "typical America."

Like Raj and Malati, Saleem and Salina deeply valued the lives they built for themselves in Muncie. Saleem balanced his personal success against a wish in some ways to recapture a life in India that he had enjoyed in childhood alongside a growing anxiety about the plight of Muslims in a Hindu-dominant India. When asked to recall his childhood, Saleem's eyes lit up as he spoke of a memory from the 1950s of doing mathematics sums and practicing Urdu calligraphy with chalk on a slate. But he also remembered the India of his young adulthood in the late 1960s and early 1970s as a place that lacked opportunities for Muslims. Muncie was where he and his family prospered. He could accept the city as his home for what it had given him and what he was willing, as well, to give back.

As I considered how to interpret the stories that Saleem and Salina and Raj and Malati each shared with me, I found myself also reflecting my relationship with Muncie as well as my own position as a middle-class participant in America's postindustrial economy. Just as my interviewees had grown up in India and left it without intention to return, I had grown up in Muncie and then left it after graduating from high school with no desire to return. Although I began a career in journalism, I left that pursuit because the workplace demands and corporate influence on the shaping of news had made me cynical and had tired me out. Reading the stories the younger Muncie immigrants shared from this vantage point led me to theorize that the very opportunities that opened America up to immigrants like Saleem and Salina and Raj and Malati also produced the feeling of being dehumanized that Eugenides alluded to in his depiction of the Fordist factory. In one of my discussion groups, eight of the elder immigrants reminisced together about their arrivals to Muncie and their years of building their careers, raising their children, and forming friendships with each other that had led to the present-day Muncie South Asian community. "We were the lucky ones," one of these immigrants remarked. "We got in [to the United States] when it was still easy."

Building the "Muncie Family"

Neither Saleem nor Malati came to Muncie with an expectation that there might be other South Asians in the community. Soon, however, separately their lives became interwoven with those of the elder generation of South Asians who had come to Muncie in the 1960s and 1970s. During the period I lived in Muncie in 2003, I spent a great deal of time in their homes. I interviewed not only each of them individually but also spoke with Raj's mother and father and Saleem and Salina's older daughter, who was beginning her own medical career as an undergraduate at Indiana University. During this time Saleem and Malati as well as several other younger immigrants were at my parents' home often. Sometimes they came to attend the discussion groups I organized, but more often they came for more informal reasons, to drop in and visit my parents.

These encounters intrigued me, at least partly because they occurred so rarely in my own life. Even though I had many friends, I usually spent my time at home alone, unless friends and I had arranged for a get-together, usually a few weeks in advance. Nobody dropped by uninvited. At my parents' house, dropping by was common. Many of my interviewees associated this practice with their lives in India, recalling their homes as welcoming spaces where the door always was open to family and close friends.

I considered these relationships quite a bit during my observations of my interviewees' interactions with one another as well as how my own rapport developed with them in the years following the initial project. Over time, I came to interpret these everyday encounters as a process that served to build familial bonds among the community members and in doing so helped cement the community solidarity among these individuals. This sense of family was especially reinforced in the second decade of the twenty-first century, as my interviewees celebrated weddings of their children as well as the passing of some elder community members, and during which many in the community would speak fondly of "their Muncie family."

I also came to see how these relationships resonated with studies on the growth of such family-based entrepreneurial networks in the South Asian diaspora as Dunkin Donut franchises, 7-Eleven outlets, and lower-budget motels. By the early twenty-first century, the ability to sponsor family members to emigrate had led to the creation of more of the extended networks of the traditional South Asian family. Similarly, several entrepreneurial-minded South Asians had begun in the 1990s and early twenty-first century to rely on kinship ties and adult immigrant family members to provide the capital and labor for such successful small businesses. Such enterprises also drew professional expertise and mentoring from fellow South Asian Americans.[14] These entrepreneurial endeavors are not particularly characteristic of the Muncie South Asians I interviewed. Still, the network of kinship, mentoring, and resource availability that characterizes these enterprises parallels the sentiment of Malati's feelings of reassurance upon discovering a Gupta-ji in Muncie and her desire to see the Muncie South Asian community thrive through inviting new families for dinner.

Saleem attributed the closeness to an affinity with shared cultural practices. Even as he and Salina participated in a multiracial community of Muslims that had begun to form in Muncie, he said, "We feel most comfortable culturally with the Indians here. Sometimes you feel like you want to speak your own language with someone who understands it. Sometimes you simply want to share a common type of food." Salina reiterated the sentiment, saying that while she enjoyed interacting with the multiracial community of Muslims in Muncie, she felt closer to Indians. She particularly enjoyed my father's fondness for *ghazals*, poetic couplets usually sung in Urdu that were associated with her home state, and she remarked to me that she was always impressed with his familiarity with Urdu in that respect. For Malati, the explanation was an experience of "landing in a place where you don't know anyone" and being able to form friendships with those who did the same thing. Like my mother, she was willing to reach out to non–South Asians in Muncie and was active in a number of social and civic groups. Yet she pointed to the value of knowing "her own people" in giving her a feeling of home.

House Calls

One piece of popular culture that emerges in both Saleem's and Malati's narratives is the image of the Indian doctor. While the arrival of doctors from South Asia did not occur widely in Muncie until the 1980s, the prevalence of Indian doctors became a frequent occurrence in other cities in the United States and a common motif in American popular culture. Think, for instance, of such examples as the cameo appearance of a bumbling Indian orderly in the popular 1980s film *Adventures in Babysitting*. In college and in my early years as a journalist, I often encountered queries from new acquaintances as to whether I might be related to "the Dr. Gupta" in, say, Omaha. "No, I am not related to the Dr. Gupta in Omaha," I would respond to these kindly inquiries with a vexed humor. "Nor to the Dr. Gupta from Orlando, Austin, or Roanoke, Virginia." A further explanation that Gupta was a common name—"almost like Smith"—usually would be greeted with a sort of curious disbelief.

Nevertheless, the social production of an Indian doctor was of a specific type. Rarely was the immigrant doctor portrayed as a "family doctor," the kindly jack-of-all-trades physician who kept his own office but also made house calls. Rather, the Indian doctor was more like an assembly-line physician who worked in hospitals, often on unattractive shifts, or was an individual quickly steered into a specialization that others were fearful of, such as infectious diseases. The body of the doctor also was most often male. This contrasting portrayal of the Indian immigrant doctor against the "typical family practitioner" can be related to the domestication of the Cold War period. As U.S. political leaders were proclaiming that victory in the Cold War would come not on battlefields but in kitchens and living rooms, women were celebrated for an almost patriotic willingness to fill a role of housewife. What often is concealed in this archetype of housewife is how much women work, not only at home but also externally. The immigrant wife similarly deploys a strategy of selective forgetting about such work.

In Muncie, in 2003, I observed Raj making "house calls." He came over occasionally to my parents' home to administer basic medical care, such as an examination for fever following a bee sting when doctors' offices had closed for the day. At one point, when my parents were traveling and had forgotten to bring a needed medication, they called Raj and he authorized a refill at a local pharmacy. Following fieldwork, when I would speak with my mother over the phone, she would occasionally mention an ailment afflicting my father or her. Although both of them had different doctors who filled the role of primary-care providers, my mother would add that Raj had come over to make sure "there was no emergency." Neither Malati nor Raj spoke of these "calls" when I interviewed them. Yet within the framework of the archetypal role of the doctor in small-town America, Raj's role was significant. He played the role of the neighborly pillar of the community, the doctor who made house calls for his people.

In a slightly different fashion, Malati and Salina would drop by my parents' home frequently, often with a gift of a food they had prepared or some item such as a film they had borrowed from an Indian store in Indianapolis. All of these gestures point in a sense to the manner in which race, ethnicity, and gender have coded the construction of the South Asian community in Muncie. The wives of the primary income-earning immigrants domesticated the meaning of community, holding it together with housewifely acts of warmth and kindness while subtly helping to keep it separate from the public domain of civic and economic life in Muncie itself. If the worth of a (male) immigrant lay in improving the life of a "local person" externally, the value of the wives of the immigrants rested in created spaces outside that discourse for all of the members of the immigrant community to forget—temporarily, at least—that this was their function in Muncie.

As men do the work of bettering the lives of the external community, women support them and their families in roles that are often isolating. Salina, Saleem's wife, took on the task of informing his parents that her son had rushed to America to get there before the preference offered to immigrant physicians had ended. She told that story in an interview with me, separate from my interview with Saleem. Saleem also told me that story when I interviewed him; the details of the two versions matched almost exactly. Not mentioned in either narrative was the anxiety that Salina, like many wives of post-1965 immigrants, might have faced at having to be left behind. Similarly, Malati narrated the story of how her three-year-old asked her, "What does dad look like?" during Raj's grueling, around-the-clock residency work within an overall description of the hardship that the family endured. In doing so, she said almost nothing about what kind of an effect Raj's long absences from home might have had on her personally.

No Place to Call Home

In *My Own Country: A Doctor's Story*, Abraham Verghese writes of a futile attempt to bring to fruition the relationship between his sense of self and the places in the United States where he resided and worked. The story opened as one of journey: Verghese, who had spent much of his childhood and early adult years in transit, found himself recently married and at home with his wife in a small Tennessee community. Within the first one-third of his memoir, it seemed as if the story had found its ending. Verghese had found success: he had arrived in America, completed his medical training, settled in a comfortable community, and was married to a beautiful, intelligent woman he had met in India.

However, both Verghese's relationship with his wife and his romance with his new American community grew fragile as the memoir continued. Verghese started to see patients diagnosed with AIDS. In the 1980s, most of these patients were gay men whose sexual orientation had forced them to dwell in the margins of small-town Tennessee life. Many of them had left the town to find acceptance in gay communities in larger cities and then, after contracting AIDS, had returned to die. Their marginalization in small-town America became an experience Verghese could relate to on a personal level because he, as a lone Indian doctor in a small community, felt a similar level of loneliness. He bonded with his patients, becoming not only their doctor but also their confidant. As intimacy with the AIDS patients grew, a sense of alienation from the seemingly settled life he had created for himself in the United States began to build. He grew distanced from his wife, who regarded the disease he was treating with fear and distaste. He lost standing with some medical colleagues outside the infectious-diseases specialty who were wary of the perceived contagion of AIDS. He started to remove himself from the society of other Indian immigrants in the region and ultimately within the town he had started to call home. *My Own Country*'s narrative ends with Verghese on the road, uprooted once again. He had lost the sense of belonging that allowed him to be at home within both small-town America and the immigrant community in that space.

Muncie residents who represented what the Middletown studies depicted as typical Americans struggled in the 1980s through early twenty-first century to make ends meet. The narrative of the postindustrial typical American was one of trying to survive in an America where something, as journalists Donald Barlett and James Steele had observed in the early 1990s, had gone terribly wrong.[15] Saleem, Malati, Raj, and other South Asian medical professionals stood outside this normative framework. On one hand, they were individuals who symbolized a new, more prosperous side of the city. Following the example of civic participation set by my parents and others, they, like many other South Asian Americans in Muncie, devoted much of their energy to improving the overall health and welfare of Muncie. Saleem and Salina donated generously to public radio, participated in both the city's Islamic center and interfaith coalitions, and were active in the South Asians of Muncie Association. Malati was among several South Asian immigrant women who provided and delivered food to clients of a local food pantry. Other immigrants of this generation were working with African American community organizations to raise money for children's health programs and to improve after-school opportunities for youth. Still others had joined voter organization drives and phone banks for the national Democratic Party. On the other hand, however, being outside the normative framework also carried a price. Many said the general community continued to view them as foreign. In this sense, their place in America resonated with Pawan Dhingra's characterization of Asian immigrants as perpetually foreign, thus reinforcing the constructs of what was American and what was other.

In 2009 I was invited to speak in Muncie at a summit on diversity organized by a consortium of university and community groups. Before my talk, I sat in the audience and listened to a presentation on the difficulties Muncie's working poor faced. The presentation, delivered by a white social-services worker, highlighted these struggles by making several references to jobs that were being taken outside the United States, mentioning India frequently as a place that was benefiting from Muncie's problems. An Indian immigrant sitting next to me wondered quietly why Indians always got such a bad name in this context.

As I considered the question, my mind returned to a suggestion that Kamal, an elder Indian immigrant, had posed during my interview with him in November 2003. He said, "Go to your interviewees and ask them, 'How many times have you been invited to dinner at the home of a non-Indian for a completely non-work-related matter?'"

I asked Raj that question.

"The answer to that question," said Raj, "is once in our own neighborhood. Once or twice every year because of some neighborhood gatherings. In ten years, I can count two other instances where someone has called us out of an interest in friendship. In both cases, these people had traveled a lot, were familiar with India."

His voice trailed off, as he tried to think of an explanation. "Maybe it's because we don't eat meat. Maybe that makes it more difficult."

For many of the elder immigrants in Muncie, the diminishing dream of returning permanently to India was accompanied in part by a reconciliation of life in America but also with traces of the kind of sadness that seemed to feed both Kamal's suggested question and Raj's response. These traces of sadness brought both generations of immigrants together, revealing a sense that, for all of them, life in the United States was satisfying in an economic sense but lonely on a personal level. To overcome this loneliness, the immigrants turned inward toward their American homes and sought out the company of other South Asians, hoping to recapture something of the cultural practices and way of life that coming to America had made them give up.

But has that camaraderie been enough?

Raj went on to state: "As long as I am useful to the hospital, I am a good doctor. If I grow older, if I am no longer able to carry out my tasks, they won't care. They'll just find someone else."

His words paralleled the thought from Jeffrey Eugenides that opened this chapter: "People stopped being human in 1913. That was the year Henry Ford . . . made his workers adopt the speed of the assembly line."

"At first, workers rebelled," Eugenides added. "Then they learned to adapt."

"I know a doctor," Raj said, continuing his reflection. "When he falls into these moods, he buys himself cars to comfort himself."

"[My wife]," he added wryly, "won't let me do that."

"What do you do?" I asked.

Raj responded: "I work; it's my way of not having to think about these things that we're talking about."

CHAPTER 6

Knowing Your Place

Religious Identities and Differences

Knowledge is not made for understanding; it is made for cutting.
—Michel Foucault, "Nietzsche, Genealogy, History," 1971

The festival Diwali celebrates Ram's return to the mythic kingdom of Ayodhya after fourteen years of exile in the forest. The festival occurs in late fall on a night with no moon. As one story goes, the sky on that night was so dark that the people of Ayodhya feared Ram would not be able to find his way out of the forest. So the people lit their homes with candles and small oil lamps to create a pathway for their king. Ram ruled for many years and as an incarnate of the Hindu God Vishnu, he ascended to heaven upon his death, accompanied by followers.

Hundreds of millions of people in India remember the exiled Ram during Diwali. Like many traditions, how Ram's story is told and retold varies from region to region and among Hindus, Muslims, Sikhs, Jains, and Buddhists. South Asians worldwide also celebrate Diwali, using the festival to remember Ram and their ancestral homelands.[1] In keeping with these traditions, the South Asians of Muncie Association (SAMA) has celebrated Diwali annually since the late 1990s with Hindus, Muslims, Jains, Sikhs, and Christians coming together to share food, camaraderie, and dances, songs, and comedic acts. The celebrations evoke the multiple ways in which Diwali and the story of Ram have been understood among people of South Asian ancestry.

In the 1980s and 1990s the figure of Ram returned to India's public culture in an angry, militant form, claiming to represent a righteous Hindu majority who sought to protect India from desecration by so-called Muslim invaders.

The Hindu nationalists made the modern-day pilgrimage community of Ayodhya a focal point. They claimed that a mosque known as Babri Masjid that was built in 1528 by the Mughal emperor Babur was sitting on Ram's birthplace. Under a consortium known as the Sangh Parivar (family of associations), Hindu militants had mounted an aggressive effort to gain political control of India by demanding that Ram's birthplace be restored.

After a decade of building support for Hindu nationalism through a crescendo of anti-Muslim sentiment, the Sangh Parivar declared December 6, 1992, as a day for prayers and fasts. More than three hundred thousand people gathered in Ayodhya at the mosque, which the Sangh Parivar had rechristened as Ramjanmabhoomi, or birthplace of Ram. As shouts of "Jai Sri Ram" erupted, stones began to fly and people clawed past police. A teenage boy scaled one of the mosque's three red domes and plunged a grappling hook into it. He sent down a rope, which allowed others to climb up. Clouds of dust arose as rods and chisels speared the brick. The first dome fell, then the second. By late afternoon, the final dome caved in. Smoke rose from nearby Muslim homes that some of the Hindu militants had set on fire. Construction of a Ram temple began that night while bricks collected from Hindu nationalist supporters in South Africa, the Caribbean, Canada, and the United States lay in a pit.[2]

As the demolition of the Babri Masjid was underway, the father of Muncie South Asian resident Saleem witnessed the violence from Saleem's childhood home in Faizabad, a town adjacent to Ayodhya. Saleem's father could not sleep because of anxiety and the next morning suffered a heart attack. Family members tried to get him to the hospital, but police would not let their car through a blockade and he died en route. Saleem, who is Muslim, told me this story when I first met him.

I was working as a journalist in Seattle when the mosque fell. I had followed coverage in the late 1980s about the rise of a Hindu fundamentalist political party known as the Bharathiya Janata Party (BJP) and had read some reports about a campaign to replace the mosque with a temple. While visiting India early in 1992, I discovered that the rhetoric for Hindu rights was much stronger in India than it had appeared in the United States. In the decades since, that rhetoric has intensified. It claims that Muslims in India take advantage of Hindus and provoke violence, even as media coverage and activism among social-justice groups often report the opposite.[3] I spoke with my mother in the days after the mosque destruction and was surprised to hear her express an anti-Muslim view. She was sorry the mosque had been destroyed and that people had been hurt but said the Muslims had gotten what they deserved. Surprised by her words, I reminded her of her Muslim friends in the United States and of the kind face of religious tolerance that Hinduism was said to espouse. Her reply was that her friendships and Hinduism were not related to the strife.

You cannot understand, she told me. You are not Indian like me.

Religious Nationalism

The Hindu nationalist movement is one of the oldest, largest, and most aggressive right-wing movements in the world.[4] It bears many similarities to Christian fundamentalist politics in the United States and fundamentalist religious movements worldwide. Its participants have worked across the globe to unite Hindus under a separatist banner of religiously defined cultural supremacy. This supremacy extends beyond the restoration of sites claimed to be sacred to Hindus and has come to be articulated in rewriting textbooks on India's history, in renaming cities, and in promoting public policies that align with a chauvinistic, singular Hindu view. Overseas Hindu responses to the movement raise a range of issues on the role of religion in establishing one's sense of self and one's understanding of what it means to affiliate with particular national, religious, ethnic and racial, and cultural communities in the early twenty-first century. This chapter discusses some ways the movement has woven itself into the lives of South Asian Americans.

The assertion that Muslims had gotten in Ayodhya what they deserved implies that conjoining religious and national identities is normal and perhaps desirable. It echoes claims that members of differing religious groups should not mix, as my future sister-in-law had implied in stating that singing a Hindu mantra alongside Christian prayers in a wedding ceremony would be a sin. And it resonates with racially coded claims from some post-9/11 Americans that such markers of Muslim identity as women wearing burqa or Muslims praying in public spaces should be restricted. These statements all underscore the challenges of imagining America as multiracial and multireligious, a challenge that has heightened since the September 11, 2001, terrorist attacks with an increase in religiously motivated hate crimes in the United States against Muslims, Sikhs, and Hindus.[5] In doing so, they also call attention to how such events as Diwali and India's Independence Day are celebrated among diaspora communities in the United States as nominally secular but at their base are Hindu, even as the numbers of Muslim and Sikhs émigrés have risen substantially in recent years.[6] Such Hindu codings convey an impression that to be a proper Indian one must be Hindu, in a way that it is implied that being a proper American is equated to being a Christian. Within this framework, one need not be a religious extremist to start to believe that a marginalized group like Muslims had gotten what they deserved.

Stories like Ram's return from the forest have long helped Hindu Indian immigrants pass on to their children an understanding of their ancestral ties and have helped establish a sense of community membership defined on religious terms.[7] Like many Hindu-born children, I first learned about Ram through bedtime stories. Those stories helped me imagine a connection to my Indian heritage and to regard Hinduism as being a faith that welcomed all. Yet against that template of inclusivity have come violently imposed policies and practices in India that at times have favored Hindus and maligned persons of other faiths, particularly Muslims. In the United States this violence has often used religious oppression to racialize the South Asian American body. This confluence of racism and religious oppression has come to inform how South Asian Americans' encounters with race also define their interactions with religion, making them compassionate sympathizers of each other at times, regardless of religious affiliation, and antagonists at others.[8] In this way, Hindus by virtue of being a numeric majority of the diasporic Indians can choose to align themselves with South Asians who are Muslim or Sikh at some times while distancing themselves from these groups at others.

The challenge that the Ram story presents is determining how to value the story. Like diaspora celebrations of Diwali, it offers great potential to cultivate multifaith fellowship. However, ignoring the Hindu dominance in these articulations of fellowship allows animosity toward non-Hindus being expressed in India and among some South Asian diaspora communities to go unchecked. Among the multireligious South Asian Americans in Muncie and elsewhere, religious fellowship has long served as an important space for immigrants to come together and find solace in the companionship of others. But religion also can divide people within and across communities through its forceful power as a knowledge-creating process to impose some idea of what is the truth. These truth-seeking practices made their presence felt in the mixing of Hindu-derived traditions and Christian practices at my wedding. They surface as well in growing violence against Muslims and Sikhs and in the efforts among some Hindu Indians to marginalize non-others as being "less Indian" than they.

Outreach in the United States

The Hindu nationalist movement grew through the 1990s with the conservative Hindu-aligned BJP becoming one of India's largest political parties by the early twenty-first century. An electoral victory in 2014 put the national government into the party's control and made longtime Hindu fundamentalist and Gujarati state chief minister Narendra Modi the prime minister. News media since 2015 have reported increases in repressive police and governmental actions against women, non-Hindus, and noncaste Hindus, often with Modi or other top officials citing Hindu texts as justification.

The movement's outreach in the United States began in the 1970s as the numbers of Indian immigrants increased. This outreach took place under the guise of cultural and religious education for young Hindu immigrants displaced from their home practices. In doing so, the movement's followers evoked its historical roots as a spiritual awakening in the early to mid-nineteenth century among upper-caste Hindu communities in northern and eastern India.[9] This awakening came partly as a reaction to Christian missionary proselytizing in India as well as the growing grip of British control over India's economic and educational systems. Control of commerce and schooling produced an orientalizing discourse that portrayed Indian people as weak and as having lost touch with a once-strong but no-longer-viable cultural past. The awakening sought a rekindling among Hindus of that cultural past to regain personal and collective strength. This spiritualized Hindu response came to be aligned with Indian independence as well as an assertion of an Indian self that was neither Christian (as epitomized in the body of the British colonizer and European missionary) nor Muslim (as characterized as a descendent of an "invader" from what is today known as the Middle East).[10]

The conflation of Muslim with invader helped Hindu nationalists win sympathy among both Indians and non-Indians because it enabled a distorted understanding of Muslim aggression. Many Muslims in India are longtime descendants of people who converted to Islam, partly because Hindu caste practices had oppressed them. In formulating an identity that defined the Indian as neither Christian nor Muslim but simply Hindu, Hindus conflated Islam with foreignness and in doing so developed a means of separating themselves and "their" India from the centuries of Muslim interaction and influence that have contributed to India's society and cultural heritage. These tensions culminated with the creation of separate nations of India and Pakistan in 1947. Mahatma Gandhi opposed this separation and was assassinated on January 30, 1948, by a member of the Rashtriya Swayamsevak Sangh (RSS), an almost-century-old grassroots social-services organization and one of the main Hindu nationalist organizations in India. This led to a ban on several Hindu organizations, which prompted them to begin cultivating overseas support.

Into the early twenty-first century, support for Hindu nationalism has led to destructive rioting, killings, and forcible reshapings of India's public culture. Proponents of this militant Hinduism have targeted Christian, Buddhist, Sikh, and even noncaste Hindu groups in Indian society. However, Muslims, who compose about 184 million of India's estimated 1.32 billion residents, have been particularly vilified.[11] Thousands of Muslims have been killed in communal riots in India. Mosques have been ransacked. School history texts have been revised to depict centuries of Islamic interaction in India in negative ways; cities such as Bombay, Madras, and Calcutta have been renamed as Mumbai, Chennai, and Kolkata to imply restoration of an ancient Hindu India untouched by Muslim and British and foreign influence; and songs with a pro-Hindu theme have been proposed as national anthems.

These changes in India's public culture occurred alongside the growth of the South Asian immigrant population in the United States. Among Indians particularly, Hindus (who make up about 80 percent of the population of India) were numerically dominant, even though their overall percentage (59 percent, as of 2012) is proportionately smaller in the United States in relation to Indians of other religious affiliations, particularly Sikhism and Christianity.[12] This numeric dominance has enabled the conflating of Indian with Hindu. Hindu temples have been built in cities throughout the United States with a stated goal of serving as community centers for all South Asian Americans but are structured around key events in the Hindu religious calendar and offer activities that reflect primarily Hindu traditions. While these practices serve the majority religious community of South Asian Americans, they subtly ignore the presence and potential needs of other religious followers.[13] Similarly, public-school districts throughout the United States have increasingly sought the assistance of Indian American cultural experts in preparing or revising curricula on India for American students. Yet many such cultural experts who have offered assistance have had ties to the Hindu nationalist movement and have attempted to shape the curricula in a way that is uncritical of Hinduism. These experts have tried to change textbooks so that oppression in India's history and social structures is downplayed, allowing such ideas as the caste system to go uninterrogated.[14] These efforts have come as Hindu South Asians have taken steps to differentiate Hinduism from Islam and Sikhism in the wake of the September 11, 2001, terrorist attacks in ways that presented Hindus as loyal, peace-loving citizens of the United States in contrast to the perceived terrorist threat that followers of Islam and Sikhism were said to represent.[15]

Questioning Boundaries in Muncie

I organized a discussion group among Muncie South Asian residents to discuss Ram and how Hindu nationalism might have politicized religious identities and differences among them. It drew nine participants: four elder immigrants, three of whom were Hindu and one Muslim; four younger immigrants, two of whom were Hindu, one Muslim, and one Christian; and one American-raised Hindu. As the group settled in, I explained that I was interested in exploring the overseas support for the Hindu nationalist movement and wanted to get a sense of their points of view.

We spent the first hour of our session watching a documentary film *Ram Ka Nam* (In the Name of God) on the 1980s rise of Hindu nationalism in India's politics. Some of the younger immigrants were still living in India during this time, and they spoke during the film of incidents they remembered. After I turned the film off and invited the group to comment, a flurry of responses arose.

"This is not good for the country, for India," said the younger Muslim. "We need to organize some like-minded people: Hindu, Muslim, Christian. We can begin in this country. If you write to your Congressman here about what is happening, they'll answer."

"There was a particular train stop," remembered the elder Muslim immigrant, who had grown up in Kenya as a result of family migrations from Punjab in the nineteenth century. "A Muslim man would pray there. Now, everybody goes there and prays at the stop in their own way. Muslim, Hindu, Christian, everyone. The train has to stop at that spot because people insist on doing their prayers."

"My family is Muslim, but in our community, we were always well-respected," added the younger Muslim.

Other participants called the pro-Hindu and anti-Muslim rhetoric expressed by political leaders in the film disgusting. While scenes that described the diaspora support for the Hindu nationalist movement bothered them, the bulk of the discomfort centered on the politicians' articulations of India's heritage and culture. The politicians were not describing the India they knew or remembered as their former homes. In response, I asked the group: "What was it like back home? What was India like for you?"

"We had a common practice when I was a child," said an elder Hindu, who had grown up in New Delhi both before and after the 1947 Partition. "In my family, when a son was born, we would take him to a Muslim holy man first for worship. We were taught not to tease Muslim children. The Muslim children were taught not to tease us. These dramatic acts that these politicians display are not what it's like."

"We can coexist, if we have respect for each other," said another elder Hindu, who had been born in what is present-day Pakistan and whose family had migrated to India following the Partition. "In India, we did coexist."

"But we have to understand the boundaries," added one of the younger Hindus, who had grown up in eastern India. "For instance, I am very liberal in some ways and very conservative in others. I come from a Hindu Brahmin family, and I married a Brahmin. . . . When it comes to marriage, the values have to be the same."

"What do you mean by values?" asked the Christian immigrant.

"Religion is how values are transmitted," replied the Hindu.

"All religions carry some values," said the Christian.

"One of those values is coexistence," said the Hindu. "Coexistence is not the same thing as melting pot."

As the conversation continued, the question of coexistence began to trouble me. Growing up not in India but in Indiana, I had been well aware of myself as a non-Christian and had been told that if I did not believe in the divinity of Jesus, I would go to hell. Those statements provoked shame, confusion, and, later, anger. As I grew older, I tended to treat all religions with some disdain. At the same time, I did agree with the Christian immigrant that all religions held values. As an adult, I had gained respect for the strength that such faith practices as prayer and self-discipline had given to people who were seeking strength, solace, and a way to build meaning into their lives. I could also see power in the communities that emerged through participation in religious rituals. In Muncie, Hindus gathered for group prayers at each others' homes and to sing Hindu devotional songs known as *bhajans*. Muslims participated in a community mosque. Sikhs joined the monthly Hindu bhajan gathering and traveled to Indianapolis to worship at a gurdwara. Alongside studies of the long, varied histories of Hinduism and Islam as well as how I had seen political activists frame pursuits for social justice in terms of a Christian ethic, these practices had further reinforced my understanding of faith as a valuable mode of self-identification and community building for individuals.

What I could not understand was the need for separation to achieve coexistence. Didn't separation create miscommunication, misunderstanding, and, ultimately, strife? Out loud, I asked the group: "Can we have peace in a diverse society if diversity is based on boundaries between groups divided by differences in race, in religion, or other means?"

The Hindu who had brought up coexistence was politically active as a college student in India and, after settling in Muncie, had become involved with community activists who were working to create cross-racial alliances. The individual answered my question by contrasting daily life in India with that of Muncie. Back home, the Hindu said, the way of life was more simply defined. Everyone knew their places within the society and respected each other. People could live in extremely close quarters in peace. But that peace resulted from an understanding that certain boundaries should not be crossed. "Here, apart from religion and maybe caste, the values of all of us in this room are very similar," the individual said. But in India, "we all knew each other and what was expected. You understood your place and you stayed there."

"Yes, don't impose your values on someone else," the younger Muslim immigrant responded. "That is important. Back home, it was beautiful. We lived that way. But now, with this movement, it's being changed. All references to Muslim culture are put into a negative context. I talk to people back home. They tell me, 'If you say you're Muslim, immediately there's a barrier.' Now, even when people ask you your name, they assume you are one religion or another, based on your name. That is what has changed."

These ideas of barriers and boundaries speak to how religion helps organize nonwhite and non-Christian immigrant lives in a white, Christian-dominant America. Against a template in which Christianity and whiteness are hegemonic, the practice of religion in private spaces is seen as a desirable means for enacting ethnic and cultural difference.[16] Religion in this sense enables non-Christians to be themselves without intruding into the sociocultural fabric of an America that Christianity has defined. The difference in this case was that my discussion group participants represented what they had come to see as shared ethnic and national affiliations but different religious ones. Did boundaries established by practices from India make sense in this scenario?

Among Muncie's South Asian Americans, regional, linguistic, and religious diversity predominates. I had been aware of this diversity growing up in Muncie and had noticed it repeatedly during my months of fieldwork. In ensuing years, I've seen that sense of comingled difference continually reenacted at weddings of the children of my interviewees, at funerals, and in casual gatherings. Yet that diverse participation is continually enacted against a singular dominant force as an organizing matrix. In some cases, like my own wedding, that force was Christianity. In many South Asian American events, it is Hinduism. Was there anything wrong with this? Perhaps not. But I could not help remembering that a lack of awareness of this dominance would taint perceptions of the other in moments of duress: in my wedding, the prospect of singing a Hindu mantra was treated as a sin; in Ayodhya, Muslims had gotten what they deserved.

From Hinduism to Hindutva

Much of present-day Hindu nationalism operates through organizations affiliated with the Rashtriya Swayamsevak Sangh. The group, formed in 1925, envisioned the RSS as a volunteer cadre of upper-caste Hindu boys and young men who would participate in daily neighborhood-based *shakas*, or training groups. Organized as a decentralized entity, much as the Boy Scouts in the United States, RSS shaka members would participate in trainings aimed at building mental and physical discipline.[17] While the early agenda of the RSS was directed toward resisting British rule in India, the organization's rhetoric often blamed followers of Islam and Christianity for weakening Hinduism through forced conversions. The RSS established use of the term Sangh Parivar to refer to its shakas and other allied organizations. It also popularized the term Hindutva, or the beingness of Hindu, as a key characteristic of its mission. As its network of followers grew, many of its members began to affiliate with a pro-Hindu political party known as the Jan Sangh.

The practices, values, and tenets associated with Hinduism throughout its centuries of evolution have been varied with traditions differing among linguistic, ethnic, and caste-defined groups.[18] Through the mid- to late twentieth century, however, organizations aligned with Hindu-nationalist groups began to put forth a more nationalized and homogenized understanding of being Indian through their articulations of Hindutva. This redefining of Hinduism as Hindutva and of Indian as Hindu has not found widespread acceptance among Hindus worldwide, and it seems of lesser interest among American-raised South Asians than their parents.[19] However, as Khyati Joshi has argued, Hindutva presents an understanding of a stripped-down, simple Hinduism that offers American-raised children of Hindu immigrants who are growing up in a Christian-dominant society an alternative religious identity that can be regarded as "equal" to Christianity in offering a clear dogmatic set of beliefs and practices.[20]

With the increased circulation of Hindutva came a streamlining of the Hindu-nationalist network. By the late 1980s, the Sangh Parivar was composed of three major organizations, each of which also maintained ties with a number of other affiliates. In addition to the RSS was an organization known as the Vishwa Hindu Parishad (VHP) that dedicated its efforts to cultural outreach, and the BJP, which was founded in 1980 after the breakup of the Jan Sangh. These groups have worked both independently and together to promote a Hinduized ethnic and religious understanding of national identity and patriotism among resident and overseas Indians alike. The globalization of mass media and the establishment of an affluent diasporic community aided this strategy of defining "nation" less as a geographic entity and more with the spiritual affiliation that the term Hindutva encompassed. By 1992, the Hindu militants who gathered in Ayodhya had a worldwide following of Indians who had left India but still nurtured a love for their homeland. Just as leaving a light burning through the night for Ram could help South Asians living overseas connect with the soil of their roots, donating bricks to a campaign for a temple in his name could let them cement that identity in a politicized, territorial sense. India came to represent a culturally pure land that was Hindu at its essence.

Hindutva in Muncie

"I always like to log into the BBC and find out what's going on in India because it gives you news about South Asia," said one Hindu woman in Muncie who had told me that she and her husband had received mailings from the Vishwa Hindu Parishad's American office. "This [rise of Hindu fundamentalism] is something that started in the late '80s. I was sorry to see that Hindus were getting so fanatical. I always took pride in the fact that Hinduism was so accepting of all religions."

When I asked her how she had responded to the mailings, she said, "I'm sure there are a lot of regional centers to try to spread Hinduism to the people who are growing up here. Or to portray the right picture of what Hinduism is all about. But many times it is all, in a way, self-serving. I was always raised with a very broad mind. So it's hard for us to embrace that kind of attitude."

This interviewee's views resonated with others. Few, if any, of my interviewees were believers of the kind of Hindutva view of Hinduism that the Hindu-nationalist movement supported. Many of the elderly Hindu men I interviewed in Muncie, my father among them, told me that they had participated in the RSS shakas during their childhood and early adolescent years. Some of these men connected that participation to political involvement as youths in the struggle for India's independence and noted that they had appreciated the organization's emphasis on the building of self-discipline, moral integrity, and camaraderie. Most lost interest after reaching adulthood and felt that the RSS had taken on a more fanatic turn in recent decades. Because they had left the RSS, they expressed surprise when I told them of its outreach in the United States.

Most of these men also did not remember the RSS of their childhood years as being anti-Muslim, only pro-Hindu. Many attributed the fundamentalist turn the organization took in the 1980s to threats from Muslim fundamentalists. "India always has been a very secular country, right from the beginning," said one of the elder Hindu male interviewees. "Gradually . . . after the making of Pakistan and with encouragement from Pakistan, Muslims have started becoming more Islamic than they were before. To counteract this, Hindus are starting to be like them."

Another interviewee, a male born in 1954 in India after his parents had left Pakistan following the 1947 Partition, stated, "A Hindu by himself cannot be a fundamentalist. He only becomes fundamentalist when he gets resistance from other groups, when there's no tolerance from others." This interviewee had supported the BJP financially in the past and had donated money to a scholarship fund in India that was established by an RSS office in New Delhi. His college-age daughter was a member of a U.S. college-campus organization started by the RSS, known as Hindu Student Council, while his son was involved with an east-central Indiana chapter of an RSS-affiliated group called Hindu Swayam-sevak Sangh. He saw his children's role in these activities in ways similar to the elder immigrants who had participated in RSS shakas as youths. The groups were helping his children gain self-worth. How this individual expressed his own support for Hindu nationalism also was not anti-Muslim. It was more about supporting the growth of Hinduism as part of a developing India.

"As a young man, I had never heard of BJP. Until 1980, you know, even the party did not exist. My father was always a government servant, so he was always a supporter of Congress. Congress always opposed Jan Sangh. But my parents also had migrated to India from Pakistan; like so many people, they lost everything they had. The message of Hindus united . . . that was a message we could understand."

These comments from Muncie Hindus show an overt disavowal of the motives of the Hindu right, particularly its more militant aspects. Yet the comments also acknowledge and accept Hindutva's role in defining the place of Hindus, Muslims, and the followers of other religions in South Asian diaspora life. In doing so, the comments deflect responsibility for religious fundamentalism away from Hindus and onto the targeted Muslims themselves. Like my mother who had remarked that in Ayodhya in 1992 the Muslims had gotten what they deserved, they were able to speak from a position of being members of a dominant faith. It is in this way that Hindutva reveals its strength. Whatever overt support for Hindu nationalism may have existed among Muncie South Asians might be entrenched in the past and hold little relevance on the surface. Yet the comments also indicate that efforts by groups such as the Hindu Student Council to promote a Hindu agenda in the name of cultural development or community building could be sanctioned because they did not appear to be harmful on the surface. Harm would arise within this discourse only when those who did not understand their place as inferior asserted themselves.[21]

The dismissal of the power of Hindu nationalism outside India among my interviewees also comes against documentation of broad, if diffuse, support for the movement among overseas Hindus. The VHP has claimed it has chapters in forty U.S. states and has reached out to more than eight hundred thousand Hindus in America. The RSS has established a variety of affiliates, including the Hindu Student Council on college campuses, the Hindu Sevika Samiti for wives in immigrant families, and the Hindu Swayamsevak Sangh, which organized youth camps in communities across the United States.[22] The presence of such organizations suggests Hindu-nationalist groups could gain a fairly powerful presence among South Asian Americans who are seeking an alternative to Christian dominance. Some scholarly experts argue that the movement's activities have been particularly successful in the United States because the U.S. multicultural ethos encourages non-Christian immigrants to forge ethnic community ties through participation in religious activities.[23] These factors make Hindutva potentially appealing among U.S.-born Hindus.[24]

Hindutva in the Midwest

In mid-September 2003, I learned that one of the Midwest branches of the Hindu Swayamsevak Sangh was organizing a weekend gathering for Hindu youth at a Boy Scouts of America camp about five hours northwest of Muncie. I contacted the organizers, and upon receiving word that I was welcome to attend, I drove up on a Saturday.

I arrived while the camp participants were away from their meeting spot for lunch. While waiting for the group to return, I looked around the room. It was decorated with images of Hindu deities, and literature published by well-known proponents of Hindu nationalism lay on tables. I was examining a biography of an early RSS organizer when the participants returned. A young man in his twenties greeted me warmly and invited me to observe and participate in the group's activities and to ask any questions I had. For several hours, I watched a series of games that emphasized knowledge of Hindu deities and religious practices as well as a need for physical toughness. One game left a teenage boy needing ice and bandages for minor injuries. While watching this game from the sidelines, I spoke with a couple of women who told me they had emigrated recently from India, where they had been members of the women's group Rashtriya Sevika Samiti and were pleased to find a chapter in the United States with which they could affiliate. I videotaped a flag-bearing ritual that resembled practices by the RSS's shakas in India, until one of the organizers asked me to stop.

The organizers grew increasingly less receptive to me as the day went on, and even though I had planned to stay overnight, I ended up leaving after about six hours. Two young men pulled me out of a talk in which a VHP representative from Chicago was making a link between consumer consumption of gasoline and control over petroleum supplies by Muslim Arabs in the Persian Gulf. One of the men escorted me to a separate room and then disappeared under the pretext of bringing me a cup of tea while the other man began asking me questions about what I knew of Hindutva. As I tried to summarize what I had learned of the movement's history and contemporary activities, he repeatedly interrupted me, telling me that I had been misled by communists. The same man also ordered me to strike the comments by the VHP speaker from my notebook, and to hand over any videotapes and audio tapes that I had used during my time at the event. Although he eventually dropped his request, it, along with the activities that I observed and the interrogation that I was subjected to, matched similar accounts that South Asian American activist-scholars had published on such weekend gatherings.[25]

In the weeks that followed I shared my experience with several of my interviewees, including some of the elderly Hindu men in Muncie who had taken part in RSS activities in India as children. While most of them were curious about what had transpired, few felt as if the organization itself was advocating a form of Hinduism that parents would want their children to be exposed to. Most also still said they felt that the movement had little significance in the United States. The fact that my interviewees were unaware of this level of activity of Hindu nationalism highlights how hegemonic truth formations can create a semblance of full-on normalcy. Just as the Ku Klux Klan was normalized as an American organization in the Middletown studies, so has Hindutva worked to normalize the culture of India as Hindu. By establishing footholds in the United States as apparent experts on Indian culture, supporters of Hindu nationalism have been able to use their presence on college campuses, in temple organizations, and through mailings and other outreach to immigrant Hindus to present education on a homeland that many are eager to remain in touch with. Within this scenario, even if one disagrees that India is Hindu, it becomes difficult to dispute that India is Hindu first. In this process, the equating of Indian with Hindu becomes a discursive truth that Indians who are non-Hindu cannot easily challenge.

Being Muslim in Muncie

My first visit with Saleem and his wife, Salina, took place in September 2003. They invited me to their home, which was located down the road from my parents' house and had picture windows in their sitting room looking out onto cornfields, trees, and a creek bed where a couple of deer were grazing. Salina told me the view reminded her of her family's home in India. I brought copies of my project proposal and a list of interview questions. Saleem studied the material as Salina and I chatted. Finally, he looked up. "This is a really important issue that you're writing about. This is something that people need to know about, to know about what's happening in India."

"That government, that BJP government, it is a fascist government," Saleem said. "It is very hard to share how I feel with other Indians here. That is a bad thing."

"We don't bring it up with our friends," added Salina, "but we feel it ourselves."

"A Hindu fellow lives very close to my uncle [in India]," Salina went on. "So close that at night my uncle can hear him coughing. One night he began coughing so loudly that my uncle shouted out that he was making too much noise. The neighbor responded, 'Why don't you go back to Pakistan if my coughing is too loud for you? If you go to Pakistan, you will not even hear me cough.'"

"'Go back to Pakistan,'" said Saleem, picking up the thread from Salina's story. "As if we are not also from India."

Saleem and Salina's story highlights one way Hindutva had become by the early twenty-first century an acceptable aspect of India's national identity, much as a "love it or leave it" defense of patriotism in the United States has been used by Americans since the mid-twentieth century to stifle dissent. Muslims who did not appreciate a Hindu India could go back to Pakistan, to a non-Indian space to which, regardless of where they were born, they were perceived as rightfully belonging. When voiced against the practices of rewriting history textbooks, changing the names of Indian cities, and turning Hindu songs into national anthems, "go back to Pakistan" is like a threat, implying that being born and brought up in India does not necessarily make one an Indian, especially if one is Muslim. Having family in India for generations could make one an Indian, but it would be an Indian who is forever foreign. As non-Hindu Indians, Muslims would be characterized as appendages to a Hindu-first credo, not as integral elements of India's cultural polity. The appendages can be broken off—sent back to Pakistan—just as blacks and the foreign born could be excluded from a typical America.

Saleem and Salina's depiction of Muslims as always outsiders to India resonated with my memories of childhood. Even though I was born and brought up in the United States, I could not be seen or accepted by the wider society as an American. Like them, I, too, was perceived as foreign. The call to "go back to Pakistan" in this sense illuminates how religious hegemonies enact nationalistic rhetoric in microaggressive ways to assert which racial, ethnic, and cultural communities would be tolerated as participants in the late-twentieth and early-twenty-first-century nation.

Saleem recalled in his childhood that he would see RSS members practicing militaristic drills in schoolyards and public squares. The uniforms and maneuvers the members would enact would frighten him. At night, he said, he would have nightmares of riots breaking out between the militarized Hindus and Muslims. "Most of those nightmares would be Technicolor," he said. "Bright red."

Salina remembered her daughter coming home from high school on the afternoon following the September 11, 2001, attacks. "She was upset," she said. "Some kids had said things, you know, about violence and Muslims."

In a separate interview, their daughter recounted an experience of driving to Friday prayers after the attacks on the World Trade Center and Pentagon. She was dressed in burqa. She stopped at a four-way intersection, and a pickup truck bearing a Confederate flag pulled up beside her. The driver gave her the finger.

Neither Saleem nor Salina nor their daughter harbored any ill will toward other Indians, especially those in Muncie whom they counted as being among their closest friends. Additionally, none of the three expressed anger or resentment toward the people in Muncie, regardless of race or religious affiliation. For them, their memories and experiences of prejudice against Muslims in India put the insults they had experienced as Muslims in the immediate aftermath of the September 11 attacks into a different perspective. It highlighted the importance of finding strength in their faith and the value of being a part of Muncie's civic sphere and its South Asian community.

"That white-picket fence, two-car garage that the American Dream describes," their daughter said. "I believe in it, too. I believe it exists in Muncie."

Defining Coexistence

Hindus in the discussion group I organized acknowledged how Hindutva discourses were marginalizing Muslims. These Hindus also claimed a sense of powerlessness to act. When a Muslim participant urged the others to write letters to U.S. lawmakers to pressure the United States to condemn the cultural-religious impulses of Hindu nationalism, Hindus demurred. They could not affect what was happening in India, many of them said. Since they had left, their opposition would be seen as an assertion of unwanted interference. I suggested that the mere act of not taking a stance might be what gives rise to such dangerous politics as Hindu nationalism. I then asked the group if they thought the growing size of the South Asian community in Muncie was giving them a reason not to comingle with persons of other races and ethnicities in Muncie on more than a superficial level.

For a few seconds the room was silent. Then a couple of people murmured that coexistence in a multicultural society was better than hostility.

"What would happen," I asked the group, "if one of your children wanted to marry someone of a different race or religion, or someone who perhaps did not believe in God?"

"I would have some difficulty," one participant said in response. "But if [my child] were happy . . ."

"That they're happy. That is all that matters," another participant broke in, someone whose children had married whites brought up as Christians.

"But you asked how we felt, for ourselves," a third person said. "It's different in this country. For us, it takes some adjustment because it's not how it was done at home."

To grasp the line between coexistence and outright separation, it helps to again review Michel Foucault's essay "Nietzsche, Genealogy, History." The essay suggests in part that traditional ways of comprehending knowledge are built on a false belief that one learns in order to understand. Viewing knowledge as "not made for understanding" but "for cutting," as Foucault puts it, allows one to un-silence alternative views and voices that are embodied in all knowledge-producing practices in a manner that leads to a new way of being with a particular view of the world. To know something is to express certainty. Certainty is like authority, a power to dominate and comment. Another approach to knowing is to acknowledge how relationships of power put authority to voice certainties into the hands of some while denying it to others.[26]

My interviewees' conversations on Hindu nationalism have shown that one condition they perceive is necessary to life both inside and outside India is a need to maintain walls of separation. These walls shield Hindus particularly from a mainstream American society, where Christianity is dominant. This allows them to use religious beliefs and practices to capture a sense of safety they felt as members of the majority group in India. These same walls, however, also have potential to create exclusivist spaces where Hindus as a majority group among South Asian Americans can self-define an authentic Indianness in a manner that regards Muslim, Sikh, Buddhist, Jain, and Christian Indians as less-relevant minority groups within the Hindu template. If the non-Hindu groups upset the majority in some way, the Hindus can retaliate as they did in Ayodhya and justify their actions on the basis of Muslims getting what they deserve.

Such walls of separation, however, are not necessarily rigid in the South Asian American community in Muncie or among South Asian Americans elsewhere. Friendships that grew out of long experiences of living in smaller,

Midwest American communities where any South Asian face could be a welcome reminder of home often break down the walls. Foucault's statement that "knowledge is not made for understanding; it is made for cutting" presents a challenge, in a sense: one of evading certainty in favor of continual dialogue. Like Christian fundamentalism in the United States, the Hindu-fundamentalist movement tries to freeze the walls of separation by linking what it has defined as the trauma of emigrating away from a homeland to a spiritually defined vision of connecting through nationalism back to the home. A more fluid understanding of home can be a way of resisting the violence of religious hegemony, even as such an understanding risks reifying that violence, as both the repudiations of Hindu nationalism's strength among my interviewees and the persistent continuation of Hindutva in rearticulating religious and ethnic identities among overseas Hindus suggests. Thus, it is important to keep in mind the fact that Hindutva has kindled both strident aggression for its cause as well as outright dismissal among overseas Hindus of its validity as an organizing force. This duality helps to contextualize the statement my mother made, that I "could not understand because I was not Indian" like she. It also might offer an opening dialogue to resisting the strident fundamentalism that Hindutva espouses in favor of seeking a path toward a more nuanced multireligious and multiracial America.

Conclusion

Race, Religion, and the Limits of Tolerance

> I take issue with the word "toleration." If somebody's just going to
> tolerate you, then there is still some anti-Semitism.
>
> —Ben Hertz, "I'm the Jew You're Talking About," 1979

May 1, 2003
Muncie, Indiana

About three hundred Muncie residents gathered at City Hall on this first Thursday in May to celebrate the National Day of Prayer in two ceremonies. These ceremonies were organized as separate events so that Christians who wished to pray only as Christians would not have to comingle with those of other faiths. The first event, which took place at noon, was a Bible reading led by Rev. William Keller of the Full Gospel Temple before approximately 125 observers. The second event, at 4 P.M., was led by Muncie's Unitarian Universalist Church leader, Rev. Thomas Perchlik, and included an array of songs, prayers, and tributes from a variety of religious and cultural traditions. Both events celebrated the National Day of Prayer under the directive of the city mayor. Among the 180 residents who joined the second ceremony were some Muncie South Asians.[1]

I learned about the separated services shortly after arriving in Muncie in August 2003, when my mother showed me newspaper articles with photos of her and Malati's mother-in-law, Leila, performing a Hindu puja. She also told me about an Indiana Public Radio segment that had featured Malati singing a Hindu devotional. From her, I learned that the reason behind these separated services had been the Christian minister Keller's reluctance to pray in a service that would include prayers from Jews and Muslims, whom he characterized as heathens. As my interest in the event deepened, several of the South Asians who took part agreed to share their thoughts, including my parents, Malati, Leila and her husband Ramesh, and Saleem.

My initial plan was to study only how my interviewees' participation in what I had perceived to be a politically charged religious event might speak to how Hindus and Muslims placed themselves and were placed in Muncie's predominantly white and Christian social framework. Over time, however, I began asking myself other questions pertinent to the event. Whereas I had seen my interviewees' participation as a political stance, they described it as being only about prayer, which led me to question how and where boundaries between private activities and public stances came to be drawn. I also found myself connecting Muncie's decision to separate the services to the questions of religion that had surfaced through my engagement and subsequent marriage to my husband Jim. After our engagement, Jim and I had begun attending weekly services at a Presbyterian church in Honolulu. There, I found myself being drawn toward aspects of Jesus's teachings that seemed to advocate social justice. As my investment in these teachings deepened, many of my past perceptions of Christianity as a strict, one-sided faith whose adherents' warnings that those who did not accept Jesus would go to hell started to change. Against my evolving understanding of Christianity as a practice of socially just behaviors, Keller's depiction of the followers of non-Christian faiths as heathens seemed a bigoted misinterpretation of biblical statements. My views on Christianity came into question again, however, as my future sister-in-law intervened in the wedding ceremony that Jim and I had planned. As I have noted in previous chapters, she felt that bringing a Hindu mantra into Christian nuptials would be a sin, and had recommended separate ceremonies.

My sister-in-law's reaction bore no direct relationship to the National Day of Prayer dispute. However, her stance continued to disturb me over the years, leading me to see how Jim and I chose to celebrate our wedding and how we have continually conversed on religious difference throughout our marriage share similarities with Muncie's dispute. In this chapter, I discuss those similarities. I show how the blendings of faith that Jim and I carry out and the dispute over a public blending of faith can be highly charged political acts. Both challenge the idea that it is okay to separate peoples by faith and to call such separations harmless practices of tolerance. Both also reveal the quiet but powerfully insidious way religion can align with exclusivist social behaviors to sanction and perpetuate racist hostilities and anti-immigrant antagonisms well into the twenty-first century. These themes have been an undercurrent throughout this study as I have sought to highlight the persistence of the myth of the typical American image that the *Middletown* studies provoked. Therefore, understanding the workings of religious oppression is incumbent to attempting to unravel that image in order to ask what it means to be an American in the twenty-first century.

It has been said that the hour of Sunday worship is the most racially segregated hour in America. What is not said in that statement is that that Sunday hour is a Christian hour. It leaves no space available for non-Christians to fit. Is it possible to create that space? By situating the interfaith celebration within the template of Muncie's typicality, I offer a somber critique of Christian dominance that nevertheless holds a glimmer of hope. I show that even as the interfaith service expressed a challenge to Christian normativity, the hegemonic formation of Christianity trumped the effort. Still, I suggest that such challenges might provide one potential template for imagining a more equitable balance of religious and racial pluralism for a future America.

The National Day of Prayer

American communities began observing the National Day of Prayer in 1952, after President Harry S. Truman called for such an event. The Day of Prayer became more institutionalized with the endorsement in 1988 of President Ronald Reagan. Into the second decade of the twenty-first century it has been celebrated annually in some fifty thousand municipalities on the first Thursday in May. The idea, as ordained by American presidential policy, is to pray in public, often at governmental buildings, in honor of self, community, city, state, and nation.

Continuing that spirit, President Barack Obama issued an annual presidential proclamation in 2013 that defined prayer as a uniting, binding, all-American force. "On their voyage to the New World, the earliest settlers prayed that they would 'rejoice together, mourn together, labor, and suffer together, always having before our eyes our commission and community in the work,'" Obama declared. "From that day forward, Americans have prayed as a means of uniting, guiding, and healing. In times of hardship and tragedy, and in periods of peace and prosperity, prayer has provided reassurance, sustenance, and affirmation of common purpose." Obama concluded his statement by saying that on that year's National Day of Prayer, "I join the citizens of our nation in giving thanks, in accordance with our own faiths and consciences, for our many freedoms and blessings, and in asking for God's continued guidance, mercy, and protection."[2]

Obama's invocation of "our own faiths and consciences" evokes an ideal of a multireligious and multiracial America, an ideal epitomized in his own leadership as the nation's first African American president as well as his mixed-race family genealogy. At the same time, the proclamation normalized the Christian practices that European settlers introduced as natural in the New World. It ignored the presence of peoples in America praying in non-Christian ways before the arrival of European settlers, and its historic references to the prayers of the earliest settlers also set aside the rituals of prayers in which non-Christians in the United States historically have taken part.

Obama's statement echoed an endorsement of prayer that was voiced by President George W. Bush. In 2003 Bush urged Americans "to thank God for our nation's many blessings, to acknowledge our need for His wisdom and grace, and to ask Him to continue to watch over our country in the days ahead." Although Bush noted that America "welcomes individuals of all backgrounds and religions" and that "in prayer, we share the universal desire to speak and listen to our Maker, and to seek the plans He has for our lives," his use of such terms as "Maker" and capitalization of the pronouns "his" and "he" evoked specific language of the Christian tradition.[3] These statements from the first two American presidents of the twenty-first century reiterate the importance of religion—particularly Christianity—in American life across political lines. They link statements on prayer to celebrations of worship in government spaces. In doing so, they also expose the falseness of the belief that the United States is a multireligious polity that advocates a separation of church and state. As well, they show how that belief is built on a premise that Christianity sets the parameters for tolerance of all other faiths.

For Muncie, the National Day of Prayer was long observed solely as a Christian affair. Annual observances began in the late 1980s and were officiated primarily by Keller. Each year, Keller would read from the Bible on the steps of the City Hall and ask those assembled around him to pray, in accordance with what he had articulated to be a Christian way. Neither Keller's practice of limiting his prayers to the Bible nor the official policy of holding prayers in governmental spaces drew much attention until late 2002, when a multifaith, multiracial crowd of believers proposed that the annual tribute be more religiously diverse. This group formed an interfaith coalition and began planning a new celebration under Perchlik's leadership. Keller initially participated in the planning but then declared that as president of the Delaware County Evangelical Association he could not subject his godly flock to Jewish and Muslim heathens. Jews and Muslims could pray at City Hall with Christians if they wished, Keller said, but he would not pray with their gods. "This is a Christian gathering," Keller declared. "We were not comfortable with praying to Allah at the same time we're praying to Jesus."[4]

Keller's statements generated several angry letters to the *Muncie Star-Press* and a public-relations crisis for Mayor Dan Canan, who was just beginning to mount a re-election bid. In an effort to bring about a workable compromise, Canan called for two services, one that Keller would officiate for Christians and one that Perchlik would lead for everyone else. The public turmoil brought several regional and national news reporters to Muncie and subjected the town to a mass-media scrutiny of how Americans were to continue to define themselves as a nation of believers. At least some of the media coverage reiterated Muncie's place in American life as quintessentially typical. For example, *Chicago Tribune* reporter Rex W. Huppke reminded readers that Muncie not only had a longstanding reputation as typical America but also was home to more than one hundred churches. Rhetorically, he asked: "If the various religious groups can't get together in a place like Muncie, what does that mean for the prospects for religious harmony in the country?"[5]

Like the individualized maintenance of separate worship spaces for Hindus and Muslims discussed in the previous chapter, Muncie's compromise reinforced a discomforting rationale for separation at a more public level. Separate services became necessary to keep religious peace. Yet such a compromise also reinstalled the power of Christian dominance. Just as Keller invited non-Christians to pray with him to Jesus but said he would not pray with them in their traditions, the city allowed the interfaith coalition space for a nonreligiously exclusive ceremony on condition that the Christian service remain intact.

The interfaith group's service itself helps show how cross-religious cominglings might eventually displace Christian dominance if such practices were sustained. To understand how this sustained engagement might take place, however, one must look more closely at the historic roots of a value long enshrined in American life, that of tolerance. As the epigraph to this chapter states, within tolerance remains prejudice, if not discrimination. In this sense, tolerance, as feminist political theorist Wendy Brown has proposed, loses its qualities of gentleness and becomes a way of normalizing celebrations of difference without acknowledging the social hierarchies that keep those defined as nonnormative in their subordinated places.[6] This view of tolerance allows one to see how examples like my sister-in-law's protests over our co-religious wedding ceremony signaled that my husband and I were disrupting a normative way of life. While this way of viewing tolerance cannot change the treatment of non-Christians in America in and of itself, it can call attention to how subtle slights, insults, and injuries to such others are legitimized in American life.

Christian Tolerance

A right to prayer is enshrined in the First Amendment to the national Constitution with the words "Congress shall make no law respecting an establishment of religion, or prohibiting the free exercise thereof." The intent of this constitutional statement is to protect a right to pray or not pray as one desires through establishing what Thomas Jefferson described in an 1802 letter to the Danbury Baptist Association as "a wall of separation" between the government and organized religion. A right to prayer also reinforces tolerance, the idea that one should respect others' beliefs and right to do as they please, as long as no harm is done to society as a whole. That wall of separation, in the eyes of advocates of civil liberties, is what makes America tolerant.

However, for many non-Christians, tolerance historically has had a discordant ring. In the epigraph, Ben Hertz, a Jewish businessman from Muncie, suggests tolerance might contain some "anti-Semitism"—in other words, prejudice. By questioning whether tolerance is a virtuous act, Hertz's words evoke the discursive power that Christianity asserts by pointing to the unstated assumption that America is Christian first, and that a Christian America can tolerate without fully incorporating those of non-Christian faiths. This assumption is embedded in the earliest histories of European contact with the New World, as Khyati Joshi observes: "One of the most enduring and powerful misconceptions about religion in American history . . . is that America was created so that members of all religions could practice freely. In fact, the Puritans fled England in search of a place where they could practice *their* religion without fear or oppression. Their agenda for religious freedom was limited to their own freedom, which they did not extend to other religious groups."[7]

The nineteenth-century French traveler Alexis de Tocqueville notes the tight bond between Christianity and Americanness in his *Democracy in America*. In the opening to the second volume, for instance, Tocqueville asserts: "In the United States, Christian sects are infinitely diversified and perpetually modified; but Christianity itself is an established and irresistible fact, which no one undertakes either to attack or to defend."[8] This integration of Christian and American also was reinforced in *Middletown*. Among the questions that the Lynd team asked of white Muncie high-school students in 1924–25 was for a response of true, false, or uncertain to the statement "Christianity is the one true religion and all peoples should be converted to it." Of the 241 boys who responded to the query, 83 percent marked "true," as did 92 percent of the 315 girls who responded. These findings, Robert S. Lynd and Helen Merrell Lynd wrote, not only supported a general belief that Christianity was the prevailing religion of Middletown but also provided a sense that Muncie residents saw Christianity's set of tenets as offering "self-sufficiency for all mankind." The Lynds quoted a pastor as stating that "Christianity can never be supplanted by another system, for it gives the only perfect statement of right."[9]

Some seventy years later, this seemingly unvanquished support for Christianity was reflected in the PBS *First Measured Century* series on American life. The series drew on the Middletown archive and other subsequent surveys to assert the power of Christianity over Americans. A book that accompanied the series noted that even though "religious ethnocentrism declined significantly during the [twentieth] century," faith in Christianity as a true representation of God remained strong. Citing the Middletown archive, the report observed that while only 38 percent of the high-school students surveyed in 1977 in Middletown agreed with the statement that the Lynd team had asked in 1924, that figure had risen to 42 percent by 1999.[10]

Against this historic interlocking of Christian and American, Mayor Canan opened Muncie's Christian-only National Day of Prayer service on May 1, 2003, with a proclamation that "prayers unite people." The city's police chaplain offered a Christian prayer and Keller led gatherers grouped around him in prayers for the city, state, and nation. Those in attendance waved American flags, sang the national anthems "God Bless America" and "America the Beautiful," and shouted "Amen!" as Keller uttered the phrase "in the name of the Lord Jesus Christ." These gestures integrated a love for the country with a love for a God articulated to be existent in only one form—that of the Christian-defined Jesus.

After the service, Keller complained to news-media representatives that his pro-Christian stance had been misunderstood. "We got hate mail," Keller told a *Muncie Star-Press* reporter. "One letter said Keller is a bigoted, shameful S.O.B." Keller portrayed the division in the community as unfortunate, saying that while "religions, like political parties, do not always see eye to eye," he didn't "try to foster divisions." "We love everybody," he said.[11]

The *Muncie Star-Press* also reported the presence of two dissenting voices, one of which involved an encounter with police. Rashid Shabazz, a member of the Muncie Islamic Center, stood at the edge of the crowd and remarked that there should not have been a need for two services.[12] The police intervention occurred when a longtime Muncie civic activist and Islamic Center director Aamir Shabazz tried to approach Keller at the podium. As police and bystanders blocked his path, Shabazz declared that he, as an African American, knew from personal experience that "separate has never been equal."[13] A photo in the *Star-Press* the next day showed Shabazz with his fist extended toward a white man, identified in the caption as Muncie resident Greg Guinn. The caption stated, "Shabazz was protesting being denied the opportunity to voice his opposition to viewpoints expressed during the service."[14]

These disruptions highlight how tolerance asserts Christian power. All was peaceful and without incident until Aamir Shabazz tried to speak. At that point, tolerance lost its gentle face and Shabazz was denied a right to speak—for the sake, again, of a Christian-defined religious peace. His statement "separate has never been equal" furthermore evoked the historically hostile era of racial segregation. In doing so, it illuminated Brown's description of tolerance as "a code word for well-mannered racism" that came into use in the late nineteenth century era of Jim Crow laws and institutionalized discrimination of African Americans. Tolerance was a way for Americans who disagreed with such treatments to position themselves as superior to the post–Civil War South.[15]

Multiculturalism and Tolerance

The interfaith gathering began at 4 p.m., also with a welcome from Mayor Canan. Perchlik opened the event by stating that it was neither a "religious ceremony" nor a "worship service." "We will not say anything about the truth or falsehood of any religious belief," Perchlik told the 180 congregants assembled. "First and most importantly, we're celebrating tolerance."[16] The tribute included a performance of "America the Beautiful" and the Christian prayer that the Muncie police chaplain had offered at the morning gathering. Three Hindu women— my mother, Malati, and Leila—sang a Hindu hymn in Sanskrit and English; a Jewish officiant delivered a prayer in English and Hebrew; and a representative of Muncie's mosque delivered a Muslim prayer. Other reflections came from a Pagan follower, a Bahá'í, an atheist, a Buddhist, and a number of Christians representing different denominations. Participants called the interfaith tribute a nice gathering that they hoped would replace the Christian-only service in future years.

An interfaith service did replace Muncie's Christian-only National Day of Prayer celebration in subsequent years. But was this shift truly an alternative approach? Or was it like many multicultural celebrations of diversity in the United States that parade differences without interrogating the politics of or seeking to build bridges across those differences? In other words, was this service merely a celebration of tolerance? Brown argues that while tolerance initially helped Americans in the North to distance themselves from the institutionalized segregation of the Jim Crow South, its use became more widespread in the late twentieth century as multiculturalism came to dominate understandings of American democracy. Into the twenty-first century, Brown further notes, the term has been deployed to articulate "peaceful coexistence in racially divided neighborhoods, the potential fabric of community in diversely populated public schools, the corrective for abusive homophobia in the military and elsewhere, and the antidote for rising rates of hate crime."[17] This articulation suggests that tolerance in the twenty-first century works with Christianity's dominance to reinforce Christianity as a truth-creating practice. As a truth-creating practice, Christianity establishes an image of a multicultural, religiously tolerant America that implies acceptance of spaces for other religious practices within a normative Christian framework. In this framework, it is normal, for instance, to attend church on Sundays. If one does not attend church, it is appropriate that one observe the Sabbath in some way. Many retail establishments close for business or abbreviate their operating hours on Sundays; many counties and cities, including Muncie, ban the sale of alcohol on Sundays; and state holidays often occur in accordance with the Christian calendar. Followers of non-Christian faiths are expected to acculturate to Christianity's societal framework. In Muncie, for instance, a Hindu group meets one Sunday each month to sing bhajans, while others travel to Indianapolis for a larger Hindu community prayer service. Similarly, the Muncie Islamic Center holds a community service on Sundays in addition to its Friday prayers. These adaptations often go unnoticed by individuals raised within Christianity. For members of a non-Christian faith, they are felt keenly. In interviews with second-generation Indian American young adults, for instance, Joshi found that nearly every one of her research participants' exposure to Christianity had led them to a feeling of either being "different" or being made to feel different for not being Christian.[18] Being made to feel different almost always occurs within the framework of hierarchical relationships that establish the "different other" as lesser to the dominant. This positioning, as many critical race theorists and feminist theorists have argued, naturalizes those who are deemed different as subordinate and weak in relation to the other.[19]

Having a separate space for religious practices that are non-Christian offers one antidote to the affective pain that arises from being made to feel subordinate. Embrace of this antidote was reflected in many of the comments that the South Asian participants in the interfaith service shared with me. For many of them, the decision to participate in the interfaith service was grounded in an understanding of the role of religion in American life that they had accepted as a given good. Because everybody in the United States had been given a right to prayer, it was through prayer that one could reconcile one's place in America as a racial, ethnic, and/or religious minority.

Christian America routinely tolerates expressions of religious diversity at varying levels, drawing on the principles of separation of church and state as well as the idea that all people have a right to worship in any way they choose. Toleration, however, can end when the status quo is disrupted and challenges to the Christian rule of order are raised. Such a challenge arose when Aamir Shabazz tried to approach Keller. Quickly, people moved to block Shabazz, to assert the dominance of Christianity, and to clearly place South Asians, African Americans, Hindus and Muslims within the multicultural template established by Christianity. Whereas the press used photos of Hindu women praying to illustrate the seemingly gentle tolerance of interfaith diversity, their primary depiction of Islam was that of an African American male waving his fist at a white man, signifying Muslims as a threatening presence at a Christian event. The latter image particularly called up the history of Muncie in which Ku Klux Klan rallies occurred in the 1920s and cross-burnings continued to be reported through the 1970s as a way for a white majority to keep perceptions of black assertiveness in check.

South Asian Participation

The number of South Asian Muncie participants was small compared with the overall group of residents who joined the interfaith service. In the media coverage of the event, however, the presence of South Asians—particularly Hindus—stood out. Newspaper photographs showed the performance of Hindu rituals, as noted, and an Indiana Public Radio broadcast of the event featured Malati singing. The high visibility of Hinduism seemed surprising because Keller's main complaint had not been directed toward Hindus but rather Jews and Muslims.

My group of interviewees represented a well-educated, economically prosperous sector of Muncie's community, a demographic that mirrors many other South Asian communities in the United States. Like many of their counterparts elsewhere, South Asian residents of the Muncie community have tended to live quietly. While they have participated in civic and charitable activities, they have not often expressed themselves during public disputes. On a national level, this group of immigrants has often remained on the sidelines of many race- and class-oriented conflicts. This has resulted in a tendency among scholars to portray economically affluent South Asian immigrants as politically apathetic and to view this apathy as problematic because it allows South Asians to reap benefits of affirmative-action initiatives designed to support racial and ethnic minorities without engaging in a long-term effort to address the structural inequities of American society that perpetuate racial and economic oppression. The formation of separate spaces for religious worship in homes, mosques, gurdwaras, and temples also has been seen as contributing to this apathy on the grounds that wealthier immigrants are able to celebrate their cultural and ethnic differences without having to challenge the norms by which a Christian America sanctions such celebrations.[20]

Yet here in Muncie were multireligious expressions of identity taking place among a group of participants who generally were friends and seemed to have few qualms about weighing in on a highly public act. In this sense, the decisions of South Asian individuals to participate in what had become a politicized event diverged from more common patterns of participation in American civic and political life. Therefore, when I spoke with Malati, Leila and Ramesh, and my parents about the event during a gathering at Malati's home, asking them if they saw their participation as political, I was a little surprised when the general response was that it was not political at all.

"I didn't see any political side to this at all," said Leila. "I only saw faith."

"Whether it is religion A, or religion B, or C, or D, it doesn't matter," added her husband Ramesh. "All of them are using different roads to lead to one path."

"Everybody has a right to prayer, and well, we live here," my mother chimed in. "We have a right to live here, too. If expressing that is politics, well . . . that Keller . . . he stirred up the pot and brought it all out to the surface."

"The way I see it, God created everyone equally," Malati added. "This idea that only Christians can pray, it has the flavor of oppression, of slavery. One of my pet peeves is injustice. When I see it, in any form, it ticks me off."

Malati, Leila and Ramesh, and my mother all are Hindu, the numerically dominant group among South Asian Americans. In a separate interview, Saleem, a Muslim who shared much affinity with these individuals, concurred with these comments in terms of differentiating participation in a religious event from politics. He characterized his decision to participate as part of his ongoing desire to educate others in Muncie about Islam. "Although Muncie appears to have been one of the birthplaces of the [Ku Klux Klan], people here are open," Saleem said. "They are willing to listen."

These articulations alongside stories that other interviewees had shared highlighted religion as a steadying force in their lives as immigrants and/or racial and religious minorities in the United States. The elder immigrant Subhadhra, for instance, noted that helping her daughters understand that their family believed in God even if they did not attend church allowed them to gain a positive image of their selves as Hindus and Indians in a white- and Christian-dominant America. Salina, on a similar note, shared how she taught her children to embrace Islam as a part of their selves by learning Arabic and the religion's tenets through a daily after-school reading of the Quran. Salina's eldest daughter, while confessing that she "hated it when she was little," attested to the power of this practice in describing how she turned to faith when she left Muncie to attend college. Alone at a university she described as "party central U.S.A.," Salina's daughter located a community mosque, joined the college's Indian and Pakistani student associations, and leaned on the principles of the religion to guide her through her education.

My interviewees' explanations also spoke to the importance of religion in defining the place of immigrants in American life. Changing ethnic demographics that accompanied the lifting of anti-Asian restrictions on immigration also has effected changes in the United States' religious landscape. While non-Christian immigrants often encounter challenges in practicing other religious beliefs because of a lack of community space or individuals with expertise in the rituals of the faith, some—particularly the more affluent South Asian Hindus, Sikhs, and Muslims—have been able to compensate for these deficiencies by reinventing their religious practices by creating home-based rituals centered on memories of how family members practiced their religions back home. As the number of South Asians increased in the United States, home-based rituals evolved from private, individualized practices into community affairs. Over time, these community events led to a more institutionalized engagement with religion and the building of temples, mosques, gurdwaras, and other houses of worship.[21]

Given the context within which my interviewees regarded religion, their statements of public participation as being about religion and not at all about politics were consistent with their worldviews. However, they left me with a question: Was mere practice of faith enough? In the previous chapter, I recalled being told as a child that if I did not accept Jesus Christ as the one true savior, I would go to hell. Perhaps because of this early socialization, I could not understand how my interviewees could disassociate their participation in the interfaith celebration from politics. Religion indeed held incredible power as an identity-shaping and steadying force, but simply embracing one's own religion could not adequately address Christian dominance. It merely left non-Christians with a separate, subordinated space within a multicultural America organized and controlled by Christianity. Just as I had wondered if the separation of Hindus and Muslims was fueling anti-Muslim hostilities within the rhetoric of Hindu nationalism, I questioned how people of different religious affiliations could hope to live together in a nation if they did not seek commonality across differences.

As my previous discussion reveals, tolerance historically has posed as a virtuous stance that enabled the establishment of a nation of many faiths. Freedom of religion and a separation of church and state are deeply enshrined principles within this idea of tolerance. Yet despite these principles, Christianity has remained the dominant and controlling faith, setting the terms by which followers of other religions must practice their faiths and asserting control over the rhythms of daily life. Although followers of non-Christian faiths make up a small percentage of the U.S. population, the more public presence of organized religions that are not Christian has generated tensions in communities throughout the United States. City zoning boards and building and permit agencies throughout the United States have fielded complaints about requests for variances to construct such houses of worship—often on grounds that these religious sites would disrupt a traditional American way of life.[22]

Commonality across Difference

The critique of tolerance this chapter has offered might leave one with an impression that there is no recourse but to accept the dominance of Christianity and the whiteness of America as the norm. However, throughout this chapter, I also have pointed to small ways in which that dominance was challenged: through the organization of the interfaith celebration itself, through the presence of two African American Muslims at the Christian-only event. Such challenges might offer a glimpse into what a multiracial, multireligious America might look like if they were to be sustained.

How might these challenges be sustained? In search of an answer, I have turned to writings by feminist scholars of color. Many such scholars emphasize a need for coalitions across communities defined as different. They criticize feminist stances that assume that all women, by virtue of being women, share a sisterly kinship. In doing so they bring to light the range of racial, ethnic, economic, educational, religious, and other differences that exist among women. They particularly value attention to difference because inattentiveness to such differences, they argue, allows for a range of discriminations sanctioned under patriarchy to continue. Just as Christianity in the United States defines followers of all other religions as improperly religious, patriarchy defines women as non-men, as aberrations to a masculine norm.

Such arguments can establish a starting point from which one can understand the problematic aspects within religion that the idea of separate spaces advocates. In order to get to this starting point, however, one needs to understand Christianity less as a pattern of beliefs and more as a knowledge production practice that has the power to establish the parameters of normalcy in American life.

Feminist scholarship has provided a strong foundation for making this case. Donna Haraway, for instance, has likened truth-creating practices to "visualizing technologies" in her examination of the "re-workings of what counts as female in primate studies since the early 1970s." Haraway describes these re-workings as occurring alongside "worldwide re-workings of what the differences and similarities within and among women might be and might mean for any practice enforcing what counts as human and what counts as natural." Haraway's phrases "differences and similarities within and among women" and "enforcing what counts as human and what counts as natural" help show how visualizing technologies operate because they invite one to ask how it might be possible to see women outside the constructs articulated by universal man.[23] To see outside such a dominant force as Christianity, requires quieting the noise of the universalizing discourse in order to hear alternative voices and imagining instead that the production of knowledge is less unitary and more like what Evelyn Fox Keller has described as "a polyphonic chorus." Within such a chorus, "what one hears as a dominant motif depends very much on where one stands." At the same time, "there are always corners from which one can hear minor motifs continuing to sound."[24]

The idea of a polyphonic chorus serves as a metaphor for a practice of listening for alternative perspectives. I have shown throughout this book how popular reception and media promotion of the first *Middletown* studies created a distorted understanding of what it meant to be American and then have explored the ramifications that perpetuation of the typical American image have had on how nonwhite individuals of South Asian ancestry come to understand themselves: sometimes in prideful ways of standing outside the norm as different and often in shame-filled ways of not being able to fit in. In the stories I have shared, the body of the white Christian has appeared repeatedly to establish the figure of a normative American, consequently categorizing others as foreign and/or undesirable on the basis of the racial, foreign, and ethnic identity categories with which they might affiliate.

A tolerant position lets one acknowledge difference. What it often fails to do is to provide an education about other people's cultural practices, religious views, and ways of life in a way that seeks commonality and encourages engagement. Tolerant positions often fail to see differences as interdependent. Furthermore, a tolerant stance can only comprehend differences that a dominant position has defined; it is unable to go the extra step of embracing the idea of uncertainty as a central aspect of knowledge, a willingness to acknowledge that a self can never fully know its other.[25]

A state founded on principles of liberalism like the United States supports the idea of individual freedom. Such a state can create a safe, secure space in which people of different faiths, ethnicities, sexual orientations, and so on can stand together, with each group comfortably ensconced under its own umbrella. What such a state does not provide is a communal space where people can come together and share umbrellas, intermingling with one another. Is it possible to do more than merely allow for difference?

Feminist scholars of color who critique the presumed unity of womanhood offer one way to answer that question. Audre Lorde, for instance, has stated that a feminist "need for unity is often misnamed as a need for homogeny." This need for homogeny, Lorde argues, "destroys the attributes of those who are subordinate."[26] Similarly, bell hooks rearticulates the idea of "sisterhood," describing it as a space that allows for discomfort, negativity, hostility, and anger to be brought forth and worked through in the interest not so much of unity but of solidarity. Such an ethos of solidarity "requires sustained, ongoing commitment," says hooks. "In the feminist movement, there is need for diversity, disagreement and difference if we are to grow."[27] These statements call attention to how the tolerant society that liberalism envisions treats difference as something to be left alone. Instead, feminists propose, difference can be used to restage commonality, suggesting that it is not which identity one has that matters but how one identifies with what one does.

One example of how this restaging might work surfaced in a story shared by Leila, one of the Hindu women who took part in the interfaith service. She said: "I have a friend, an Indian friend, a Muslim. One day she was here at my home and others were here and she wanted to leave at 1 P.M. because she wanted to do namaz. I told her to do it here, and to come back again and do it here as many times as she would like. Because that would bring even more blessing to my home."

Leila's words extend an invitation from a Hindu self to a Muslim other. In that invitation lies the possibility of a sustained dialogue that bridges difference. These kinds of dialogues create the conditions of possibility for a multireligious, multiracial alliance to evolve.

Epilogue

An Unraveled America?

My husband Jim and I celebrated our tenth year of marriage in 2015 by running the same marathon in Minneapolis/St. Paul that we ran on the eve of our wedding in 2005. Even as we were ten years older, we both finished the marathon with much faster times and much healthier bodies than we had ten years earlier. We both continue to run, separately and together. I like to think of this development as a metaphor for our marriage, which is characterized still by our diffusely entangled genealogical threads of race, ethnic identity, and religious background and our willingness to confront them.

We celebrated our wedding in 2005 with the multireligious ceremony we devised. The pastor opened the ceremony by welcoming the guests. Jim and I exchanged lei, using the traditional flowers of Hawaiian ceremonies in a ceremonial Hindu Indian exchange. Jim's father, who loved to sing, performed an acapella version of "It Had to Be You" and my father and one of his longtime Muncie friends sang the mantra to the Hindu deity Ganesh that I had requested. Jim's nieces and nephews performed an instrumental piece. Jim and I recited the seven vows of the Vedic ceremony, and a Christian vow in which we promised to love, protect, and take care of each other. I put a ring on Jim's finger and he applied a red powder to my scalp, signifying myself as his wife. The ceremony closed with a passage from the First Letter of St. Paul to the Corinthians.

Most of our guests enjoyed the wedding. Several, I learned later, were not entirely sure what was going on but found a guide to following the various rituals that I had written out to be helpful. A few, I learned several years later, found the ceremony offensive.

Jim's sister delivered the latter message to me in 2010, on the morning after the Fourth of July. Jim and I had driven from our new home in northeastern New York to join a weekend gathering at his sister's family's vacation home on Michigan's Upper Peninsula. I had felt uncomfortable throughout the weekend, which included several group activities like playing softball that I felt awkward trying to join. I spent much of the time writing and reading, swimming in the lake, and talking with Jim's parents. The underlying tensions escalated after I said something to the children that the parents deemed inappropriate, which was that it was okay for children to disagree with their parents. The parents' anger culminated with Jim's brother-in-law ordering us at midnight to leave the property as soon as it got light.

We packed and went to their cabin at dawn to apologize and say goodbye. Jim's sister held the screen door shut and talked through it to me. She told me that the children had regarded me as an aunt, and that I had violated their trust and hers. She also said she did not understand how her brother could have grown into the person he did. I told her that I had never felt unwelcome in their home, but that sometimes I had felt uncomfortable and that the reasons for the discomfort went back to how she had reacted to our wedding plans. I suggested that we talk about that discomfort as a way of getting past, if not resolving, the current state of tension.

Her face hardened as I made this suggestion. "You probably don't know this, but a lot of people whom I knew for a really long time were at your wedding and they were completely freaked out by what the two of you did," I remember her saying. "I don't know why the pastor allowed it. Worlds that different don't belong together. They ought to be kept apart."

I reached for the knob of the door and tried to open it. Jim's sister held it shut.

"I'd like to think that the different faiths can be together," I said. "It's not always easy, but Jim and I live those differences and work them out every day. It's part of what makes us human. It's part of what makes our marriage and our lives together strong."

"Say goodbye," I heard her husband bellow from a back room. "Now."

I let go of the handle I had been clutching and, with Jim, walked away.

Even as I had attempted in my wedding to assert a sense of identity as a woman of Indian ancestry in a multiracial and multireligious America, some members of my husband's family countered my moves. By having their own bodies marked with mehndi paintings of the image of the Christian fish, they had subtly enacted a hegemonizing practice of using symbols to establish meaning and to regain control. As much as I sought to define my wedding as a multireligious event, Christianity established the parameters by which such pluralism would be allowed.

Such hegemonizing efforts occur without apparent intention on the part of their perpetrators. The initiators of the efforts might not mean harm. No more harm than my husband's nieces intended when they stroked the silky folds of my dress without considering whether I would like such touching. No more harm than Robert S. Lynd and Helen Merrell Lynd intended when they chose to eliminate considerations of the experiences of African Americans and Muncie's foreign-born residents from their 1920s and 1930s studies of American culture. The power of such no-harm-intended actions was further reinforced in the Muncie mayor's 2003 sanctioning of two separate services for the National Day of Prayer, and the proposal to split a wedding marrying individuals of two different backgrounds into separate services where differing traditions are acknowledged but not allowed to affect one another. In these ways and others, it becomes clear that a society that is tolerant remains racist. It is holding true to the idea evoked by the African American writer James Baldwin that a truce with reality is the best one can hope for.

Is this the America we want to leave to the next generation?

Silencing difference helped Muncie maintain the reputation of American typicality that it procured through the popularity of the first *Middletown* study. The interfaith coalition's proposal for a multireligious Day of Prayer service, like the filming of interracial dating in the long-censored film *Seventeen*, challenged that very practice. In this way, the coalition revealed that the typical America of *Middletown* was not the kind of America that most would outwardly advocate for today. Along these lines, the participation of Muncie South Asians alongside non-Christians and Christians in a multireligious event such as the 2003 inter-faith service offered one example of how a multireligious, multiracial and mul-tiethnic America might be imagined in a way that did not separate differences but rather engaged with them. But, as the example of the National Day of Prayer suggests, such a vision is not easy to attain. Creating a more diverse America takes more than occasional assertions of one's presence. It requires a sustained effort on the part of many people to forge connections across difference.

· · ·

More than a decade has passed since the National Day of Prayer dispute. An interfaith service did replace the Christian-only National Day of Prayer celebration in Muncie in subsequent years. It was accompanied by renewed efforts among civic activists—Aamir Shabazz and Rev. Thomas Perchlik among them—to initiate citywide dialogues on Muncie's tortured history of racial division and religious difference in an effort to foster a public healing. Those dialogues continued after Perchlik's departure from Muncie in 2011 and Shabazz's death following a battle with pancreatic cancer in 2013. While I have not been able to ascertain whether Rev. William Keller took part in these community conversations before his death in 2011, I have seen the dialogue continue through a decision made by the city in 2013 to close Southside High School and to make Muncie a one-high-school city—the proposal that Hurley Goodall and other community activists had advanced as a way to integrate the city racially and economically in the 1960s.

Against these promising changes, my mind goes back to July 2009.

My parents were celebrating their fiftieth wedding anniversary and had asked the members of our family residing in the United States to come to Muncie to celebrate with them. I was in Seattle preparing to board a flight to Indianapolis when text messages, email messages, and Facebook notifications began to light up my cell phone. It was 8:30 A.M. in Muncie, and my rendition of "The Lost Suitcase" story was playing on Indiana Public Radio.

"One Sunday morning, my mother, Shailla, went into her attic to sort through junk," the story, audio-recorded in my voice, began. "As she moved through piles of boxes and clouds of dust, a pale-blue vinyl suitcase in the corner interrupted her thoughts. The bag she had brought from home, India, in 1961. The bag that was lost, then found, in the journey from India to America."

My parents, sisters, brothers-in-law, and nieces were gathered in my parents' kitchen, listening to the story. Knowing that my parents regularly listened to public radio in the morning, I had written and recorded the story earlier in the week and worked with the station manager of the public-radio affiliate in Muncie to air the story.

"Hey, it's on now," my sister Nisha wrote to me via Facebook. "We are all listening, almost like a family gathered around the old-fashioned radio again."

In between flight changes, I responded to text messages, emails, and Facebook notifications from friends in Muncie who heard the story live. When we arrived in Muncie, my mother told me her phone had been ringing all day as friends called to congratulate her and my father and to talk about the story that aired. What surprised her the most, she said, was how many people with whom she had been friends for numerous years commented that they had known nothing about her journey from India to America or of the immigrant experience of Indians.

I was pleased by the response and simultaneously puzzled. My parents had lived in Muncie for more than four decades. How could their friends not know their story?

That question took me back further in time to 2006 and my twenty-five-year high-school reunion. This was the first reunion I had attended after graduating in 1981 and fleeing the small town in which I had grown up. For five, ten, fifteen, even twenty years I had had little desire to return. The prospect of going to a high-school reunion even after embarking on this project of telling my story of Muncie still made me nervous. But a few minutes into the event and I was enjoying myself. More people remembered me than I would have guessed. I remembered more of my classmates than I had expected to, as well. But one encounter stood out.

"It's so good to see you again," remarked one classmate, a man with whom I had attended nursery school, elementary school, junior high, and high school. "So many people like you just left. You left and never returned."

Why did we leave?

This book has offered several possible answers to the question of why we left: no jobs, no future, no opportunities, and no desires, particularly among children of South Asian immigrants, to stay. Into the twenty-first century, Muncie remained, in some ways, the small-city that the Middletown archive portrayed: a small town, lacking opportunities for the well-educated and not-so-well educated, somewhat resistant to change. Are these characteristics representative of small-town American life? To what extent are they ramifications of categorizing individuals of non-European and non-Christian backgrounds as non-representative of a society composed of people from a multitude of ethnic and racial cultures?

The door of my sister-in-law's cabin remains shut to my husband and me. She has not opened it, and I have to admit that in this particular case I am not willing to try. As much as I would like to move beyond tolerance, I find that I cannot do so alone. The commitment to multiracial and multireligious pluralism needs to come from people representing all facets of American life, not just one's own.

Appendix

Table 1 provides information about the South Asian immigrants in Muncie who were interviewed for the book or who took part in discussion groups organized by the author. It includes data on each interviewee's gender, birthplace, first language, religious affiliation, year of arrival in Muncie, and occupation and age at the time the interview took place.

Table 1. Immigrant Interviewees and Discussion-Group Participants

#	Year of Arrival in Muncie	Age in 2003	Occupation	Birthplace (India, unless specified)	Gender	First Language	Religious Affiliation
1	1966	71	University professor	Haryana	Male	Hindi	Hindu
2	1966	67	Business owner	Himachel Pradesh	Female	Hindi	Hindu
3	1967	71	University professor	Karnataka	Male	Kannada	Hindu
4	1968	63	Housewife	Karnataka	Female	Kannada	Hindu
5	1970	66	University professor	East Bengal (present-day Bangladesh)	Male	Bengali	Muslim

#	Year of Arrival in Muncie	Age in 2003	Occupation	Birthplace (India, unless specified)	Gender	First Language	Religious Affiliation
6	1970	60	Mental-health counselor	East Bengal (present-day Bangladesh)	Female	Bengali	Muslim
7	1971	60	Housewife	Punjab	Female	Punjabi	Hindu
8	1971	68	University professor	Himachel Pradesh	Male	Punjabi	Hindu
9	1972	63	Physician	Hyderabad	Male	Marathi	Hindu
10	1972	57	Housewife	Hyderabad	Female	Marathi	Hindu
11	1976	65	University professor	Bangalore	Female	Tamil	Hindu
12	1976	55	Not provided	Bangalore	Female	Tamil	Hindu
13	1976	63	Housewife	Kenya	Female	Punjabi	Muslim
14	1976	68	Retired engineer	Kenya	Male	Punjabi	Muslim
15	1983	53	Surgeon	Uttar Pradesh	Male	Urdu	Muslim
16	1983	45	Housewife	Uttar Pradesh	Female	Urdu	Muslim
17	1984	48	Physician	Bangalore	Male	Kannada	Hindu
18	1986	49	Hotel manager	Uttar Pradesh	Male	Punjabi	Hindu
19	1986	48	Housewife	Uttar Pradesh	Female	Punjabi	Hindu
20	1989	51	University professor	Mumbai	Male	Punjabi	Sikh
21	1989	48	Housewife	Mumbai	Female	Punjabi	Sikh
22	1990	41	Software engineer	Chennai	Male	Tamil	Hindu
23	1990	39	Systems analyst	Chennai	Female	Tamil	Hindu
24	1994	47	Counselor	Uttar Pradesh	Female	Hindi	Hindu
25	1994	50	Physician	Uttar Pradesh	Male	Hindi	Hindu

#	Year of Arrival in Muncie	Age in 2003	Occupation	Birthplace (India, unless specified)	Gender	First Language	Religious Affiliation
26	1994	70	Retired teacher	Uttar Pradesh	Female	Hindi	Hindu
27	1994	76	Retired military officer	Uttar Pradesh	Male	Hindi	Hindu
28	1998	33	Programmer/ Analyst	Rajasthan	Male	Hindi	Jain
29	1998	42	Psychiatrist	Assam	Female	Assamese	Hindu
30	1999	25	Systems analyst	Nepal	Male	Nepalese	Christian
31	1999	26	Escrow reporter	New Delhi	Female	Hindi	Jain
32	2000	Did not provide	Housewife	Maharashtra	Female	Marathi	Hindu
33	2001	33	Physician	Kerala	Female	Malayalam	Christian
34	2001	34	Student	Andhra Pradesh	Female	Telegu	Hindu
35	2001	24	University professor	Mumbai	Male	Marathi	Hindu
36	2002	30	Physician	New Delhi	Male	Hindi	Hindu
37	2002	29	Dietitian	North India	Female	Hindi	Hindu
38	N/A	Did not provide	Hotel owner	Mumbai	Male	Gujarati	Hindu
39	N/A	Did not provide	Housewife	Punjab	Female	Hindi	Hindu

Table 2 provides information on South Asian Americans interviewed for the book or who took part in discussion groups organized by the author. It includes data on each interviewee's gender, birthplace, religious affiliation, year of their family's arrival in Muncie, and occupation and age at the time the interview took place.

Table 2. American-Raised Immigrant Interviewees and Discussion-Group Participants

#	Year of family's arrival in Muncie	Age in 2003	Occupation	Birthplace	Gender	Religious affiliation
1	1966	37	College counselor	Cleveland, Ohio	Female	Hindu
2	1966	36	Actuary	Muncie	Female	Hindu
3	1968	43	Physician	Karnataka, India	Female	Hindu
4	1968	38	Chemist	Madras, India	Female	Hindu
5	1970	43	Organization director	Bangladesh	Female	Muslim
6	1970	40	University professor	Karachi, Pakistan	Female	Muslim
7	1971	34	Physician	Muncie	Male	Hindu
8	1976	27	Musician	Muncie	Female	Hindu
9	1983	19	College student	Muncie	Female	Muslim
10	1989	24	Quality-assurance analyst	Bombay, India	Female	Sikh
11	1989	23	College student	Bombay, India	Male	Sikh
12	N/A	15	High school student	New Castle, Indiana	Female	Hindu
13	N/A	16	High school student	New Castle, Indiana	Male	Hindu

Notes

Introduction

1. Gloria Anzaldúa, *Borderlands/La Frontera: The New Mestiza* (San Francisco: Aunt Lute, 1999), 23.

2. Benjamin Bryce and Alexander Freund, *Entangling Migration History: Borderlands and Transnationalism in the United States and Canada* (Gainesville: University of Florida Press, 2015), 1–3.

3. Warren Blumenfeld, "Christian Privilege and the Promotion of 'Secular' and Not-So-'Secular' Mainline Christianity in Public Schooling and in the Larger Society," *Equity and Excellence in Education* 39 (2006): 195.

4. Sunaina Maira, *Desis in the House: Indian American Youth Culture in New York City* (Philadelphia: Temple University Press, 2002), 6.

5. Min Zhou and Jennifer Lee, "The Making of Culture, Identity, and Ethnicity Among Asian American Youth," in *Asian American Youth: Culture, Identity, and Ethnicity* (New York: Routledge, 2004), 9–11.

6. Candace Fujikane, "Foregrounding Native Nationalisms: A Critique of Anti-nationalist Sentiment in Asian American Studies," in *Asian American Studies after Critical Mass*, edited by Kent A. Ono (London: Blackwell, 2005), 74–75, 79.

7. Michel Foucault "The Order of Discourse," in *Untying the Text: A Post-Structuralist Reader*, edited by Robert Young (Boston: Routledge/Kegan Paul, 1981); Foucault, "Nietzsche, Genealogy, History," *The Foucault Reader*, edited by Paul Rabinow (New York: Pantheon, 1984); Stuart Hall, "The West and the Rest: Discourse and Power,"

Modernity: An Introduction to Modern Societies, edited by Stuart Hall, David Held, Don Hubert, and Kenneth Thompson (London: Blackwell, 1996).

8. Jennifer Brady, "Cooking as Inquiry: A Method to Stir Up Prevailing Ways of Knowing Food, Body, and Identity," *International Journal of Qualitative Methods* 10, no. 4 (2011): 325; Sally Denshire and Allison Lee, "Conceptualizing Autoethnography as Assemblage: Accounts of Occupational Therapy Practice," *International Journal of Qualitative Methods* 12 (2013): 222–23; and Amani Hamdan, "Autoethnography as a Genre of Qualitative Research: A Journey Inside Out," *International Journal of Qualitative Methods* 11, no. 5 (2012): 586–87.

9. Shahram Khosravi, *Illegal Traveler: An Auto-Ethnography of Borders* (New York: Palgrave Macmillan, 2011), 4–5.

10. "2015 American Community Survey," *American Fact Finder*, United States Census Bureau, http://factfinder.census.gov/faces/tableservices/jsf/pages/productview .xhtml?src=bkmk (retrieved December 6, 2016). See also Wei Li and Lucia Lo, "New Geographies of Migration? A Canada-U.S. Comparison of Highly Skilled Chinese and Indian Migration," *Journal of Asian American Studies* 15, no. 1 (2012): 17

11. Jeremiah 29, *American Standard Version*, http://asvbible.com/jeremiah/29.htm (retrieved February 15, 2012).

12. Jigna Desai, "Planet Bollywood: Indian Cinema in Asian America," *East Main Street: Asian American Popular Culture*, edited by Shilpa Dave, Leilani Nishime, and Tasha Orens (New York: New York University Press, 2005), 55–56; and Ashis Sengupta, "Staging Diaspora: South Asian American Theater Today," *Journal of American Studies* 46, no. 4 (2012): 832.

13. See Sathi Dasgupta, *On the Trail of an Uncertain Dream: Indian Immigrant Experience in America* (New York: AMS, 1989); Maxine Fisher, *The Indians of New York City* (New York: Heritage, 1980); Karen Leonard, *Making Ethnic Choices: California's Punjabi Mexican Americans* (Philadelphia: Temple University Press, 1992); and Parmatma Saran, *The Asian Indian Experience in the United States* (Columbia, Mo.: Schenkman, 1985).

14. Monisha Das Gupta, *Unruly Immigrants: Rights, Activism, and Transnational South Asian Politics in the United States* (Durham, N.C.: Duke University Press, 2006); Khyati Joshi, *New Roots in America's Sacred Ground: Religion, Race, and Ethnicity in Indian America* (Rutgers, N.J.: Rutgers University Press, 2006); Shalini Shankar, *Desi Land: Teen Culture, Class, and Success in Silicon Valley* (Durham, N.C.: Duke University Press, 2008); Nitasha Sharma, *Hip Hop Desis: South Asian Americans, Blackness, and a Global Race Consciousness* (Durham, N.C.: Duke University Press, 2010).

15. Vivek Bald, *Bengali Harlem and the Lost Histories of South Asian America* (Cambridge, Mass.: Harvard University Press, 2013); Joan Jensen, *Passage from India: Asian Indian Immigrants in North America* (New Haven, Conn.: Yale University Press, 1988); and H. Brett Melendy, *Asians in America: Filipinos, Koreans and East Indians* (Boston: Twayne, 1977).

16. Melendy, *Asians in America*, 207.

17. Migration Policy Institute, "The Indian Diaspora in the United States," July 2014, 1.

18. Erika Lee, "The Contradictory Legacy of the 1965 Immigration Act," September 29, 2015, http://www.zocalopublicsquare.org (retrieved October 1, 2015); Sarah D. Wald, *The Nature of California: Race, Citizenship, and Farming since the Dust Bowl* (Seattle: University of Washington Press, 2016), 10–12.

19. Sharon M. Lee, "Asian Americans: Diverse and Growing," *Population Bulletin* 53, no. 2 (Washington, D.C.: Population Reference Bureau, June 1998), 16; Jessica S. Barnes and Claudine E. Bennett, "The Asian Population: Census 2000 Brief" (Washington, D.C.: U.S. Census Bureau, February 2002), 9; and "2011 Community Survey Results," in American Fact Finder, U.S. Census Bureau, http://factfinder2.census.gov/faces/tableservices/jsf/pages/productview.xhtml?src=bkmk (retrieved September 14, 2013).

20. "A Demographic Snapshot of South Asians in the United States," South Asian Americans Leading Together (SAALT), December 2015, 1.

21. "Indian Diaspora in the United States," 1.

22. Emily Skop, "Asian Indians: Community and Identity," in *Contemporary Ethnic Geographies in America*, edited by Ines M. Miyares and Christopher A. Airriess (Lanham, Md.: Rowman and Littlefield, 2007), 271–73; Li and Lo, "New Geographies of Migration," 10–11.

23. Li and Lo, "New Geographies of Migration" 15.

24. See Padma Rangaoswamy, *Namaste America: Indian Immigrants in an American Metropolis* (College Station: Pennsylvania State University Press, 2000); and Khyati Joshi, *New Roots in America's Sacred Ground: Religion, Race, and Ethnicity in Indian America* (Rutgers, N.J.: Rutgers University Press, 2006).

25. Leonard, *Making Ethnic Choices*, 186–87.

26. Khyati Y. Joshi and Jigna Desai, "Discrepancies in Dixie: Asian Americans in the South," in *Asian Americans in Dixie: Race and Migration in the South*, edited by Khyati Y. Joshi and Jigna Desai (Urbana: University of Illinois Press, 2013), 2.

27. Abraham Verghese, *My Own Country* (New York: Vintage, 1995), 202–3.

28. Surinder Bhardwaj and N. Madhusudana Rao, "Asian Indians in the U.S.: A Geographic Appraisal," in *South Asians Overseas: Migration and Ethnicity*, edited by Colin Clarke, Ceri Peach, and Steven Vertovec (Cambridge: Cambridge University Press, 1990), 207.

29. Pawan Dhingra, *Life behind the Lobby: Indian American Motel Owners and the American Dream* (Palo Alto, Calif.: Stanford University Press, 2012), 208.

30. Dhingra, *Life behind the Lobby,* 19–20.

31. Leslie Bow, "Racial Interstitiality and the Anxieties of the 'Partly Colored': Representations of Asians under Jim Crow," in Joshi and Desai, *Asian Americans in Dixie*, 55.

32. Yolanda Moses, "Foreword," in *The Other Side of Middletown: Exploring Muncie's African American Community*, edited by Luke Eric Lassiter, Hurley Goodall, Elizabeth Campbell, and Michelle Natasya Johnson (Walnut Creek, Calif.: AltaMira, 2004), ix.

Chapter 1. Creating a Typical America

1. *South Asian Americans in Illinois: Making Data Count*, South Asian American Policy Research Institute and Advancing Justice–Chicago, 2013, p. 12, http://www.advancingjustice-chicago.org/wp-content/uploads/2015/10/SAAPRI-2013-Making-Data-Count.pdf (retrieved May 17, 2016).

2. Bruce Geelhoed, "The Enduring Legacy of Muncie as Middletown," in *The Other Side of Middletown: Exploring Muncie's African American Community*, edited by Luke Eric Lassiter, Hurley Goodall, Elizabeth Campbell, and Michelle Natasya Johnson (Walnut Creek, Calif.: AltaMira, 2004), 47–48.

3. Theodore Caplow, Howard M. Bahr, and Bruce A. Chadwick, *All Faithful People: Change and Continuity in Middletown's Religion* (Minneapolis: University of Minnesota Press, 1983), 42–43, 51; Richard Springer, "Analysis of the Indian American Community from Census 2010 Data," *India West*, March 30, 2012, http://www.indiawest.com/news/3783-analysis-of-the-indian-american-community-from-census-2010-data.html (retrieved August 23, 2013); Geelhoed, "Enduring Legacy of Muncie," 32–35; and Anthony O. Edmonds and E. Bruce Geelhoed, *Ball State University: An Interpretive History* (Bloomington: Indiana University Press, 2001), 53–54.

4. Foucault, "Nietzsche, Genealogy, History," 86.

5. Ibid., 75.

6. Robert S. Lynd and Helen Merrell Lynd, *Middletown: A Study in Modern American Culture* (New York: Harcourt, Brace and World, 1929. reprint 1956), 3.

7. Helen Merrell Lynd, *Possibilities* (Ohio: Ink Well, 1983), 29–30.

8. H. Lynd, *Possibilities*; Staughton Lynd, "Making Middletown," *Indiana Magazine of History* 101, no. 3 (September 2005): 226, 229; and Ben Wattenberg, "Staughton Lynd Interview," *The First Measured Century*, (BJW/New River Media, 2000), http://www.pbs.org/fmc/interviews/lynd.htm (retrieved April 6, 2012).

9. H. Lynd, *Possibilities*, 34.

10. Ibid., 37.

11. Richard Jensen, "The Lynds Revisited," *Indiana Magazine of History* 75, no. 2 (1979): 307–9.

12. Henry Yu, *Thinking Orientals: Migration, Contact, and Exoticism in Modern America* (London: Oxford University Press, 2002), viii, 7–10.

13. Sarah Igo, *The Averaged American: Surveys, Citizens, and the Making of a Mass Public* (Cambridge, Mass: Harvard University Press, 2007), 80.

14. Jensen, "Lynds Revisited," 303–4.

15. H. Lynd, *Possibilities*, 35.

16. Ibid., 38.

17. Sarah E. Igo, "From Main Street to Mainstream: Middletown, Muncie, and 'Typical America,'" *Indiana Magazine of History* 101, no. 3 (September 2005): 240–41; "Reviews and Notices," *Indiana Magazine of History* 25, no. 2 (1929): 178.

18. H. Lynd, *Possibilities*, 40.

19. Igo, *Averaged American*, 10–12, 77.

20. Lynd and Lynd, *Middletown*, 32–33.

21. Igo, "Main Street to Mainstream," 239–40.

22. Robert S. Lynd and Helen Merrell Lynd, *Middletown in Transition* (New York: Harcourt Brace, 1937), xi–xii; and Jennifer Parchesky, "Melodramas of Everyday Life: 1920s Popular Fictions and the Making of Middle America," PhD diss., Duke University, Durham, N.C., 1998, 258–59.

23. Lynd and Lynd, *Middletown*, 9.

24. H. Lynd, *Possibilities*, 34.

25. Ibid., 34.

26. Lynd and Lynd, *Middletown*, 8.

27. Jensen, "Lynds Revisited," 306.

28. James Connolly, "A Retrospective on Middletown Research," *Indiana Magazine of History* 101, no. 3 (2005): 215.

29. Erika Lee, *The Making of Asian America: A History* (New York: Simon and Schuster, 2015), 5, 65, 163–66; Mae M. Ngai, *Impossible Subjects: Illegal Aliens and the Making of Modern America* (Princeton, N.J.: Princeton University Press, 2004), 17–21, 37; Sarah D. Wald, *The Nature of California: Race, Citizenship, and Farming since the Dust Bowl* (Seattle: University of Washington Press, 2016), 10–12.

30. "Bellingham and Everett Anti-Hindu Riots, 1907," Asian American Curriculum and Research Project of Western Washington University, http://www.wce.wwu.edu/Resources/AACR/lessons.shtml (retrieved May 30, 2015); Mary Lane Gallagher, "1907 Bellingham Mob Forced East Indian Workers from Town," *Bellingham Herald*, September 2, 2007, http://www.bellinghamherald.com/2007/09/02/170095/1907-bellingham-mob-forced-east.html (retrieved May 30, 2015).

31. Lee, *Making of Asian America*, 167, 171–73.

32. Sucheng Chang, *Asian Americans: An Interpretative History* (New York: Twayne, 1991), 196; Lee, *Making of Asian America*, 5–9.

33. As quoted in Abigail Delpha and Cari Peterson, "Making a Home," in Lassiter et al., *Other Side of Middletown*, 123–24.

34. Yu, *Thinking Orientals*, 8, 93.

35. Jensen, "Lynds Revisited," 306.

36. Yu, *Thinking Orientals*, viii, 7–10. See also Ian Haney Lopez, *White by Law: The Legal Construction of Race* (New York: New York University Press, 2006), particularly the preface to the revised and updated edition, xiv–xvi.

37. Igo, *Averaged American*, 73.

38. Yu, *Thinking Orientals*, 7.

39. Igo, *Averaged American*, 64–65.

40. Howard M. Bahr, Mindy Judd Pearson, and Leif G. Elder, "Erasure, Convergence, and the Great Divide: Trends in Racial Disparity in Middletown," *City and Community* 6, no. 2 (2007): 95–97.

41. Luke Eric Lassiter, "The Story of a Collaborative Project," in Lassiter et al., *Other Side of Middletown*, 1–2.

42. Delpha and Peterson, "Making a Home," in Lassiter et al., *Other Side of Middletown*, 123–24.

43. Hurley Goodall and Elizabeth Campbell, "A City Apart," in Lassiter et al., *Other Side of Middletown*, 51–55; and Jack S. Blocker Jr., "Black Migration to Muncie, 1860–1930," in *Indiana Magazine of History* 92, no. 4 (1996): 299.

44. Delpha and Peterson, "Making a Home," in Lassiter et al., *Other Side of Middletown*, 118.

45. "Mss. 90, Hurley Goodall Papers, 1946–1980," Archives and Special Collections, University Libraries, Ball State University, Muncie, Indiana, http://www.bsu.edu/libraries/archives/findingaids/MSS090.pdf (retrieved April 25, 2012); and Michelle Anderson, Anne Kraemer and Ashley Moore, "Getting a Living," in Lassiter et al., *Other Side of Middletown*, 79.

46. Blocker, "Black Migration to Muncie, 1860–1930," 313.

47. Vivek Bald, *Bengali Harlem and the Lost Histories of South Asian America* (Cambridge, Mass.: Harvard University Press, 2013), 118–21.

48. See *Middletown Jews: The Tenuous Survival of an American Jewish Community*, edited by Dan Rottenberg (Bloomington: Indiana University Press, 1997), xxvii–xix; 3; 8–14, 15–20.

49. Blocker, "Black Migration to Muncie," 317.

50. Geelhoed, "Enduring Legacy of Middletown," 36; Blocker, "Black Migration to Muncie," 308–9; Goodall and Campbell, "City Apart" in Lassiter et al., *Other Side of Middletown*, 58–60.

51. Lynd and Lynd, *Middletown*, 200.

52. Ibid., 482–3.

53. S. Lynd, "Making Middletown," 226–27.

54. Lassiter et al., *Other Side of Middletown*, 257.

55. Pawan Dhingra, "Introduction to *Journal of Asian American Studies*, Special Issue on the Midwest," *Journal of Asian American Studies* 12, no. 3 (2009): 239–46.

56. Erika Lee, "Asian American Studies in the Midwest: New Questions, Approaches, and Communities," *Journal of Asian American Studies* 12 (2009): 247–73.

57. "Muncie, Ind. Is the Great U.S. 'Middletown' and This Is the First Picture Essay of What It Looks Like," *Life*, May 10, 1937, 16.

58. Ibid., 16.

59. Geelhoed, "Enduring Legacy of Muncie," in Lassiter et al., *Other Side of Middletown*, 42–43.

60. Igo, *Averaged American*, 101.

Chapter 2. Marring Typicality

1. Vijay Prashad, *The Karma of Brown Folk* (Minneapolis: University of Minnesota Press, 2000), 4–6; Monisha Das Gupta, *Unruly Immigrants: Rights, Activism, and Transnational South Asian Politics in the United States* (Durham, N.C.: Duke University Press, 2006), 34–35; and Johanna Lessinger, *From the Ganges to the Hudson: Indian Immigrants in New York City* (Needham Heights, Mass.: Allyn and Bacon, 1995), xii.

2. Anthony O. Edmonds and E. Bruce Geelhoed, *Ball State University: An Interpretative History* (Bloomington: Indiana University Press, 2001), 8–11, 53–54, 104, 133, 142, 157.

3. Edmonds and Geelhoed, *Ball State University*, 177–79.

4. Das Gupta, *Unruly Immigrants*, 34–5.

5. Gopinath Pillai and Hema Kiruppalini, *Political Economy of South Asian Diaspora: Patterns of Socio-Economic Influence*, edited by Gopinath Pillai (New York: Palgrave Macmillan, 2013), 3.

6. Sandhya Shukla, "South Asian Migration to the United States: Diasporic and National Formations," in *Routledge Handbook of the South Asian Diasporas*, edited by Joya Chatterji and David Washbrook (New York: Routledge, 2014), 166.

7. Erika Lee, *The Making of Asian America: A History* (New York: Simon and Schuster, 2015), 358.

8. Sandhya Shukla, *India Abroad: Diasporic Cultures of Postwar America and England* (Princeton, N.J.: Princeton University Press, 2003), 34; Lessinger, *From the Ganges to the Hudson*, xii–xiii.

9. Joya Chatterji and David Washbrook, *Routledge Handbook of the South Asian Diaspora* (New York: Routledge, 2014), 1.

10. Surinder Bhardwaj and N. Madhusudana Rao, "Asian Indians in the U.S.: A Geographic Appraisal," in *South Asians Overseas: Migration and Ethnicity*, edited by Colin Clarke, Ceri Peach, and Steven Vertovec (Cambridge: Cambridge University Press, 1990), 204–5.

11. "The Indian Diaspora in the United States," *RAD Diaspora Profile*, prepared by the Migration Policy Institute for the Rockefeller Foundation–Aspen Institute Diaspora Program, July 2014.

12. Erika Lee, "Asian American Studies in the Midwest: New Questions, Approaches, and Communities," *Journal of Asian American Studies* 12 (2009): 247.

13. Jigna Desai, "Planet Bollywood: Indian Cinema in Asian America," *East Main Street: Asian American Popular Culture*, edited by Shilpa Dave, Leilani Nishime, and Tasha Orens (New York: New York University Press, 2005), 55.

14. Karen Leonard, *Making Ethnic Choices: California's Punjabi Mexican Americans* (Philadelphia: Temple University Press, 1992), 86–87.

15. "What's India Abroad?" http://www.specials.rediff.com/us/what.htm (retrieved January 27, 2007).

16. Shukla, "South Asian Migration," 172.

17. Benedict Anderson, *Imagined Communities: Reflections on the Origin and Spread of Nationalism* (London: Verso, 1983, reprint 1991).

Chapter 3. Fitting In

1. J. Hector St. John de Crèvecoeur, *Letters from an American Farmer* (New York: Penguin, 1782 reprint 1986), 68–70.

2. Marcus Rediker, *The Slave Ship: A Human History* (New York: Viking, 2007), 5–6.

3. Vivek Bald, *Bengali Harlem and the Lost Histories of South Asian America* (Cambridge, Mass.: Harvard University Press, 2013), 15.

4. Trinh Minh-Ha, "Other than Myself/My Other Self," *Travellers' Tales: Narratives of Home and Displacement*, edited by George Robertson, Melinda Mash, Lisa Tickner, Jon Bird, Barry Curtis, and Tim Putnam (London: Routledge, 1994), 9–24.

5. Yen Le Espiritu, *Asian American Panethnicity: Bridging Institutions and Identities* (Philadelphia: Temple University Press, 1992), 5–6, 15.

6. Dina G. Okamoto, *Redefining Race: Asian American Panethnicity and Shifting Ethnic Boundaries* (New York: Sage Foundation, 2014), 4–5.

7. Bich Minh Nguyen, *Pioneer Girl* (New York: Viking, 2014).

8. Aaron Terrazas, "Indian Immigrants in the U.S.," *Migration Information Source* (New York: Migration Policy Institute, 2008), http://www.migrationinformation.org/usfocus/display.cfm?ID=687 (retrieved August 6, 2012); M. Gail Hickey, "Asian Indians in Indiana," *Indiana Magazine of History* 102, no. 2 (2006): 124.

9. Hickey, "Asian Indians in Indiana," 124–27. This 1960 figure is an estimate, as no census category existed for Asian Indians at the time.

10. Khyati Joshi, *New Roots in America's Sacred Ground: Religion, Race, and Ethnicity in Indian America* (Rutgers, N.J.: Rutgers University Press, 2006), 21, 67; Sunaina Maira, *Desis in the House: Indian American Youth Culture in New York City* (Philadelphia: Temple University Press, 2002), 4–7; Bic Ngo, "Learning from the Margins: The Education of Southeast and South Asian Americans in Context," *Race, Ethnicity and Education* 9, no. 1 (March 2006): 59; Bandana Purkayashta, "Interrogating Intersectionality: Contemporary Globalisation and Racialised Gendering in the Lives of Highly Educated South Asian Americans and Their Children," *Journal of Intercultural Studies* 31, no. 1 (February 2010): 33.

11. Leah Snyder, "Remembering MLK: Ball State's First Black Faculty Member Recalls Muncie's Racism, Discrimination," *BSU Daily News*, January 19, 2004, http://www.bsudailynews.com/2.14316/remembering-mlk-ball-state-s-first-black-faculty-member-recalls-muncie-s-discrimination-racism-1.2019656 (retrieved July 25, 2012).

12. Robert S. Lynd and Helen Merrell Lynd, *Middletown: A Study in Modern American Culture* (New York: Harcourt, Brace and World, 1929, reprint 1956), 8.

13. Purkayashtha, "Interrogating Intersectionality," 34.

14. Hurley Goodall and Elizabeth Campbell, "A City Apart," in *The Other Side of Middletown: Exploring Muncie's African American Community*, edited by Luke Eric Lassiter, Hurley Goodall, Elizabeth Campbell, and Michelle Natasya Johnson (Walnut Creek, Calif.: AltaMira, 2004), 66–67.

15. Arthur Christy, *The Orient in American Transcendentalism: A Study of Emerson, Thoreau and Alcott* (New York: Columbia University Press, 1932); Carl T. Jackson, *The Oriental Religions and American Thought: Nineteenth Century Explorations* (Westport, Conn.: Greenwood, 1981); Vijay Prashad, *The Karma of Brown Folk* (Minneapolis: University of Minnesota Press, 2000).

16. Karen Isaksen Leonard, *The South Asian Americans* (Westport, Conn.: Greenwood, 1997), 42.

17. Roger Daniels, *History of Indian Immigration to the United States: An Interpretative Essay* (New York: Asia Society, 1989), 14–17; Bill Ong Hing, *Making and Remaking Asian American Through Immigration Policy, 1850–1990* (Palo Alto, Calif.: Stanford University Press), 31; Leonard, *South Asian Americans*, 42–43.

18. Susan Koshy, "Historicizing Racial Identity and Minority Status for South Asian Americans," *Asian Pacific American Collective History Project*, http://www.sscnet.ucla.edu/history/faculty/henryyu/APACHP/teacher/research/koshy.htm (retrieved August 9, 2012); Lopez, *White By Law*, 90; Sridevi Menon, "Disrupting Asian-America: South Asian American Histories as Strategic Sites of Narration," *Alternatives* 31 (2006), 353–54; Crystal Parikh, "Minority," in *Keywords for Asian American Studies*, edited by Cathy J. Schlund-Vials, Linda Trinh Võ, and K. Scott Wong (New York: NYU Press, 2015), 162.

19. Karen Leonard, *Making Ethnic Choices: California's Punjabi Mexican Americans*, (Philadelphia: Temple University Press, 1992), 62–83.

20. Ibid., 208–9.

21. Bald, *Bengali Harlem*; Maira, *Desis in the House*; Nitasha Sharma, *Hip Hop Desis: South Asian Americans, Blackness, and a Global Race Consciousness* (Durham, N.C.: Duke University Press, 2010).

22. Arthur Helweg and Usha Helweg, *An Immigrant Success Story: East Asians in America* (Philadelphia: University of Pennsylvania Press, 1989), 18; Ravindra Jain, *Indian Communities Abroad: Themes and Literature* (New Delhi: Manohar, 1993), 38; Harry H. L. Kitano and Roger Daniels, *Asian Americans: Emerging Minorities* (Englewood Cliffs, N.J.: Prentice Hall, 1995), 105.

23. Leonard, *Making Ethnic Choices*, 205–9.

24. George Lipsitz, *The Possessive Investment in Whiteness: How White People Profit from Identity Politics* (Philadelphia: Temple University Press, 1998), 152–54.

25. "Indian Diaspora in the United States," 3–4.

26. Bharati Mukherjee, "American Dreamer," *Mother Jones* (January/February 1997), http://www.motherjones.com/politics/1997/01/american-dreamer?page=1 (retrieved August 11, 2012).

27. Menon, "Disrupting Asian America," 346–47.

Chapter 4. Navigating Rebellion and Respect

1. Sunaina Maira, *Desis in the House: Indian American Youth Culture in New York City* (Philadelphia: Temple University Press, 2002), 38–45; Shalini Shankar, *Desi Land: Teen Culture, Class, and Success in Silicon Valley* (Durham, N.C.: Duke University Press, 2008), 47–55.

2. Shankar, *Desi Land*, 55; Nitasha Sharma, *Hip Hop Desis: South Asian Americans, Blackness, and a Global Race Consciousness* (Durham, N.C.: Duke University Press, 2010), 19, 21.

3. Mary Yu Danico, *Asian American Society: An Encyclopedia* (New York: Sage) 526–29; and Rifat Anjum Salam, *Negotiating Tradition, Becoming American: Family, Gender, and*

Autonomy for Second Generation Asian Americans (El Paso, Tex.: LFB Scholarly, 2014), 63–64.

4. Dwight Hoover, *Middletown: The Making of a Documentary Film Series* (New York: Routledge, 1992), 186–88.

5. Ibid., 109–10.

6. Dwight Hoover, "Changing Views of Community Case Studies: Middletown as a Case Study," *Journal of the History of Behavioral Sciences* 28 (April 1989): 114–15.

7. Lynd and Lynd, *Middletown in Transition*, 164, 237, 311.

8. Hoover, "Changing Views," 117.

9. Ibid.

10. Theodore Caplow, Bruce Chadwick, and Howard M. Bahr, *Middletown Families: Fifty Years of Change and Continuity* (Minneapolis, University of Minnesota Press, 1982), 5.

11. Caplow et al., *Middletown Families*, 4, 14–15, 34, 56–59, 162–63.

12. Gregory Howard Williams, *Life on the Color Line: The True Story of a White Boy Who Discovered He Was Black* (New York: Plume, 1996), 190.

13. Susan Koshy, "Historicizing Racial Identity and Minority Status for South Asian Americans," *Asian Pacific American Collective History Project*, http://www.sscnet.ucla.edu/history/faculty/henryyu/APACHP/teacher/research/koshy.htm (retrieved August 9, 2012); and Monisha Das Gupta, *Unruly Immigrants: Rights, Activism, and Transnational South Asian Politics in the United States* (Durham, N.C.: Duke University Press, 2006), 28–33, 38–42.

14. Caplow et al., *Middletown Families*, 159.

15. Ibid., 14.

16. Ibid., 34.

17. Hurley Goodall and Elizabeth Campbell, "A City Apart," in *The Other Side of Middletown: Exploring Muncie's African American Community*, edited by Luke Eric Lassiter, Hurley Goodall, Elizabeth Campbell, and Michelle Natasya Johnson (Walnut Creek, Calif.: AltaMira, 2004); 68–69.

18. Taylor A. Marrow III, *Reconciling the Past: A Brief History of Race Relations in Muncie, 1827–2004* (Muncie, Ind.: Teamwork for Quality Living, 2004), 35–37.

Chapter 5. Cowpath Crossings

1. Abraham Verghese, "The Cowpath to America," *New Yorker* 73, no. 17 (1997), 74.

2. Pawan Dhingra, *Managing Multicultural Lives: Asian American Professionals and the Challenge of Multiple Identities* (Palo Alto, Calif.: Stanford University Press, 2007), 16–17.

3. Michel de Certeau, *The Practice of Everyday Life* (Berkeley: University of California Press, 1984), 68–70.

4. Gary Colombo, Robert Cullen, Bonnie Lisle, *Rereading America: Cultural Contexts for Critical Thinking and Writing* (Boston: Bedford/St. Martin's, 2001), 535; and "The American Experience: Henry Ford Transcript," *Public Broadcasting Corporation*, 16–17, http://www-tc.pbs.org/wgbh/americanexperience/media/uploads/special_features/download_files/henryford_transcript.pdf (retrieved November 18, 2013).

5. Priya Agarwal, *Passage from India: Post-1965 Immigrants and Their Children* (Palos Verde, Calif.: Yuvati, 1991), 22; Surinder Bhardwaj and N. Madhusudana Rao, "Asian Indians in the U.S.: A Geographic Appraisal," in *South Asians Overseas: Migration and Ethnicity*, edited by Colin Clarke, Ceri Peach, and Steven Vertovec (Cambridge: Cambridge University Press, 1990), 199–200; Catherine Choy, *Empire of Care: Nursing and Migration in Filipino American History* (Durham, N.C.: Duke University Press, 2003), 3–4; James Ciment and John Radzilowski, *American Immigration: An Encyclopedia of Political, Social, and Cultural Change*, 2nd edition (Florence, Ky.: Taylor and Francis, 2015), 250–51.

6. "Plight of Foreign Doctors," *Time*, December 5, 1960.

7. Abraham Verghese, *My Own Country* (New York: Vintage, 1995), 17–18.

8. Choy, *Empire of Care*, 117.

9. James Connolly, "Can They Do It? The Capacity of Small Rust-Belt Cities to Reinvent Themselves in a Global Economy," in *After the Factory: Reinventing America's Industrial Small Cities*, edited by James Connolly (Blue Ridge Summit, Penn.: Lexington, 2010), 4; and Max Fraser, "Down and Out in the New Middletowns" *Dissent* (Winter 2012), 27–30.

10. Fraser, "Down and Out," 28–30.

11. See "Changing Gears," http://idee.iweb.bsu.edu/work/changinggears.html; "Muncie Chevrolet Plant Photographs," Digital Media Repository, Ball State University Libraries, https://libx.bsu.edu/cdm/landingpage/collection/ChevyPlant (retrieved November 18, 2013); "The History of the Delco-Remy Division of General Motoros," http://www.delcoremyhistory.com/theplants.htm (retrieved November 18, 2013).

12. Fraser, "Down and Out in the New Middletowns," 28–30.

13. Catherine Casey, *Work, Self, and Society: After Industrialism* (London: Routledge, 1995), 86, 93, 97–99.

14. Padma Rangaoswamy, "South Asians in Dunkin' Donuts: Niche Development in the Franchise Industry," *Journal of Ethnic and Migration Studies* 33, no. 4 (2007): 672–73, 677–80; Pawan Dhingra, *Life behind the Lobby: Indian American Motel Owners and the American Dream* (Palo Alto, Calif.: Stanford University Press, 2012), 4–5; Jennifer Parker, "Ethnic Social Structures and Mainstream Capital: The Ethnic Anchoring of 'American' Franchise Growth," *Journal of Asian American Studies* 16, no. 1 (2013): 34–36, 42, 45, 47.

15. Donald L Barlett and James B. Steele, *The Betrayal of the American Dream* (Philadelphia: Public Affairs, 2013), 3–8; and *America: What Went Wrong* (Kansas City: Andrews and McMeel, 1992), which was based on the journalists' series for the *Philadelphia Inquirer*.

Chapter 6. Knowing Your Place

1. Bhikhu Parekh, "Some Reflections on the Hindu Diaspora," *New Community* 20, no. 4 (1994): 613–14. See also Sherry-Ann Singh, "The Ramayana in Trinidad: Socio-Historical Perspectives," *Journal of Caribbean History* 44, no. 2 (2010): 201–3; Mandakranta Bose, *Ramayana Revisited* (London: Oxford University Press, 2004), 4; Marina

Carter and Khal Torabully, *Coolitude: An Anthology of the Indian Labour Diaspora* (London: Anthem, 2002), 128–29.

2. Himanee Gupta, "Illuminating India: How a South Asian Diaspora Helps Build a Hindu Nation," *Sagar: A South Asia Research Journal* 6 (1999): 14–15; and Christophe Jaffrelot, *Hindu Nationalism: A Reader* (Princeton, N.J.: Princeton University Press, 2007), 280–82.

3. See, for instance, Mandakini Gahlot, "India's Hindu Fundamentalists," *al-Jazeera–English*, October 8, 2015, http://www.aljazeera.com/programmes/peopleandpower/2015/10/indias-hindu-fundamentalists-151008073418225.html (retrieved May 26, 2016).

4. Matthew N. Lyons, "Hindu Nationalism: An Annotated Bibliography of Online Resources," http://comminfo.rutgers.edu/~lyonsm/hindunatbib.html (retrieved February 7, 2014).

5. See "Post 9-11 Backlash," SAALT (South Asian Americans Leading Together), for a log of hate crimes against South Asians in the United States since 2015, http://saalt.org/policy-change/post-9-11-backlash (retrieved May 26, 2016); Sameera Hafizz and Suman Ragunathan, "Under Suspicion, Under Attack: Xenophobic Rhetoric and Hate Violence against South Asian, Muslim, Sikh, Hindu, Middle Eastern, and Arab Communities in the U.S.," *SAALT* (2014), http://saalt.org/wp-content/uploads/2013/06/SAALT_report_full_links1.pdf (retrieved May 26, 2016), 2.

6. Prema Kurien, "Immigration, Community Formation, Political Incorporation, and Why Religion Matters: Migration and Settlement Patterns of the Indian Diaspora," *Sociology of Religion* 75, no. 4 (2014): 527.

7. Parekh, "Some Reflections on the Hindu Diaspora," 613–14.

8. Sylvia Chan-Malik and Khyati Y. Joshi, "Asian American Religions in a Globalized World," *Amerasia Journal* 40, no. 1 (2014): viii; Kurien, "Why Religion Matters," 529.

9. Gupta, "Illuminating India"; Christophe Jaffrelot, *The Hindu Nationalist Movement in India* (New York: Columbia University Press, 1998) and *Hindu Nationalism: A Reader*; Prema Kurien, *A Place at the Multicultural Table: The Development of an American Hinduism* (New Brunswick, N.J.: Rutgers University Press, 2007); Rajeswari Sunder Rajan, "The Politics of Hindu 'Tolerance,'" *boundary 2* 38, no. 3 (2011): 72–74; John Zavos, "The Shapes of Hindu Nationalism," in *Coalition Politics and Hindu Nationalism*, edited by Katherine Adeney and Lawrence Saez (London: Routledge, 2005), 36–54.

10. Partha Chatterjee, *Nationalist Thought and the Colonial World: A Derivative Discourse* (Minneapolis: University of Minnesota Press, 1993), 30; and Rajan, "Politics of Hindu 'Tolerance,'" 77–80.

11. "Population of India, 2016," *India Online Pages*, http://www.indiaonlinepages.com/population/india-current-population.html (retrieved March 28, 2016).

12. Kurien, "Why Religion Matters," 528.

13. Himanee Gupta, "Staking a Claim on American-ness: Hindu Temples in the United States," in *Revealing the Sacred in Asian America*, edited by Jane Iwamura and Paul Spickard (New York: Routledge, 2003), 193–96.

14. Jaffrelot, *Hindu Nationalism: A Reader*, 363–65.

15. Prema Kurien, "Mr. President, Why Do You Exclude Us from Your Prayers: Hindus Challenge American Pluralism," in *Nation of Religions: The Politics of Pluralism in Multireligious America*, edited by Stephen R. Prothero (Chapel Hill, N.C.: University of North Carolina Press, 2006), 119–21.

16. Vanaja Dhruvarajan, "Ethnic Cultural Retention and Transmission among First-Generation Hindu Asian Indians in a Canadian Prairie City," *Journal of Comparative Family Studies* 24, no. 1 (1993): 64–65; Kurien, "Why Religion Matters," 529–30.

17. Walter Anderson and S. D. Damle, *The Brotherhood in Saffron: The Rashtriya Swayamsevak Sangh and Hindu Revivalism* (New Delhi: Vistaar, 1987); and Jaffrelot, *Hindu Nationalist Movement in India*.

18. Diana Eck, *India: A Sacred Geography* (New York: Three Rivers, 2012), 100.

19. Kurien, "Why Religion Matters," 532.

20. Khyati Joshi, *New Roots in America's Sacred Ground: Religion, Race, and Ethnicity in Indian America* (New Brunswick, N.J.: Rutgers University Press, 2006), 87–88.

21. Ibid., 87–88.

22. Gupta, "Illuminating India," 16–17.

23. Jaffrelot, *Hindu Nationalism: A Reader*, 363.

24. Joshi, *New Roots in America's Sacred Ground*, 88.

25. Sadanand Dhume, "No Place Like Home: Hindu Nationalism Draws Strength from U.S. Supporters," *Far Eastern Economic Review*, February 25, 1999; Rukmini Callimachi, "The Scars of Nationalism: Suburban Hindu Nationalists Say Their Shakas Promote Pride, but in India Similar Groups are Linked to Atrocities," *Daily Herald*, May 7, 2003, http://www.dailyherald.com/special/passagefromindia/hindu.asp (retrieved March 17, 2007); and Anita Khandelwal, "Long Distance Sectarianism: Summer in a Hindu Nationalist Camp," *Samar* 14 (2001).

26. Deborah Osberg, "'Knowledge Is Not Made for Understanding; It Is Made for Cutting,'" *Complicity: An International Journal of Complexity and Education* 7, no. 2 (2010): iv.

Conclusion

1. Judith Cebula and Liza Renz-Rhodes, "Groups Give Separate Prayers for Unity," *Indianapolis Star*, May 2, 2003 (accessed via http://wwrn.org/articles/4535/?&place=united-states&section=other on February 9, 2014).

2. "Proclamation 8974–National Day of Prayer, 2013, May 1, 2013," *Administration of Barack Obama*, Office of the Federal Register, 2013.

3. "Proclamation 7672–National Day of Prayer, 2003, April 30, 2003," *Administration of George W. Bush*, Office of the Federal Register, 2003.

4. "Prayer Day Fuss Proves Some Haven't Learned," *Muncie Star-Press* editorial, April 20, 2003.

5. Rex W. Huppke, "Day of Prayer Turning into Day of Discord," *Chicago Tribune*, April 27, 2003.

6. Wendy Brown, *Regulating Aversion: Tolerance in the Age of Identity and Empire* (Princeton, N.J.: Princeton University Press, 2006), 204–5.

7. Khyati Y. Joshi, "Guest Editor's Introduction," *Equity and Excellence in Education* 39 (2006): 177.

8. Alexis de Tocqueville, *Democracy in America Vol. II*, translated by Henry Reeve, third edition (Cambridge: Sever and Frances, 1863), 5–6.

9. Robert S. Lynd and Helen Merrell Lynd, *Middletown: A Study in Modern American Culture* (New York: Harcourt, Brace, and Jovanovich, 1929), 316.

10. Theodore Caplow, Louis Hicks, and Ben J. Wattenburg, *The First Measured Century: An Illustrated Guide to Trends in America, 1900–2000* (Washington D.C.: AEI, 2000), 106, 116; Lynd and Lynd, *Middletown*, 316.

11. Cebula and Renz-Rhodes, "Groups Give Separate Prayers for Unity," and Keith Roysden, "Keller: No Apologies for Split in Events," *Muncie Star-Press*, May 2, 2003.

12. Keith Roysden, "Devout Divided: Christian, Multifaith Day of Prayer Services Celebrated Separately," *Muncie Star-Press*, May 2, 2003.

13. Brian Beaver, "Muncie's Day(s) of Prayers," Indiana Public Radio, May 2, 2003.

14. Roysden, "Devout Divided."

15. Brown, *Regulating Aversion*, 2.

16. Keith Roysden, "Inter-faith Group Offers Variety of Prayers," *Muncie Star-Press*, May 2, 2003.

17. Brown, *Regulating Aversion*, 2.

18. Khyati Joshi, *New Roots in America's Sacred Ground: Religion, Race, and Ethnicity in Indian America* (New Brunswick, N.J.: Rutgers University Press, 2006), 21–22.

19. Judith Butler, *Undoing Gender* (New York: Routledge, 2004), 24.

20. Monisha Das Gupta, *Unruly Immigrants: Rights, Activism, and Transnational South Asian Politics in the United States* (Durham, N.C.: Duke University Press, 2006), 14, 21–22, 27–54.

21. Prema A. Kurien, *A Place at the Multicultural Table: The Development of an American Hinduism* (New Brunswick, N.J.: Rutgers University Press, 2007), 8–12.

22. Jaideep Singh, "The Racialization of Minoritized Religious Identity: Constructing Sacred Sites at the Intersection of White and Christian Supremacy," in *Revealing the Sacred in Asian and Pacific America*, edited by Jane Iwamura and Paul Spickard (New York: Routledge, 2003), 90–91.

23. Donna Haraway, *Primate Visions: Gender, Race and Nature in the World of Modern Science* (New York: Routledge, 1989), 285–86, 289.

24. Evelyn Fox Keller, *A Feeling for the Organism: The Life and Work of Barbara McClintock* (New York: Freeman, 1983), 174.

25. David Campbell, *National Deconstruction: Violence, Identity, and Justice in Bosnia* (Minneapolis: University of Minnesota Press, 1998), 205; Morton Schoolman and David Campbell, "An Interview with William Connolly 2006," in *The New Pluralism: William Connolly and the Contemporary Global Condition*, edited by David Campbell and Morton Schoolman (Durham, N.C.: Duke University Press, 2008), 307–9.

26. Audre Lorde, "Age, Race, Class and Sex: Women Redefining Difference," in *Dangerous Liaisons: Gender Nation, and Postcolonial Perspectives*, edited by Anne McClintock, Aamir Mufti, and Ella Shohat (Minneapolis: University of Minnesota Press, 1997), 377–78.

27. bell hooks, "Sisterhood: Political Solidarity Between Women," in McClintock, Mufti, and Shohat, *Dangerous Liaisons*, 410–11.

Index

HIMANEE GUPTA-CARLSON is an associate professor at SUNY Empire State College.

THE ASIAN AMERICAN EXPERIENCE

The Hood River Issei: An Oral History of Japanese Settlers
  in Oregon's Hood River Valley *Linda Tamura*
Americanization, Acculturation, and Ethnic Identity:
  The Nisei Generation in Hawaii *Eileen H. Tamura*
Sui Sin Far/Edith Maude Eaton: A Literary Biography *Annette White-Parks*
Mrs. Spring Fragrance and Other Writings *Sui Sin Far; edited by Amy Ling and
  Annette White-Parks*
The Golden Mountain: The Autobiography of a Korean Immigrant, 1895–1960
  Easurk Emsen Charr; edited and with an introduction by Wayne Patterson
Race and Politics: Asian Americans, Latinos, and Whites
  in a Los Angeles Suburb *Leland T. Saito*
Achieving the Impossible Dream: How Japanese Americans Obtained Redress
  Mitchell T. Maki, Harry H. L. Kitano, and S. Megan Berthold
If They Don't Bring Their Women Here: Chinese Female Immigration
  before Exclusion *George Anthony Peffer*
Growing Up Nisei: Race, Generation, and Culture among Japanese Americans
  of California, 1924–49 *David K. Yoo*
Chinese American Literature since the 1850s *Xiao-huang Yin*
Pacific Pioneers: Japanese Journeys to America and Hawaii, 1850–80 *John E. Van Sant*
Holding Up More Than Half the Sky: Chinese Women Garment Workers
  in New York City, 1948–92 *Xiaolan Bao*
Onoto Watanna: The Story of Winnifred Eaton *Diana Birchall*
Edith and Winnifred Eaton: Chinatown Missions
  and Japanese Romances *Dominika Ferens*
Being Chinese, Becoming Chinese American *Shehong Chen*
"A Half Caste" and Other Writings *Onoto Watanna; edited by Linda Trinh Moser
  and Elizabeth Rooney*
Chinese Immigrants, African Americans, and Racial Anxiety
  in the United States, 1848–82 *Najia Aarim-Heriot*
Not Just Victims: Conversations with Cambodian Community Leaders
  in the United States *Edited and with an introduction by Sucheng Chan;
  interviews conducted by Audrey U. Kim*
The Japanese in Latin America *Daniel M. Masterson with Sayaka Funada-Classen*
Survivors: Cambodian Refugees in the United States *Sucheng Chan*
From Concentration Camp to Campus: Japanese American Students
  and World War II *Allan W. Austin*
Japanese American Midwives: Culture, Community, and Health Politics *Susan L. Smith*
In Defense of Asian American Studies: The Politics of Teaching
  and Program Building *Sucheng Chan*
Lost and Found: Reclaiming the Japanese American Incarceration *Karen L. Ishizuka*
Religion and Spirituality in Korean America *Edited by David K. Yoo and Ruth H. Chung*

The University of Illinois Press
is a founding member of the
Association of American University Presses.

Composed in 10.25/13 Marat Pro Regular
with Trade Gothic display
by Kirsten Dennison
at the University of Illinois Press
Cover design by Megan McCausland
Cover illustration: ©iStock.com/realPHOTO

University of Illinois Press
1325 South Oak Street
Champaign, IL 61820-6903
www.press.uillinois.edu